# 实习教师初级英语教学能力提升的培训模块开发研究

## Development of A Training Module to Improve Initial ELT Proficiency of Student-teachers

肖友兴　张玉红　著

中国纺织出版社有限公司

**图书在版编目（CIP）数据**

实习教师初级英语教学能力提升的培训模块开发研究：
英文／肖友兴，张玉红著. --北京：中国纺织出版社
有限公司，2023.10
　　ISBN 978-7-5229-1121-2

Ⅰ. ①实… Ⅱ. ①肖… ②张… Ⅲ. ①中小学－英语
－师资培养－研究－英文 Ⅳ. ①G633.412

中国国家版本馆CIP数据核字（2023）第 194711 号

---

责任编辑：韩　阳　郭　婷　　责任校对：王蕙莹
责任印制：储志伟

---

中国纺织出版社有限公司出版发行
地址：北京市朝阳区百子湾东里A407号楼　邮政编码：100124
销售电话：010—67004422　传真：010—87155801
http://www.c-textilep.com
中国纺织出版社天猫旗舰店
官方微博 http://weibo.com/2119887771
北京虎彩文化传播有限公司印刷　各地新华书店经销
2023年10月第1版第1次印刷
开本：710×1000　1/16　印张：16.75
字数：200千字　定价：88.00元

---

凡购本书，如有缺页、倒页、脱页，由本社图书营销中心调换

# Introduction

This study aimed to investigate the current needs of student-teachers' professional development, develop a training module to improve their initial ELT proficiencies and determine its effectiveness. The mixed methods research design with convergent parallel strategy, starting with the quantitative and following by the qualitative research methods were employed in eliciting various sets of research data. Numerous instruments were utilized in different stages with 168 respondents (student-teachers and English teachers), 18 informants (parents, kindergarten English teachers, principals and stakeholders) and 58 participants (student-teachers). The ADDIEM training process was adopted as a guideline for the framework to develop the training module.

The study resulted in the following outcomes: ① fourteen prioritized topics within the four transformed training modules (Linguistic Basis, Lesson Design, Teaching Techniques and Teaching Demonstration) were identified as the challenges facing current student-teachers; ② training objectives and its syllabus, lesson plans, instructional strategies, training participants and location, delivery of the training, and training evaluation and improvement were defined sequentially in each phase as the specific components of the training activities; ③ the ADDIEM Training Process, constituting of the six phases of need analysis, design, development, implementation, evaluation and modification, was merged systematically to develop a feasible training module, and the training program was highly accepted because of the effectiveness of great benefit and satisfaction. It was discovered that the participants' improvements from the training evaluation forms were mainly categorized as follows: ① enhanced learning interests and confidence; ② improved comprehensive English pronunciation, practical spoken English and listening ability; ③ well-acquired application skills and techniques upon instructional design; ④ positive self-reflected awareness of the disadvantages. Additionally, two types of evidence could be obviously identified from the two practical assignments in terms of better legibility and fluency of English handwriting by comparing their formative progress, and good fulfillment of the present teaching contextual standards or patterns for effective lesson design by checking their summative assessment of lesson plans.

Finally, the constructive recommendations in view of focusing on establishing a pleasant teaching and learning environment, ensuring sufficient training periods, identifying the trainer's professional traits and competences, specifying trainees' background knowledge, altering training models at the in-service level were made for future practice and research.

**Keywords:** Training module; professional development; ELT proficiency; student-teachers; multi-ethnic groups

# CONTENTS

**CHAPTER 1    INTRODUCTION** ················································· 1

  1.1  Background of the Study ······································· 1

  1.2  Statement of the Problem ······································ 5

  1.3  Significance of the Study ······································ 8

  1.4  Purposes of the Study ········································ 9

  1.5  Research Questions ·········································· 9

  1.6  Conceptual Framework of the Study ······················· 10

  1.7  Contribution to Knowledge ··································· 10

  1.8  Scope of the Study ·········································· 12

  1.9  Definition of Terms ········································· 13

  1.10  Summary ················································ 14

**CHAPTER 2    LITERATURE REVIEW** ································· 15

  2.1  Overview of Bilingual Education in China ·················· 15

      2.1.1  Definition of Bilingual Education ···················· 15

      2.1.2  Bilingual Education in Multi-ethnic Communities ········· 16

  2.2  Overview of Multilingual Education in China ················ 20

      2.2.1  Definition of Multilingual Education ·················· 20

      2.2.2  Background of Multilingual Education in China and Yunnan ········ 20

      2.2.3  Minorities' Attitudes to Multilingual Education ··············· 22

      2.2.4  Instruction of Multilingual Education in China ·········· 23

      2.2.5  Development of Multilingual Education in China ········· 25

  2.3  Overall Situation of EFL Education in China ················ 27

  2.4  The Controversy of EFL Education ························· 29

      2.4.1  Overseas' Perceptions of EFL Education ··············· 29

    2.4.2   Domestic Debate of EFL Education ·············31

2.5   Teacher Quality and Professional Development ·············34

2.6   Professionalism of Kindergarten English Teachers·············38

2.7   English Language Teaching Proficiency ·············41

    2.7.1   Importance of English Language Teaching Proficiency ·············41

    2.7.2   Components of English Language Teaching Proficiency ·············43

    2.7.3   Linguistic Proficiency ·············46

    2.7.4   Teaching Proficiency ·············49

2.8   Patterns of Teacher Training and Development ·············50

    2.8.1   Rationale of Teacher Training and Development ·············50

    2.8.2   Overview of English Teacher Training Programs·············52

    2.8.3   Pre-service and In-service Teacher Training Programs ·············53

    2.8.4   Foreign Patterns of English Teacher Training Programs ·············56

    2.8.5   Chinese Application of English Teacher Training Programs·············62

    2.8.6   Teaching and Training Module ·············65

2.9   Instructional Design ·············66

2.10   The ADDIE Model ·············67

    2.10.1   The Analysis Phase ·············68

    2.10.2   The Design Phase·············70

    2.10.3   The Development Phase ·············70

    2.10.4   The Implementation Phase·············70

    2.10.5   The Evaluation Phase·············71

2.11   Related Research ·············72

2.12   Summary ·············75

CHAPTER 3   RESEARCH METHODOLOGY·············76

3.1   Research Paradigm and Rationale·············76

3.2   Research Design·············77

3.3   Research Process and Training Phases ·············80

3.4   Research Methods ·············83

    3.4.1   Context of the Study ·············83

    3.4.2   Quantitative Research Design·············85

3.4.3　Qualitative Research Design·············································89

3.4.4　Linkage between Data Collection and Data Analysis···············94

3.5　Ethical Considerations·······················································96

3.5.1　Harmfulness ································································97

3.5.2　Informed Consent ··························································97

3.5.3　Privacy and Confidentiality ···············································98

3.6　Summary ·······································································98

**CHAPTER 4　FINDINGS** ································································ **100**

4.1　Context of the Present Study ···············································100

4.2　Findings of Research Question 1·············································101

Results of the Needs Analysis Phase ·········································102

4.3　Findings of Research Question 2·············································110

4.3.1　Results of the Training Design Phase ·····································110

4.3.2　Results of the Training Development Phase ·····························117

4.3.3　Results of the Training Implementation Phase ·························121

4.3.4　Results of the Training Evaluation Phase ······························124

4.3.5　Results of the Training Modification Phase·····························137

4.4　Findings of Research Question 3·············································139

4.4.1　The Development of the Training Process······························139

4.4.2　The Improvements of the Student-teachers' ELT Proficiency ······140

4.5　Summary ·······································································146

**CHAPTER 5　CONCLUSION, DISCUSSION AND**

**RECOMMENDATIONS**·······························································**147**

5.1　Summary of the Results ·····················································147

5.2　Discussion of the Findings ··················································150

5.3　Implications of the Study ····················································170

5.4　Recommendations of the Study···············································171

5.4.1　Recommendations for Future Practice····································172

5.4.2　Recommendations for Future Research·································174

5.5　Summary ·······································································176

**ACKNOWLEDGEMENTS** ················································ **177**

**REFERENCES**··············································································· **178**

**APPENDICES**··········································································· **203**

    APPENDIX A·····························································203

    APPENDIX B·····························································205

    APPENDIX C·····························································206

    APPENDIX D·····························································213

    APPENDIX E·····························································219

    APPENDIX F·····························································220

    APPENDIX G·····························································222

    APPENDIX H·····························································223

    APPENDIX I·····························································228

    APPENDIX J·····························································237

    APPENDIX K·····························································245

    APPENDIX L·····························································248

    APPENDIX M·····························································250

# CHAPTER 1

# INTRODUCTION

This chapter introduces a general background of the research, and the chapter is divided into ten sections as follows:

1.1    Background of the Study

1.2    Statement of the Problem

1.3    Significance of the Study

1.4    Purposes of the Study

1.5    Research Questions

1.6    Conceptual Framework of the Study

1.7    Contribution to Knowledge

1.8    Scope of the Study

1.9    Definition of Terms

1.10    Summary

## 1.1    Background of the Study

As an ethnically and linguistically diverse country with 56 minority nationalities (the majority Han and the rest are 55 minority groups) and over 80 languages, bilingual education policies in China were typically of two formulations: (1) the development of ethnic minority (home) languages and Mandarin (Putonghua) for ethnic minority groups; (2) the development of Chinese and an additional foreign language (mainly English) for non-ethnic minority groups (Wang, 2015). However, the extent of implementation was differed for various ethnic minority groups in different locations, with a sharp disparity of teaching resources and socioeconomic development (Adamson & Feng, 2008). China was encountering problems in improving the quality and effectiveness of bilingual education for minorities. Postiglione (1999) indicated that the number and diversity of languages used by the non-Han peoples of China were a formidable barrier to popularising education in China's rural and remote frontier regions. Yunnan is a frontier province in Southwest China with a great diversity of language, culture, and ethnicity; it is home to 25 officially identified ethnic minority groups speaking 26 languages and using 22 scripts (Dao, 2005). Therefore, given the differences in living environment, population size, community distribution, and socioeconomic development, the language use of ethnic communities was very diversified and complicated (Wang, 2015). Johnson and Chhetri (2002) also indicated that bilingual education in multi-ethnic community schools was directed at young language minority students, who were required to be proficient in their native language as well as Mandarin. According to different languages used in bilingual education, normally it was distinguished into two categories in the Chinese context, bilingual education for minorities (*local ethnic language and Chinese*) and bilingual education for foreign languages (*Chinese and English)* (Li, Liu, & Ghil'ad, 2014). Although minorities had the right to use their languages, most of the decisions on language usage and language of instruction in the schools were still made by regional and local officials who are mostly Han Chinese (Gil, 2005). This fact created a wide variety of the goals and methods of bilingual education in China and it made difficult to evaluate the overall effectiveness of bilingual education programs in minority areas. In addition, the biggest obstacle to bilingual education in China was the lack of qualified teachers (Johnson & Chhetri, 2002). This is in accordance with Postiglione (1999), he stated that the scarcities of human resources (qualified minority language teachers) and material resources (texts and materials in minority languages) were obstacles to the implementation and effectiveness of bilingual education policies. Over the last 20 years, various measures have been implemented to encourage graduates from teacher's education colleges to work in minority regions (Lin, 1997). To compensate for the teachers' willingness to work in minority areas, improved working conditions and higher wages were used as rewards including having a second child (Johnson, 1999; Lin, 1997). Unfortunately, the incentives have done little to improve the situation and the trend of minority teacher shortages will likely to continue for some time.

To reduce the exclusionary nature of the language policy, China needed to construct a strong bilingual education program (Postiglione, 1999). On the one hand, China could not possibly enroll and keep monolingual linguistic minority children in schools without mother-tongue instruction; but on the other hand, the Chinese government could not socialize these children into the political, cultural and economic mainstream of Chinese society without providing minority children instruction in Mandarin. To be successful, the Chinese educational system needed to produce people who were *"both ethnic and expert"* (Postiglione, 1999, p.124).

At the beginning of the 1980s, English was introduced into the secondary school curriculum. In the early 2000s, English became a compulsory course in the national elementary school curriculum, and schools with the necessary qualified English teachers were required to teach English from grade three. At present, English is not only a required subject at almost all levels of school curricula, but also a yardstick for talent selection and quality evaluation of higher learning institutions. Under the encouragement of the government, more and more Chinese have begun to accept English as their main foreign language, and more and more young Chinese have begun to learn English. As for the youngest ethnic minority people, Chinese was a pathway to social mobility and personal development, and English was a passport to the globalized world. But due to a lack of qualified English teachers, it is still a long way for English language to become effectively used in communication among Chinese and non-Chinese in China (Zhang, 2012). Additionally, it could be attributed to the lack of funding and resources which are critical for the development of English proficiency in the ethnic minority communities (Wang, 2015).

The quality of teachers secured the attainment of the national educational objectives, but to achieve these goals, strict criteria about teacher quality must be utilized. However, it was quite clear that whatever measures were to be adopted to deal with these educational issues, it was always the teachers who would have to put these objectives into reality (Ahmed, 2011). The same was applied to the EFL field of education; a sufficient number of qualified English teachers played the key role. Teachers' low language proficiency had a direct impact on students' target language performance and language development. In an EFL context like that of

China where English is neither the official language nor the language of daily use, language teachers and language classrooms might be students' only access to the English language. Therefore, teacher role modelling is important when teachers are the only English speakers and English classes are the only target language resources which students might encounter (Ahmed, 2011). Hence, mastering sufficient English language proficiency in order to provide target language models effectively has become one of the main concerns for teachers in China (Tang, 2007).

Some Western countries, such as the USA, England and New Zealand, have put forward the goal of improving the quality of preschool education, and giving priority to the development of preschool education in the educational field with a series of reforms with respect to management, funding, teacher training, curriculum and evaluation and so on (Wang & Mi, 2014). With the continuing development of preschool education in a Chinese context, the popularity of international bilingual kindergarten and all kinds of special classes of preschool education have become a mainstream trend in preschool educational markets (Shen & Zhao, 2010). In order to meet the requirements of the social development, bilingual education gradually extended to the preschool stage, and the younger age of bilingual education will inevitably become the main trend of education development (Wang & Mi, 2014).

Bilingual education at the beginning level is the first step in lifelong learning as it is the foundation for successful progress through one's later life. Children's experiences in their early years heavily influence their development and learning; therefore, the quality of early childhood programs is of a great concern (Frede, 1995). As the communities realize the significance of bilingual education and the importance of English as an international communicative tool, parents have started to enroll their children at a younger age in preschool bilingual or multilingual programs. This could happen regardless of whether those kindergartens have been approved quality-wise or whether the curriculum is appropriate for children's development. This happens only because many parents are aware that the early onset of bilingual education is an opportunity for their children's future (Liu, 2011).

The teaching reform of second language has shown the tendency of younger age in combination with educational research, permeation with all disciplines have tremendously influnced on Chinese children's English teaching (Li, 2007). Under the such social context of China, English language teaching via a variety of ways has been initiated in many kindergartens, and have made great progress in the social controversy.

*Teaching Guidelines for Preschool Education* (MOE, 2001a) stated not only the role and status of kindergarten teachers, but also more comprehensive and specific requirements for the quality of kindergarten teachers (Wang, 2012). This meant a qualified bilingual teacher should have not only the general qualities about preschool education, but also a solid foundation of English knowledge with a diverse cultural background and advanced English teaching methods and skills (Deng, 2010; Li, 2007; Ren, 2009; Wang, 2012). The high quality of preschool bilingual education teachers is the fundamental guarantee for English education and teaching activities in kindergartens and the improved quality of preschool bilingual education (Yao & Li, 2010).

## 1.2 Statement of the Problem

Under the present context of the Chinese educational reforms, Tan (2006) highlighted that the goal of bilingual teaching practice is difficult to achieve due to the lack of qualified bilingual teachers especially in preschool education, and not yet practically functioning professional training system for kindergarten teachers. Liu (2011) confirmed the same standpoint that the shortage of qualified bilingual teachers is the main bottleneck restricting the development of bilingual education in kindergartens; the fundamental solution to the shortage of teachers should depend on training (Wang, 2012).

In terms of the current situation of initial bilingual education in multi-ethnic community schools in Yunnan province, it seems that bilingual teaching is complying with the developing trend of internationalization and the requirements of current educational reform. However, limited by the ethnic pluralism, language complexity and low professionalism of English teachers which exists in the remote and frontier regions of Yunnan province, such conflicts between the integration of national education and ethnic diversity, and disjoint between teaching practice and weak qualified teachers are ubiquitous, which still remain far from the corresponding standards (Ji, Ju & Zhang, 2015).

However, the interdisciplinary preschool teachers and talents, who could be competent both in English bilingual teaching and skills, are very scarce at present context of Chinese education (Wang, 2007; Yao & Li, 2010). Many kindergartens face the dilemma of single educational resources and shortage of qualified bilingual teachers (Ren, 2009). The overall number of current preschool teachers in China's bilingual education field is not high. Three kinds of bilingual teachers, i.e., the school-trained teachers, recruited local English teachers, and foreign native speakers (English) are obviously insufficient (Shen & Zhao, 2010). According to Wang and Mi (2014), approximately 72% of the kindergarten schools require employees with both good Chinese and English language proficiency, so as to launch better bilingual education. Some bilingual kindergartens hire native English speakers and English majors as English teachers, and most kindergartens recruit preschool education majors as bilingual teachers. However, it seems unfortunate that students majoring in preschool education can not teach English with appropriate English language teaching methods, while English majors do not understand preschool psychology and pedagogy well (Wang & Mi, 2014). Although students who majored in preschool education are familiar with basic theoretical knowledge and professional skills of Chinese education, their English language proficiency especially in pronunciation, is problematic in performing their roles in bilingual education (Tan, 2014). It is difficult for them to organize effective English teaching activities, and therefore children's English learning in the future will be affected detrimentally under such situation (Shen & Zhao, 2010). On the contrary, the English-native speaking teachers and English majors hired in bilingual kindergartens might have good knowledge and comprehensive English, but most of them have not received professional training in preschool education. Therefore, it is difficult for them to design and organize children's activities according to their age and learning level, much less to include the development of integration in the bilingual curriculum. They only teach English as an independent subject, which is unsuitable for the current role and demand of kindergarten English teachers (Wang & Mi, 2014).

Many kindergartens have raised claims on possessing basic professional skills, solid professional knowledge, familiarity with the characteristics of children's development, and understanding of the requirements of children's psychological development (Li, 2007). The kindergartens emphasize bilingual teachers to have a solid basic foundation of English knowledge: namely, comprehensive English pronunciation, normative English spoken expressions and rich vocabulary (Ren, 2009). Deng (2010) suggested that the professional quality of a bilingual teacher should be based on that of a general discipline teacher with higher English language proficiency, and creative bilingual education and teaching competencies, and so on. Similarly, Shen and Zhao (2010) further highlighted that qualified preschool bilingual teachers should have the scientific concepts about preschool bilingual education, professional knowledge, strong teaching abilities in preschool bilingual education. Moreover, they should also have feasible design ability of English games and an understanding of the differences between Chinese and western cultures, so they should also have an advanced educational ideology and better teaching proficiency, can animate the classroom atmosphere and let the children learn while playing (Yu, 2012). The practice of preschool bilingual education indicated that knowledge of a bilingual teacher's education, language proficiencies, mastery of teaching skills, values and educational attitudes has a direct influence on the future development of children's education (John, 1975, cited in Lv, 2016).

Therefore, it should supplement and cultivate English preschool teachers by strengthening the preschool English education and curriculum to develop formal and qualified preschool English teachers by following the regulations of children's physical and mental development, and the special requirements of kindergarten curriculum (Wang, 2007; Wang, 2012; Yao & Li, 2010). Equally, it is urgent to cultivate qualified kindergarten teachers and explore an effective pre-service training model for bilingual teachers (Zhu, 2007; Wang, 2012). As a professional department specialized in kindergarten teacher training, such colleges and universities should further hold the basic direction of the kindergarten teachers' professional levels and development; and also do in-depth research in pre-service training of English language teaching proficiency for the kindergarten level (Wang, 2012; Gu, 2016).

The main teaching objective of preschool English education is to develop preschool education majors' English teaching proficiency, and the emphasis of teaching content is to acquire practical English teaching proficiency in preschool children's English education (Fu & Zhong, 2013). However, the great dilemma between the enormous demand of English preschool teachers and the severe lag of pre-service teacher training for preschool bilingual education in colleges exists naturally. Therefore, cultivating professional English preschool teachers in colleges or universities became the focused task of pre-service training (Gu, 2016); vice versa, improving the pre-service training strategies of preschool bilingual teachers can help preschool teachers better adapt to the needs of career development, and at the same time, also guide normal universities to optimize the bilingual teaching levels (Zhang, 2017).

Therefore, how to equip these bilingual teachers with better language abilities and teaching proficiency has become the focus of the teacher training and practice (Wang, 2007; Wang & Mi, 2014). Based on the current situation of lacking qualified English teachers and no prepared pre-service training program, a proposed suitable training for preschool education majors and primary school education majors in university are aiming at effectively cultivating qualified English teachers for beginning levels within the required hours, is of great necessity (Jin, 2016). This proposed training module is consistent with the ultimate goal of English education in order to cultivate suitable talents for the development of society, furthermore, for the current reform of the teaching model of English curriculum in professional preschool and primary education fields. Using this teaching and training pattern, the professional pre-service training course can be combined with the English language course, which align with the trend of bilingual education and teaching (Wang, 2014).

## 1.3    Significance of the Study

The study examined the challenges facing the current student-teachers in teaching English at the beginning level in multi-ethnic community schools, and investigated their perspectives towards the one-semester training program in ELT proficiency. At the same time, it provides the evidence of insights into how the student-teachers have changed based on their teaching practicum experiences, feelings, attitudes, and beliefs about the training program. Simultaneously, the comprehensive professional qualities of both the preschool education majors and primary school education majors are expected to be improved by implementing the proposed training and teaching module. Even though the present effectiveness of professional development of preschool English teachers is still far from being satisfied, cultivating more and better qualified English teachers with practical ELT knowledge and proficiency still remains a thorny issue within the Chinese EFL college teaching context (Tan, 2014). Under this circumstance, this topic being addressed is of great theoretical and pragmatic significance for both English teaching and relative research in China.

## 1.4   Purposes of the Study

There are three purposes of this study.

① To investigate the student-teachers' professional development needs, especially their English language teaching (ELT) proficiency.

② To develop a training module for a one-semester course to improve proficiency in beginning level ELT among student-teachers in multi-ethnic communities of Yunnan province.

③ To determine both the training process and the effectiveness of the training module.

## 1.5   Research Questions

The study focused on the following research questions.

① What are the challenges facing the current student-teachers in teaching English to beginning learners in multi-ethnic community schools in Yunnan Province?

② What are the specific components of training activities for student-teachers in teaching English effectively in multi-ethnic community schools in Yunnan Province?

③ How does the training process develop and to what extent does the training module improve student-teachers' ELT proficiency?

## 1.6    Conceptual Framework of the Study

The main purpose of the study was to develop a feasible training module to improve ELT proficiency of student-teachers in such a setting, according to the ADDIE process of training and development (Richard & Elwood, 2009). Six different but related phases among the ADDIEM training process were involved in the central research problem (see Figure 1.1). The ADDIEM training process included: Phase 1: Needs Analysis; Phase 2: Training Design; Phase 3: Training Development; Phase 4: Training Implementation; Phase 5: Training Evaluation; Phase 6: Training Modification. All phases consist of a complete training process of the study, and each phase plays its uniquely important role for the final training module which focused on the ELT proficiency.

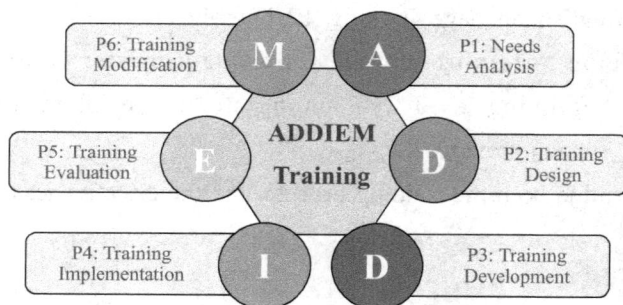

Figure 1.1    The Conceptual Framework of the ADDIEM Training Process
(*Source*: Adapted from Richard & Elwood, 2009)

## 1.7    Contribution to Knowledge

Reviewing the relative research studies, I noticed that although there were some research achievements about teacher training, professional development, pre-service and in-service training, most of the research studies remained on the conceptual level of theorization, policy, institutionalization and formalization; very few were operationalized in practice. Thus, this study is expected to add both theoretical and practical contributions to the professional development of bilingual education. The research findings are expected to provide valuable detailed information on the student-teachers' professional qualities especially their ELT proficiency; therefore, the study might also benefit the trainers and trainees for them to be aware of current training implementation and other factors that they would face during the one-semester course of learning and training. The results would be a source of information for responsible administrators and stakeholders to make sound decisions based on evidence for the ELT proficiency training program.

Due to the inconsistencies between the employees of preschool education, primary school education and employees of English majors under the special context of multi-ethnic areas in Yunnan province, insufficient qualified teachers exist in most bilingual schools in China. Thus, in spite of general qualities for preschool education major and primary school education majors, or advanced English teaching methods and skills for English majors, this study hopes to bridge the gap between these majors in order to provide both theoretical and practical exemplification for establishment of curricula and major areas of the study.

Furthermore, the professionals of preschool and primary English education majors are urgently needed because of the *"promising employment prospects"* in recent years according to Lv's investigation report (2016, p.51). Therefore, normal universities should set up special preschool or primary English education majors in order to meet the needs of professional development (Teng, 2013). The study's findings study might provide theoretical support for the current reform of teaching, curriculum and specialization construction. It was possible to initiate a new combination of pre-school and primary education majors (English oriented) for the current reform of teaching, curriculum and specialty construction at Dali University in the future.

No matter from training development to training implementation, or from training evaluation to training modification, the adapted ADDIEM training process might become a complete and creative training framework for the study, which ultimately helped improve the academic performance of trainees and in turn teaching quality when concerned trainers continue to put the acquired pedagogical, professional and instructional skills, and knowledge into practice in their actual classrooms. Based on the above-mentioned pioneering practice, the study is also expected to shift the training framework to other majors or subjects, finally partially help either directly or indirectly generalize the training framework to other multi-ethnic communities under the similar context of Yunnan Province.

Last but not least, the real English teachers working in kindergartens and primary schools (or higher secondary levels) are proposed to be the certain participants as well as trainees from day one for future research. It is potentially necessary to enhance both the pre-service training and in-service training for the ESL and EFL levels in multi-ethnic areas and to deepen the research on bilingual or multilingual interferences in multi-ethnic communities of Yunnan Province.

## 1.8    Scope of the Study

The scope of this study was concerned about the following aspects:

First, the study examined ELT proficiency among the student-teachers from Dali University in terms of professional development. Other aspects, such as personal and social competencies, which might be equally important, are not included in the present study. Therefore, the inclusion of other traits of teacher quality could supply additional information about ELT proficiency in Yunnan province. That should be topics for further study.

Second, all participants in this study were selected from Dali Bai ethnic prefecture. Therefore, the results might not be generalized to other ethnic groups in other communities.

Third, all preschool and primary education majors who were studying at the current campus from the 2014 and 2015 academic years were asked to respond to a questionnaire while the 2016 academic year was involved in the practical training. It meant that 2014 student-teachers who had finished the teaching practicum might have different interpretations and definitions regarding the interval values and rankings provided by the scale compared with 2015 and 2016 student-teachers. To decrease varying interpretations by the participants, the scaling was made as clear as possible.

## 1.9  Definition of Terms

For the purpose of this study, the following definitions of terms are used throughout the study:

**Multilingual Education:** in the minority areas of China, it refers to the use of three different languages as the media of instruction to teach different content areas: for instance, the use of minority home language or standard Chinese, or both to teach most subjects and the use of ethnic minority language and/or Chinese or/and English to teach English (Shan, 2018).

**Professional Development:** it defined as activities that develop an individual's skills, knowledge, expertise and other characteristics as a teacher. It includes ongoing training, practice and feedback, and provides adequate time and follow-up support.

**Initial ELT proficiency:** it means the basic knowledge, skills, abilities and attitudes which English language teachers need to have in order to promote effective teaching and learning processes for beginning learners including both preschool and primary levels.

**Instructional Design:** it can be defined as the creation of instructional materials, modules or lessons. The instructional design process consists of determining the needs of the learners, defining the instructional goals and objectives, designing and planning assessment tasks, and designing teaching and learning activities to ensure the effectiveness of instruction.

**Training Module:** it's a specific instructional package or learning materials created and designed to improve the student-teachers' ELT proficiency. It refers to a process of putting different components together for effectiveness in learning and teaching English among preschool and primary education majors. It offers flexibility in the provision of professional training including possibilities of modification to those with limited English language teaching proficiency in a short period of time in the present study.

**Improve:** it means to make the student-teachers' ELT proficiency better after implementing the training.

**Student-teacher:** it is a college or university student who is teaching in a school for a limited period under the supervision of a certified teacher as part of a course/degree in education. Here in this study, it refers to the third academic year for students majoring in preschool and primary education at Dali University.

**Multi-ethnic Community:** it is a region within which different ethnic groups inhabit and live together. For this study, the community is comprised of 25 ethnic minority groups distributed in 8 municipalities and 8 ethnic autonomous prefectures in Yunnan province.

## 1.10　Summary

Under the context of multi-ethnic complexity in Yunnan province, it is widely known that the lack of qualified English teachers exists in most kindergartens and primary schools. The effectiveness of English teaching, especially ELT proficiency in bilingual kindergartens and primary schools, is becoming the main concern in the present context in China. Correspondingly, it is necessary to take the responsibility to implement pre-service training in normal universities to improve the student-teachers' ELT proficiency, which is consistent with the trend of bilingual education and teaching. Moreover, the statement of the problem, purposes of the study, research questions, significance of the study, contribution to knowledge, the conceptual framework of the study and definition of terms are presented to illustrate the basic concepts of the study. The next chapter describes the literature that can help make clear concepts of this study and provide relevant related previous studies.

# CHAPTER 2
# LITERATURE REVIEW

The purposes of this study were to investigate the student-teachers' professional qualities, especially their English language teaching (ELT) proficiency; to develop a feasible training module to improve their ELT proficiency; to determine the effectiveness of the training module in such a setting. This chapter presents the readers with the literature and theories embedded in the study being explored. The following sections state the literature reviews and previous research studies.

2.1    Overview of Bilingual Education in China
2.2    Overview of Multilingual Education in China
2.3    Overall Situation of EFL Education in China
2.4    The Controversy of EFL Education
2.5    Teacher Quality and Professional Development
2.6    Professionalism of Kindergarten English Teachers
2.7    English Language Teaching Proficiency
2.8    Patterns of Teacher Training and Development
2.9    Instructional Design
2.10   The ADDIE Model
2.11   Related Research
2.12   Summary

## 2.1   Overview of Bilingual Education in China

### 2.1.1   Definition of Bilingual Education

American National Association for Bilingual Education (NABE, 2012) defined bilingual education as "Approaches in the classroom that use the native languages of English language learners (ELLs) for instruction". The NABE was an American advocacy group that provided teacher training, educational leadership, and lobbying efforts on behalf of legislation regarding individuals learning English as a second language.

The term bilingual education had been misunderstood by many people (García, 2009). According to García, bilingual education was fundamentally different from second language (L2) and foreign language (FL) education. She made the distinction between bilingual education and L2 and FL education in that students learned the target language in L2 and FL learning contexts as "a subject"; however, the target language was used as "a medium of instruction" in a bilingual education context. In the present study, I used the term bilingual education to refer to different types of additional language education, including L2 and FL education. L2 education and FL education were quite distinguishable based on the learning environments. L2 learning took place where the target language was spoken in the society, but FL learning took place where the target language was not spoken widely in the community (García, 2009).

Consequently, in the context of FL learning, children were exposed to the target language in a limited hour of instruction in school and usually did not have a chance to speak and hear the language from other people outside of the classroom (Cameron, 2001). Even though two types of language education might be differently defined, Chinese and English are involved in the present study.

## 2.1.2 Bilingual Education in Multi-ethnic Communities

China, Characterised by its ethnic diversity, national unity and multicultural education, is a rapidly developing multi-ethnic country facing several challenges, including pollution, growing income inequality and low political participation of ordinary citizens, which might threaten the social stability (Ren, 2011). In addition, China must address ethnic conflicts, particularly in urban, autonomous and border regions. The Chinese government is advocating national unity education in the school and college curriculum to help address these issues. Multicultural education could provide a framework for addressing social, economic, political and educational inequalities in China (Ren, 2011).

As one member of multi-ethnic countries in the world, China is comprised of one majority group (Han) and other 55 ethnic minority groups. Based on the basic national situation, Postiglione (1999) pointed out that the number and diversity of languages used by the non-Han people of China is a formidable barrier to the popularization of education in China's rural and remote frontier regions. To improve the quality and effectiveness of bilingual education for minorities is the main problem which China has had to challenge for a long time (Li, 2006). Compared with mass education, the bilingual education has a specific purpose not only basically to transmit universal knowledge and educate its youth, but also to contribute to a harmoniously multicultural society via the benefit of maintenance of language diversity, language practice and language planning (Julia, 2010). According to the different languages used in bilingual education, normally bilingual education is divided into two categories in China, bilingual education for minorities and bilingual education for foreign languages (Li, Liu & Ghil'ad, 2014). This study is going to discuss bilingual English and Mandarin Chinese, the second type. Accordingly, many parents are aware that the early onset of bilingual education with prior English is an opportunity for their children's future (Li, 2007).

Johnson and Chhetri (2002) indicated that minority culture and ethnic identity are too often victimized in the development of mass education in multicultural societies and that the culture of the dominant language was established at the expense of the linguistic competence of the minority children. At present, there are various issues of languages in China, such as the effect of Putonghua (Mandarin) on dialects, the endangered minority language, single foreigner language education, etc. Therefore, it was very important and necessary to analyze the impact of language policy on the development of bilingual education for minorities in China.

In China, each group of education has its specific language differing from others in various complexities. There were some 120 spoken languages among these ethnic groups. About 60 languages of these were known to be used by less than ten thousand people and about 20 languages were used by less than one thousand people (Li, 2006). Johnson and Chhetri (2002) pointed out the current problems of bilingual education for minorities in China that they were divided into three main aspects. In the first place, a highly centralized curriculum caused by a pyramid-shaped administrative system in education, with very few autonomous rights for adjustable management of local bilingual schools even for the native curriculum and making local teaching plans. Therefore, local knowledge of minorities was seldom incorporated into the bilingual education for minority students (Li, Zhang & Edwards, 2016). Secondly, the problem was the lack of resources and textbooks in minority languages. Most reference books and educational materials were in Mandarin, one reason was that experts writing textbooks who were generally qualified in training and research often work in the official language; another reason was the potential market of minorities' textbook publication was much smaller, which was not good for a profitable business. The third problem was a severe shortage of qualified teachers and the training for minority teachers was not effective enough (Tang, 2007).

Traditional cultural elements of minorities should be introduced to bilingual education system (Li, 2007). As for the issue of the shortage of bilingual teachers in multi-ethnic areas, through language policy to ensure the good treatment for them was a feasible action, which improved the current situation of insufficient and unqualified bilingual teacher resources in the areas. To improve the conditions for teachers' political and living conditions, to create a good environment for teachers, to attract more college graduates to work in the minority areas, to strengthen the training for them both in pre-service and in-service stages, all were considered to be effective way to improve the quality of bilingual education for minorities in China (Li, Liu & Ghil'ad, 2014).

In terms of linguistics stance, Jessner (2006) highlighted the equal importance between language maintenance and language acquisition. Comparing with the absolute dominant position of Chinese and ethnic languages in children's daily lives and learning, English has a disadvantageous position both in the acquisition and maintenance (Jessner, 2006). Due to the minority children learning English involved the mutual influence and competition of the three languages (Chinese, ethnic language, and English), which means the minority children have to maintain the other two learned languages in the process of English learning. Its difficulty and complexity, predictably, was bigger than Han Chinese children (Li, 2012).

Furthermore, although minorities have the rights to use their languages, regional and local officials (who are mostly Han Chinese) made most of the decisions on language usage and language of instruction in the schools. This fact created a wide variety of cognition upon English teaching ideas and teaching methods for bilingual education (Li, 2012), and made it difficult to evaluate the overall effectiveness of bilingual education programs in minority areas (Tan, 2016). The biggest obstacle to bilingual education in China was the lack of qualified teachers (Johnson & Chhetri, 2002).

Multilingual education (encompassing ethnic minority languages, Chinese, and English) for minority students has gained popular support from local ethnic communities to redress educational inequality issues affecting majority and minority groups in China. It is expected that multilingual proficiency will improve students' confidence and expand opportunities for competition with their Han peers (Feng, 2005). The past decade has witnessed a growing demand for multilingual proficiency among ethnic groups, although the state does not coerce minority students to learn an international language (usually English) as they did the Han majority.

The government had come to realize that China's opening up to other countries not only depends on "bilingualism" but also by which the government requires English curriculum to start secondary education in minority districts (Yang, Yang & Lust, 2011). Before the intervention of English teaching, bilingual phenomenon among children in minority areas had already existed (Li, 2012). Bilingual education in China is directed at young language minority learners, namely, the general and outstanding problem in Yunnan province appeared that English was being taught by kindergarten teachers who might understand early childhood education but with low English proficiency and English language teaching proficiency. Consequently, to be successful, the Chinese educational system needs to produce people who are "*both ethnic and expert*"(Postiglione,1999, p.124) and who were required to be proficient in their native language as well as Chinese (Johnson & Chhetri, 2002).

## 2.2　Overview of Multilingual Education in China

### 2.2.1　Definition of Multilingual Education

Being multilingual was a very common phenomenon in many countries all over the world and China is not an exception. Multilingual education was the one in ethnic areas through the medium of multi-languages; it generally encompasses ethnic minority languages, Chinese, and English in the context of China. Multilingualism is an important part of Chinese national education, which plays an indispensable role in promoting the national reunification, ethnic unity and social stability, developing the ethnic culture, accelerating the ethnic civilization, and realizing ethnic modernization (Dai, 2014). In teaching contents, *"trilingualism in China mainly has three: teaching in native tongue, Mandarin and English"* (Gai, 2003, p.83). And the multilingual education in China is aimed at cultivating a large number of multilingual talents for minority areas in China (Dai, 2004). That was to say, ethnic groups with separated mother tongues (native language) in Chinese contexts would take the advantage of three languages education.

Jason, Britta and Ulrike (2001) proposed and presented a typology of multilingual education in primary school based on three criteria: ① the linguistic characteristics of the context in which multilingual education took place by distinguishing monolingual, bilingual and multilingual areas; ② linguistic distance between the languages involved; ③ the simultaneous or consecutive introduction of the three languages at school.

### 2.2.2　Background of Multilingual Education in China and Yunnan

China is a country consisting of 56 officially identified ethnic groups. The central government has issued a series of top-down laws and policies to legitimize and promote the multilingual competencies of ethnic minority learners (Wang, 2015). For example, the Constitution of the PRC declares that *"all ethnic minority groups have freedom to develop their languages"* (National People's Congress, 1982). The 1982 Constitution of China reemphasized the rights of ethnic minority groups in language use, socio-cultural development, and regional autonomy. The national constitution established the legitimate status of ethnic minority groups in China and paved the way for later bilingual education in ethnic minority areas. At present, the concept of bilingual education has been put into practice within the territory of China and guaranteed by various laws and regulations formulated by central and local governments and legislation (Wang, 2015).

Since the founding of the PRC in 1949, the Chinese government has proposed and implemented multilingual education policies. As Adamson and Feng (2008) observed, the PRC had initiated educational language policies to "*foster multilingualism in ethnic minority areas with three goals: to enhance literacy, to assure internal stability and to allow knowledge transfer in order to strengthen the nation*". To achieve these goals, the PRC had issued multilingual policies separately at different historical periods. These policies included promoting Putonghua (Mandarin Chinese) and bilingual education since the 1950s and introducing a third language, English, into the secondary and tertiary curricula in the 1980s. In 2001, English was introduced into the primary school curriculum, and schools with the necessary conditions were required to teach English starting from primary Grade 3 (MOE, 2001). At present, English is not only a required subject at almost all levels of curricula, but also a yardstick for talent selection and quality evaluation for higher learning institutions. In this sense, being multilingual in China was not only an important personal choice for ethnic multilingual learners, but also a reality reflecting the state's political will and national interests (Wang, 2015).

Multilingual education has presented great complexity and diversity because it is affected by a large number of individual and contextual factors and it combined the acquisition of several languages that present different characteristics at the linguistic and social-linguistic levels (Jasone, Britta & Ulrike, 2001). Yunnan, for example, was a frontier province in Southwest China with a great diversity of language, culture, and ethnicity, with 25 officially identified ethnic minority groups living side by side in mixed communities or in compact communities where one or two groups dominate (Yuan, et al., 2015). Among these groups, 15 could be found exclusively in Yunnan and 16 were cross-border ethnic groups, and now Yunnan had 8 minority autonomous prefectures and 29 minority autonomous counties (National Bureau of Statistics of

China, 2011). Yunnan is famous for its ethnic, cultural, and linguistic diversity. The 25 ethnic minority groups in Yunnan speak 26 languages and use 22 scripts, and they live together in a pattern of "*Dazaju Xiaojuju*" (big dispersion and small concentration) (Dao, 2005). This demographic feature had further contributed to the integration of some ethnic minority groups into the mainstream Han and other neighboring ethnic groups throughout history. Given the differences in living environment, population size, community distribution, and socioeconomic development, the language use of ethnic communities was very diversified and complicated (Wang, 2015). Because of geographic isolation and slow socioeconomic development, quite a large number of people in Yunnan cannot communicate in Mandarin till now, which is a disadvantage in seeking better education and working opportunities (Huang & Yu, 2009). Thus, multilingual education in the school curriculum was essential as it "*contributes to enhanced mutual understanding, respect as well as political and economic equality*" (Teng & Wen, 2005, p.268).

To sum up, multilingual education in China which was a government-led educational campaign and policy, aimed at developing the multilingual competence of ethnic minority learners, improving the overall literacy of ethnic minority students, and achieving progress in national socioeconomic development through the public school curriculum (Wang, 2011). The bilingual learning experience would not only help to develop the early literacy of some ethnic groups, but it also would provide them experience in acquiring new languages and access to equal educational opportunities. At the tertiary level, consequently, ethnic minority students were expected to master not only generic skills, but also multilingual proficiency in the national language (Chinese) and to some extent, English (Huang & Yu, 2009).

### 2.2.3　Minorities' Attitudes to Multilingual Education

Learning English as a third language was common in the multilingual communities of most part of China. Namely, the minority students must learn English in addition to their minority languages and standard Chinese. However, with the unbalanced distribution of educational resources, the shortage of professional English teachers and the limitation of English learning materials, most English courses led to quite difficult English learning for minority students (Feng, 2005). From the survey of multilingual education in Leshan Ebian Yi Autonomous County of China, Huang (2013) indicated that the minority students were incompetent in English communication, which contributed great influence on the minority students' interest in learning English. The multilingual education materials were not attractive since the textbooks and teaching methods were commonly designed in traditional educational approaches (Feng, 2005). Still, there were no specific multilingual educational strategies for each nationality in educational policy-making (Huang, 2013).

In sum, multilingual education was not a new phenomenon but was becoming more widespread because of the mainstream of introducing a foreign language from an earlier age and a second foreign language at the end of primary school or in secondary school and the increasing use of minority languages in education in many parts of the world (Jasone, Britta & Ulrike, 2001). It was admitted that English instruction in such ethnic minority regions had not received the deserved treatment as required, for the English teaching content could not satisfy the minority learners' thirsts for knowledge, which was contributed of their different cultural backgrounds. It was also obvious that the students' ideological knowledge systems were completely constructed from their ethnic culture and family education. From Huang's survey (2013), the attitude of minority students towards multilingual education had been badly influenced, by which could be manifested as: (1) nearly all the students preferred Chinese while many of them felt exhausted in English learning; (2) they all neglected their ethnic language learning because they thought that it was not widely used in their daily life and it was not helpful to the College Entrance Examination; (3) many minority students claimed that English was widely used as an international language but they did not need to learn it. All above indifferent attitudes to English learning have greatly influenced English teaching.

### 2.2.4   Instruction of Multilingual Education in China

Drawbacks above lead English instruction in ethnic minority regions in a predicament. When learning some foreign language, bilinguals were more pragmatic functional and productive than monolinguals (Jorda, 2005). However, it turned out that ethnic minority students failed in competing with Han students in English learning because of the following teaching instructions (Feng, 2005):

First, in China, the National English Curriculum Standards declared in 2001 was designed to promote Chinese learners' overall quality, without considering the status of minority learners (Zhang, 2012). Because they lacked interest and confidence in English learning, including lack of teaching resources, many minority learners could not meet the high learning goals designed according to the National English Curriculum Standards.

Second, compared with the mother tongue, the context problem was another barrier to second language acquisition for minority learners (Jorda, 2005). Because of the unbalanced education resource distribution, minority learners' indifferent attitude towards English learning and some incorrect English teaching approaches, it was hard to establish a suitable second language acquisition (SLA) context in ethnic minority regions (Jorda, 2005).

In fact, learning languages meant learning part of the culture that belonged to other groups and this process was influenced by inter-group relationships that were affected by social, political and historical factors (Feng, 2007). The spread of English might be viewed in terms of three concentric circles representing the types of spread, the patterns of acquisition and the functional domains in which English was used across cultures and languages (Kachru, 1996).

Some scholars (Feng, 2005; Hu, 2007; Yang, 2005; Yuan, 2007) have pointed out that the bilingual experiences of ethnic minority learners seemed to contribute little to English education in Yunnan multi-ethnic areas. Their research suggested that the English learning outcomes of ethnic minority students were unsatisfactory and that positive attitudes and motivation needed to be cultivated (Hu, 2007; Yuan, 2007). These findings agreed with Yang's argument concerning the impact of L2 learning on multilingual learning: "*Such a positive second language influence on multilingual learning does not seem to apply to many of China's minority students*" (Yang, 2005, p.26). Given the national policies on language, ethnicity, education, and socioeconomic development, it was necessary to reconceptualize ethnic minority learners in the ever changing sociocultural discourse of contemporary China.

At the tertiary level, minority students were required to acquire English as a third language in a mostly Han-dominated learning environment. Their teachers usually instructed them in the same way as they did Han students, without considering the difference in linguistic context and distance (Ytsma, 2001). As a result, the ethnic minority learners had to struggle to negotiate their identities under the tension caused by the highly demanding curriculum and unfamiliar learning environment. This information could make a solid contribution to the design of more relevant language policies, teaching practices, and learning resources. This would help pave the way for future in-depth research.

### 2.2.5　Development of Multilingual Education in China

With China's Opening up since the 1980s, ethnic minority languages have increasingly faced an assault from English challenges (Feng & Adamson, 2015). Acquisition of an international language had been strongly embraced by the state government for modernization and economic development. Although the term "trilingual education" (ethnic language, Chinese, and English) has not yet been overtly referred to in official state policies and rhetoric, it increasingly received widespread attention among ethnic groups (Zhao, 2010). Apart from Chinese, which was the national and second language, English had been promoted to a significant position as an international language. With the addition of English, language learning at schools had progressed, and subsequently, language learning is now trilingual. Language proficiency and capability were closely related to education, and the arrangement of the curriculum and the subjects included in a course of study could have a substantial effect on language acquisition and learning (Feng & Adamson, 2015). A primary reason was that parents, ethnic intellectuals, and local government officials worried that denial of international languages might exacerbate educational inequalities between the majority and minority groups (Beckett & MacPherson, 2005).

The spread of English in China and its introduction into all levels of the curriculum, together with the above-mentioned policies on promoting bilingual education, has led to a multilingual education policy for ethnic minority learners. As a result, ethnic minority learners were expected to acquire three languages: their native language, Chinese, and English. These goals were presented as a collaborative policy in the development of multilingualism (Cummins, 2009). However, the implementation of these policies faced great challenges. For example, at the primary level, the introduction of English to ethnic students was influenced by various factors such as teacher availability, curriculum organization, sustainable financing, technical support, and local attitude. Unlike the policies promoting Putonghua and ethnic minority languages, which are enforced by legislation, the teaching of English as a compulsory subject at primary school was only a proposal of the MOE (Lam, 2007), which applied to schools only when the teaching conditions permitted. Research showed that the English curriculum at the primary level had not been completely implemented even in some developed areas, such as Zhejiang and Guangdong provinces (Hu, 2008). Therefore, the degree and effect of English education for primary school ethnic learners needed further observation and evaluation.

In contrast to students in primary schools, where there is little pressure to learn English, most ethnic minority students in tertiary institutions face real challenges in acquiring English as a third language in comparison to Han students who only need to master two languages (Putonghua and English). These challenges could be detected in minority students' English foundation, impact of negative language transfer, culture shock, tension with the curriculum and psychological problems, to mention just a few.

Additionally, the exposure of minority students to the English language was far later than that of their Han cohorts, who usually started to learn English at or even before elementary school. This could be attributed to the lack of funding and resources which were critical for the development of English proficiency in ethnic minority communities (e.g., Feng, 2005; Li & Zhou, 2005; Yang, 2005; Jiang, Liu, Quan, & Ma, 2007). Groups including Tibetans, Kazakhs, and Mongols have made attempts to implement multilingual courses in primary and secondary schools, generally called an "experimental multilingual class"(Zhao, 2010). This innovative program also received criticism. Some say minority students had more burdens than the Han, others claimed their achievements in Chinese and English came at the expense of their mother tongue, and it had been said that there were shortages of qualified teachers and teaching materials (Jie'ensi, 2004; Yuan, et al., 2015).

## 2.3   Overall Situation of EFL Education in China

Foreign language education is increasingly important for the sake of preparing children to be successful and capable of a high level of social integration. English as a language, on account of its current status as a foreign language, has became a top priority of many educational systems (Habeeb, 2013). Teaching English as a foreign language (EFL) is very different from Teaching English as a second language (ESL) in China (Huang, 2006). In ESL settings, such as in the United States and the United Kingdom, English learners are learning English, the predominant language in the linguistic environment of the target language (English), but EFL learners were learning it as a subject at school in the linguistic environment of their native languages such as Chinese in China (Zhang, 2004).

Since 2001, the Ministry of Education of China has engaged in curriculum reforms of all subjects at all levels. A nine-year compulsory education system had been set up to assess students' English proficiency from third grade up to high school. Accordingly, English, as a foreign language, had gained significant status in China, especially in recent passing decades. Yan (2002, p.29) in his World Englishes stated, *"China is a big country, and the number of people who study of lessons, but also of effects on the education in China and other aspects such as our national language and social life. English has been involved in China's education. Therefore, it is necessary for people to form a macro-view of the English language in China."* The number of people who study English has rapidly grown in the past decade as the principal foreign language taught in China, receiving a high status as the global medium of education, travel, entertainment, e-communication, and business (McArthur, 2002). In our modern community, it is clear to see that so many children are studying English in primary schools, even in kindergartens. The Ministry of Education constituted and published *Guidelines on Actively Promoting English Teaching at Elementary Schools* (MOE, 2001b), which indicated that based on the personalities of primary learners, therefore, it was important to create teaching methods which gave priority to class activities. As the most important foreign language, English was widely taught in primary schools, high schools, and universities in China, even middle-aged and senior people could not reject this trend (Yan, 2002).

However, some people claimed that the English language has occupied their life too much, and they felt dissatisfied with the English teaching under the background of the examination-oriented system in China. One popular topic for discussion was the "long-time but low-efficiency" of English teaching (Yan, 2002). Moreover, the teaching of English is relatively laggard in many places in China, and even many university students could not speak fluent English, it seemed meaningless for university students to take such examinations like CET-4, CET-6 (College English Test) or TEM-4 and TEM-8 (Test for English Major) (MOE, 2004). More or less, it was too extreme for people to have such an idea, even though many Chinese people did want to study English well. However, it is urgent for Chinese people to find an effective way of studying English. There was some innovation in the forms of such examinations, and actually it was a good phenomenon (Lam, 2002).

This fact gave us an alarm as to how English teaching could be effective in China and how Chinese people should view English studying. Assessments of academic achievement are most commonly conducted through exams and tests in China (MOE, 2004). Besides the subject exam in the entrance examination to higher level schools, such as the National College Entrance Exams, other exam systems were set up to assess students' English proficiency. All non-English majors have to pass the Band Four Test before they could graduate. At the college level, non-English majors were required to take intensive reading of English for at least two years (MOE, 2004). However, intensive reading should not be taken literally; it was actually a comprehensive English course which pays attention to the skills of listening, speaking, reading, writing, translating, and vocabulary building.

With China's entry into WTO and Beijing's hosting of the 2008 Olympics, the Chinese people were even more open to external influences. The role of English in the international exchange ensured only be enhanced (Lam, 2002). It gave Chinese people not only a challenge but also the opportunity to face this situation. English, as the first foreign language which had been studied by so many Chinese people, would certainly be developed in China. Everybody learned English in the Chinese Way, it was called Chinese English (or Chinglish) (Zhang, 2004). The Chinese Way consisted of memorizing English words as translations of words and phrases in the native language. Knowing the words did not mean that learners would be able to communicate in English or understand when someone spoke to them in English. When a learner continued thinking in his native language and tried to translate his thoughts into English to produce an English sentence, he failed. While 56% of Chinese university students not majoring in English spent most of their time studying English, fewer than 5% of them could carry on a conversation in it (Lam, 2002), this was the so-called mute English in China.

The Chinese way of learning English was a classic example of passive learning. It has survived for a long time because we still are not aware of what we could gain when we move from passive to active learning of English. On the other hand, most English teachers were native Chinese speakers who had learned English in China from Chinese English teachers. And these teachers usually had to teach large classes with very little technical support. A typical class in a Chinese school had 40 to 60 students or more. The large class size made it harder to employ teaching methods that require attention to the individual student and required different classroom management techniques (Lam, 2002). Moreover, while there were at least chalk and a blackboard, access to tape recorders, VCRs, overhead projectors, language labs, or computers might be very limited or unavailable, especially in ethnic communities (Zhang, 2004). Similarly, under the encouragement of the Chinese government, more and more ethnic groups began to accept English as their main foreign language and more and more young learners began to learn English as well. But as lack of qualified English teachers and a test-oriented educational system, it was a long way to go for English as a foreign language education in China (Zhang, 2012).

## 2.4　The Controversy of EFL Education

### 2.4.1　Overseas' Perceptions of EFL Education

In this globalized world, acquiring two or more languages is undoubtedly beneficial in one's life, and there is little objection to the idea that the more languages one speaks, the better opportunities one could get in this era (Wu, 2002). However, opinions are divided on the practices in bilingual education, particularly regarding the best time to start bilingual education.

It has been widely believed that the age of onset of additional language learning is a crucial key factor to be successful (DeKeyser, 2000; Sington & Muñoz, 2011). Generally speaking, children's second language (L2) learning seemed to be relatively easy as compared to adults' L2 learning, which was regarded as more difficult (Breathnach, 1993). Breathnach (1993) described late learners' L2 learning as *"lack of success"* *"lack of inevitable perfect mastery"* and *"general failure"* (p.43~44). Even though many studies had revealed contradicting results against the common belief that earlier was better in L2 learning, it was generally less challenging for children than for adults (Muñoz, 2011). Early starting of L2 education raised concerns related to children's development, such as cognitive, emotional, language, and identity development (Sington & Muñoz, 2011). It was a pervasive idea in the past that early bilingual education entailed cognitive disadvantages (Baker, 2000). The beliefs remained in many countries that early bilingual education negatively affected children's psychological/emotional development (Wu, 2002) and confusion of national and cultural identities (Jang, 2008). Research into whether or not early bilingual education was beneficial remains controversial with conflicting results.

In terms of foreign language (FL) learning, early introduction of EFL education seemed to be regarded as one of the keys to increase successful results in FL learning. Many countries in Europe and Asia had lowered the students' age for compulsory FL learning at school (Enever, 2007). For example, Korea was one of the countries in Asia that recognizes the importance of L2 education at an early age and officially lowered students' age of starting EFL from 13 to 9 in 1995. Since then, early EFL education had received great attention from parents and had greatly expanded in the private educational market in Korea. However, along with a greater interest in EFL education, concerns had been raised. A recent issue of Guardian Weekly (Shim & Park, 2008) stated that South Korean parents told preschool English "harmful". This headline showed how EFL had been a controversial issue in Korea. According to the article, an education activist group named *World Without Worries About Private Education* had distributed pamphlets to Korean parents in order to convince the parents that teaching English before the age of ten could negatively affect children's cognitive and language development. The group has been persuading many Korean parents that they were wasting their money and effort on futile and even harmful EFL education for their children. Also, Shim and Park (2008) claimed that the Korean English fever could only cause *"class division between the 'English-rich' haves and 'English-poor' have-nots"* (p.154). Moreover, there were still anxieties about starting EFL education early, especially in terms of loss of national identity, confusion between two languages and cultures, and psychological pressure from a new language (Enever, 2007).

Although these concerns were prevalent, EFL education for kindergarten learners had been rapidly increased in Korea (Enever, 2007). A current survey found that 95.6% of 262 private kindergartens in Korea conducted EFL education (Kim, 2008). Ironically, however, most English classes in kindergartens were operated by visiting English teachers who were not qualified in early childhood education (Enever, 2007). Moreover, the Ministry of Education of Korea did not declare explicitly and authoritatively that kindergartens could provide English education and many experts in early childhood education showed a negative stance towards EFL education in kindergartens (Jang, 2002; Wu, 2002). Consequently, EFL education had been subjected to skepticism because there had been no academic review or expert consultation of EFL education in kindergartens (Wu, 2002). Given the concerns about the increasing demand for EFL education and current methodological and practical problems, some researchers (Kim, 2009) asserted that arguing about the pros and cons of EFL education should not be a subject of discussion anymore; rather, the focus should be on how to effectively implement EFL education (Ahn & Kim, 2009). Ahn and Kim (2009) even suggested that EFL education in kindergartens could be a good start toward equalizing English education opportunities for all children.

## 2.4.2   Domestic Debate of EFL Education

Varying from overseas' perspectives about EFL education in kindergarten, the development of the EFL education in China could be illustrated with three steps longitudinally.

In the first step, with regard to the controversy over the feasibility and necessity of EFL education in kindergarten, there were two groups: the supporters and the opponents (Lin, 2008).

The supporters held the following reasons for starting early: (1) Children learned English with better physical conditions (Gao, 2009; Yang, 2007); (2) Children had good psychological advantages (Wu, 2002; Yu, 2000); (3) Children could better develop other intelligence (Fu & Zhong, 2013; Jang, 2008); (4) Early acquisition of English learning could enhance children's basic English thinking habit, learning methods and learning abilities (Fu & Zhong, 2013; Wu, 2005; Yu, 2000), as a result, they were bound to show a strong momentum after they gradually accepted the systematic EFL education during the period of primary school even middle school (Fu, 2006); (5) Present social conditions, economic conditions and technical conditions had met the requirements of learning English for children in China, therefore, modern management and technical means could be utilized to create a better learning environment for children (Wei, 2005; Wu, 2002). Additionally, teaching English to young learners was different compared to teaching English to adults or young adult learners; they were more enthusiastic in the classrooms (Yu, 2000; Lin, 2008). In learning a new language, children had no awareness of grammatical mistakes and were less embarrassed to talk and they also tended to speak like natives due to their lack of inhibition (Cameron, 2001).

Early studies of second or foreign language learning argue that there is a critical period or sensitive period, prior to puberty in which children can acquire native-like proficiency in a foreign language (Oyama, 1976). That perspective found ready acceptance among adults who thought children could pick up a language easily, often remembering their frustration at not having mastered another language (Lv & Wang, 2007).

On the contrary, the opponents deemed: (1) Lack of learning environment for EFL education, which led to less efficiency (Lin, 2008; Wu, 2005); (2) Children might have a keen sense of listening, psychological and physical advantages, but also have obvious disadvantages in cognitive ability, sustainability, stability of long-term memory, learning motivation, and comprehension of social culture about English speaking countries, and so on (Yu, 2000); (3) Learning English spent too long and much time while the efficiency was not high, and easily confused with Chinese (Lin, 2008; Wei, 2005).

In the second step, some researchers (Lin, 2008; Wei, 2005; Zhou, 2004) concluded that children learning English was a symbol of China's opening to the world, and EFL education is an inevitable trend after a period of debate. Therefore, we should hold a positive attitude to promote development of children's EFL education to a mature and healthy direction (Lv & Wang, 2007). As Zhou Jing (2004), a professor from East China Normal University, said: *"With the developing trend of economic globalization, China, as the Asian economic leader, has become a multicultural society which attracts the world's eye. The potential diversity of languages is a distinct characteristic of multicultural society, and English as a global language is paid more attention. From now on, setting EFL education in the kindergarten is an irreversible trend"* (p.4).

However, the concerned administrative department of education had not brought the childrens EFL education into the whole management system (Zhu, 2007). It firstly lacked more attention on the children's EFL education, and it did not make a unified arrangement and requirements for children's EFL education, nor did it have reasonable evaluation criteria (Zhu, 2007). Concretely speaking, there was no uniform curriculum standards, teaching materials, evaluation criteria, so that children's EFL education appeared chaotic, irregular and unsystematic phenomenon, which was not conducive to the sustainable development of EFL education in China (Zhu, 2007). Furthermore, children's English teachers training had become the key to restrict the development of EFL education smoothly and effectively (Tan, 2006). At present, the domestic research on children EFL education mainly focused on the feasibility and necessity of English teaching, practical and theoretical research (Fu, 2006; Lv & Wang, 2007; Wu, 2005; Yu, 2000), while lacked of systematic research on the cultivation and training of preschool English teachers, few experts and scholars had systematically explored this issue (Tan, 2006; Wei, 2005; Zhu, 2007). English teachers' education appeared a serious lag, affecting the further development of children's EFL education (Wei, 2005).

On the other hand, the training for preschool English teachers had brought great challenges because of its particularity (Zhu, 2007). Preschool English education as a part of children's education, it required that English teachers should have professional knowledge and competence of both preschool teachers and English teachers (Lin,

2008). One has to know the rules and characteristics of children's physical and psychological development. The teachers could develop educational plans, select suitable educational contents and materials, and organize live and vivid activities according to the development status of preschool education in order to promote the comprehensive and all-around development of children's quality. The other was to possess a solid foundation of English basic knowledge, standard pronunciation, rich vocabulary and flexible use, moreover, the teachers could be familiar with the cultural background, customs, traditions of the English-speaking countries, and so on (Zhu, 2007). However, high-quality English teachers with the above knowledge and ability at the same time were very scarce, which could not meet the needs of the development of children's EFL education in China (Lin, 2008).

The third step was a stage of exploration. How to teach English teachers? How to learn for children? And what kind of EFL education was suitable for children's health development? They were becoming the hot issues in present process of children EFL education, and it was worthy of exploring for most preschool staff (Zhu, 2007). At present, the training of kindergarten English teacher in China's normal universities is still in the initial exploration period, there was no systematic, complete and effective training mode (Wang, 2012). As Luo and Lu (2003) described, a huge contradiction between the demand of training for children English teachers and the lag of training model for kindergarten English teachers in such normal universities or colleges had been formed for a long time. The preschool institutions could not find excellent English teachers while the training model for kindergarten English teachers in normal universities or colleges could not meet the demand of present kindergartens. It was imperative to reform the training model for preschool English teacher in Normal Universities (Luo & Lu, 2003; Wang, 2012).

## 2.5  Teacher Quality and Professional Development

Before addressing literature relevant to understanding standards for language teachers, it is important to clearly differentiate these two terms 'quality teachers' and 'quality teaching' (Catherine, 2015). 'Quality teachers' referred to issues relevant to teachers' knowledge and practices in language teaching and discussion, they often assumed that quality teaching was solely dependent on the levels of attainment of individual teachers. 'Quality teaching', as a critical factor in the improvement of student learning, however, saw that effective teaching relies on many factors of which the knowledge base of the teacher is only one factor. The process of effective teaching—teaching that directly leads to student learning of standards-based content—was tenuous at best and easily disrupted by contextual and behavioral factors (Catherine, 2015). Highly skilled teachers might be prevented from offering quality teaching by the situations in which they found themselves working—their teaching conditions, the fragmented nature of their employment, the restrictions placed on their language programs by timetabling, resourcing, etc (Anthony, 2006). There was no firm consensus within the field as to exactly what constitutes quality teaching or a quality teacher (Hightower, et al., 2011). However, it would be useful to establish a working definition of teacher quality for the purposes of the current research. The clearest and potentially most useful example identified in our review of the literature comes from the Center for High Impact Philanthropy (2010):

*A quality teacher is one who has a positive effect on student learning and development through a combination of content mastery, command of a broad set of pedagogic skills, and communications or interpersonal skills. Quality teachers are life-long learners in their subject areas, teach with commitment, and are reflective upon their teaching practice* (p.7).

While this definition could apply to teachers working with students of all ages, few topics in education have captured as much attention from policymakers and practitioners as the connection between teaching quality and student achievement. It has clearly shown that quality teaching matters to student's learning (Anthony, 2006). Teacher quality has been consistently identified as the most important school-based factor in student achievement (McCaffrey, Lockwood, Koretz, & Hamilton, 2003; Rivkin, Hanushek & Kain, 2000; Rowan, Correnti & Miller, 2002; Wright, Horn & Sanders, 1997), and teacher effect on student learning had been found to be cumulative and long-lasting (McCaffrey, et al., 2003; Mendro, et al., 1998).

Even though to provide quality teaching, a program should be supported with such other factors as institution, teachers, teaching process and learners, among those factors, it was the teachers who held a prominent role in teaching (Richards, 2001).

Teachers, therefore, could be said as the most important factor in determining the success of teaching-learning process (Hightower, et al., 2011). The teacher's quality of young learners could be said as the most important factor not only to bring success of the teaching process but also to promote student achievement (Habibi & Sofwan, 2015).

The concept of competence was a relatively new approach that structures the vision of teaching. According to Verma, et al. (2006, p.48), *"competencies in education create an environment that fosters empowerment, accountability, and performance evaluation, which is consistent and equitable. The acquisition of competencies can be through talent, experience, or training"*. Yusuf (2007) indicated that the improvement of teachers in terms of English proficiency should be considered as matters due to the importance of teachers' quality to produce students with high quality. In addition, Richard (2011) emphasized that a successful quality teacher should have both professional and pedagogical competence in teaching English to young learners. The professional competence includes English proficiency, teacher certification or license, trainings, etc, and the pedagogical one was about ability to teach young learners. In other words, teachers' competence included *"the right way of conveying units of knowledge, application and skills to students"* (Singh, 2015, p.1632). Singh (2015) recommended that direct information about teacher effectiveness was not available; many teacher evaluations were based on information about teacher competence or teacher performance. To sum up, teaching competence is the sum total of all the competencies possessed by the teacher that are used in the teaching situation (Singh, 2015).

The educational system in India has recently attracted the attention of educators all over the world, as it had achieved tremendous success in all fields. What was the secret behind the success of the Indian experience? Ahmed (2011) indicated that the teacher professional development of India was the result of the quality of students, and the teacher training was behind all of that success.

In the educational reform of the new millennium around the world, teachers are regarded as both the objects and subjects of change, thus making teacher's professional development became an ever-growing and challenging area that had received much focus in the past years (Ganser, 2000). On studying the recent educational literature, it could be generally concluded that teacher's professional development included opportunities for educators to discuss, think about, try out, and hone new practices in an environment that values inquiry (Guskey, 2000). Professional development included formal experiences (such as attending professional meetings, collegiate discussion and cooperation in workshops, guiding novice teachers etc.) and informal experiences (such as reading professional publications, watching teaching television documentaries related to an academic discipline, etc. (Ganser, 2000). This concept of professional development was, therefore, broader than career development, which is defined as *"the growth that occurs as the teacher moves through the professional career cycle"* (Glatthorn, 1995, p.41), and broader than staff development, which was *"the provision of organized in-service programmes designed to foster the growth of groups of teachers; it is only one of the systematic interventions that can be used for teacher development"* (Glatthorn, 1995, p.41). When looking at professional development, one must examine the content of the experiences, the processes by which the professional development would occur, and the contexts in which it would take place (Ganser, 2000).

To summarize, the new tendency of teacher professional development is the traditional in-service training being replaced by a long-term process which emphasizes regular systematically planned opportunities and activities to promote the growth and development of their profession (Ganser, 2000). This new path moved educators away from a view of teaching as a solitary activity, owned personally by each teacher. The view of teaching profession could be regarded as the activity with open access to cooperative observations, learning, and improving their teaching capability (Glatthorn, 1995). It made common teachers realize and accept the notion that they were responsible for honing not only their own practice but also the shared activities of their colleagues. For the newly explored path, however, teachers would need to open their classroom doors and study their practices as a professional responsibility, rather than only evaluating each other (Hiebert, Gallimore & Stigler, 2003). Because successful professional development experiences had a noticeable impact on teachers' teaching quality, both in and out of the classroom, especially considering that a significant number of teachers throughout the world were under-prepared for their profession (Henning, 2000).

## 2.6　Professionalism of Kindergarten English Teachers

Based on the investigation of present literature reviews, the main focus was more on the macro studies on basic elements of this occupation of English teachers in terms of the quality, while less on the English teachers' professional quality in English language teaching (Lan, 2012; Lin, 2008). Namely, there was no clear expression and definition of the requirement of professional quality for English teachers, particularly, lacked of more comprehensive and systematic exposition about the requirements of kindergarten English teachers' professional quality in the new period of an explosion of teaching English to younger learners all around the world, Chinese included.

A kindergarten English teacher was first a teacher; he/she should have ordinary qualities which included knowledge, skills, emotional maturity and other aspects of the quality. Therefore, good moral quality, broad culture and knowledge quality, experienced teaching ability, healthy physical and mental state should also be included in the basic quality structure for kindergarten English teachers (Lan, 2012; Lin, 2008).

The professional quality of kindergarten English teachers was an important part of the quality of kindergarten teachers, which was a relationship between individuality and commonness (Lan, 2012; Lin, 2008). "Professionalism" here mainly included two meanings: one refers to the special occupation of preschool teachers, and the other refers to the professional division of disciplines, namely English language subject that the teacher was teaching. According to the nature of younger learner's English education and the uniqueness of target learners during the age of 3~6 in kindergarten, the professional quality of kindergarten English teachers was defined as the sum of professional attitude, professional knowledge and professional ability and so on (Bakarman, 2011), which a kindergarten English teacher should possess while engaging in teaching the English language in kindergarten.

With regard to the professional quality of kindergarten English teachers, Lin (2008) elaborated respectively: the professional attitude includes occupational emotion and educational belief; the professional knowledge includes the knowledge of early childhood education and the knowledge of preschool English education; the professional knowledge of preschool English teachers also included the theoretical basis of English education and the comprehensive linguistic basis; the professional competence of preschool English teachers included teaching abilities and scientific research ability, among teaching ability consists of these abilities of teaching design, teaching implementation and teaching evaluation. Teaching techniques mainly included music and dance, painting and writing, acting and performance, playing games, story-telling, and other application of modern educational technology, etc. Among the classification of all professional abilities, teaching ability was the core competence of preschool English teachers had been recognized evidently (Lin, 2008).

According to the relevant knowledge of English methodology and general pedagogy, we believe that the general requirements for the professional quality of preschool are to possess a solid theoretical basis and comprehensive language proficiency, namely to master the basic English linguistic knowledge of pronunciation, vocabulary, grammar and cultural background, and so on. The English teachers could organize English teaching activities skillfully with solid and basic language functions, such as listening, speaking, reading and writing, at the same time, they could sing and dance, paint and write, act and perform as well to create a rich, authentic, harmonious English learning environment with good psychological quality. Altogether, all above mentioned are essential professional qualities for preschool English teachers (Lin, 2008).

Therefore, a framework of professional qualities for preschool English teachers could be set up as the basis for investigation, interview and observation of the study by comparing, analyzing and integrating the previous researches (Lin, 2008; Yang, 2012). Three main dimensions were distributed in the conceptual framework of professional qualities of preschool English teachers as shown in Figure 2.1, they were professional attitude, professional knowledge, and professional competence, and each had different specific branches.

Scholar Wu (2005) suggested the professional quality framework of excellent foreign language teachers consists of four dimensions: (1) the teaching ability of foreign language disciplines; (2) occupation ideology and occupation morality of foreign language teachers; (3) conception of foreign language teaching; (4) conception of foreign language teachers' learning and development. Teaching methods of English subject should not be a pure theory, but putting the cultivation of students' teaching ability in foreign language teaching in the first place, increasing the intensity of teaching practice. The initiation of theoretical knowledge should serve to the cultivation of teaching ability.

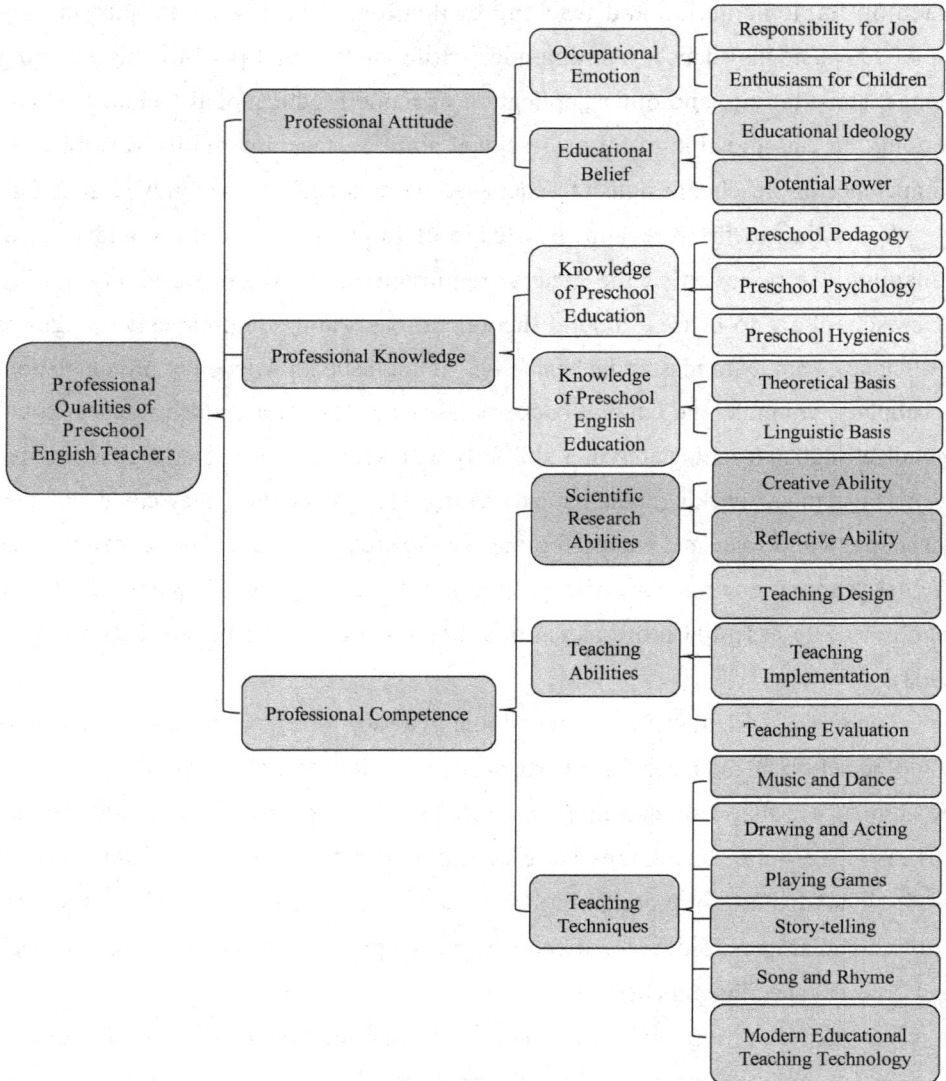

**Figure 2.1**　A Framework of Professional Qualities of Preschool English
Teachers (*Source:* Adapted from Lin, 2008; Yang, 2012)

Thus, the general requirements of professional quality of preschool English teachers could be summarized as: (1) holding the enthusiasm and passion for children, which is the most important characteristic for teachers of early childhood development (Kristine, 2017), and positive responsibility for job, steady educational beliefs and emotion for occupation affection; (2) mastering some certain knowledge of educational theories and the knowledge including pronunciation, vocabulary, grammar and English basic knowledge and cultural background knowledge; (3) having the ability not only to deal with the children's daily teaching problems, but also to manipulate the English language teaching (ELT) proficiency; (4) simultaneously, having the application ability of modern educational means and teaching technologies such as singing, dancing, painting, acting, performance, etc; (5) last but not least, possessing advanced educational and linguistic theories and creative and reflective teaching research ability (Wu, 2005).

## 2.7　English Language Teaching Proficiency

### 2.7.1　Importance of English Language Teaching Proficiency

Cullen (1994) stated the need to improve English teachers' own command of the language so that they could use it more fluently, and above all, more confidently, in the classroom. Lange (1990) concluded that English language proficiency indeed constitutes the bedrock of the professional confidence of non-native English teachers, and language competence has been rated as the most essential characteristic of a good teacher. Berry (1990) conducted a study of two groups of English teachers teaching at the secondary level in Poland. He wished to discern which of three components (methodology, theory of language teaching, or language improvement) they needed most. Language teaching improvement was ranked as the most important for both groups, and methodology was second, while the two groups rank theory a poor third. Fahmy and Bilton (1992) examined the undergraduate, teaching-English-as-a-foreign-language (TEFL) education program at Sultan Qaboos University in Oman. They found that students there were aware of their need to improve their English language skills, and they recommended language support in the program for as long as needed.

Berry (1990) also discussed the dual functions of language teaching improvement. He said that the first function was obvious, i.e., raising the teacher's level of proficiency; and the second function was very subtle and consisted of providing effective teaching models when changes were desired in teaching practices. Murdoch (1994) suggested that teacher-training programs should think more in terms of activities that would help develop both the pedagogical skills of the trainees and their language teaching proficiency. He cited the need to reduce the hours of study of other subjects in the curriculum (e.g., educational psychology and principles of education) in order to reserve more time for language study. Extracurricular reading programs that could have a significant impact on the level of competency achieved were another alternative suggested.

The results of the survey demonstrated clearly that training for language teaching proficiency should be the foundation of the trainees' ability to fulfill their professional roles. In addition, the survey suggested that in order to produce more competent teachers, training programs should place more emphasis on language training, primarily at the beginning of the training program. Buchmann (1984) claimed a foreign language teacher's lack of proficiency led students to believe that learning a foreign language consists of the completion of textbook activities rather than learning the language for the purpose of communication.

Those involved in planning teachers' programs should be concerned with the low level of English proficiency among prospective EFL teachers and should adopt approaches that would overcome the problem (Diógenes, 2001). Schrier (1994) stated that teacher-preparation programs usually divide their preparation in three ways: general, specialist, and professional education. Foreign language departments had the most influence in the area of specialist education because of the content knowledge preparation or simply the knowledge base. In the field of teacher education, content was usually the component that received the least attention, according to Lafayette (1993), he went on to say that this lacked attention to the subject matter for teacher preparation was due to the fact.

English language teaching proficiency was the most important component of content knowledge. The American Council on the Teaching of Foreign Languages' provisional program guidelines for FLT education, in the area of specialist development, stated that the FLT education program should provide students with opportunities to develop competence in speaking, listening, reading, and writing (Diógenes, 2001). Morain (1990), however, pointed out that educating the foreign language teacher is not the responsibility of a single segment of academe, (language proficiency for example) but rather the combination of four components, which are: (1) required language courses; (2) courses in the content areas; (3) courses in pedagogy; (4) in-school experiences. Schrier (1994), on the other hand, outlined four characteristics desirable in future foreign-language teachers. These were: (1) proficiency in the foreign language and its cultures; (2) proficiency in the language and culture of the school's community; (3) expertise in curricular design and its implementation; (4) technological sophistication. Schrier (1994) suggested that influences on teacher development, as well as the extent to which teachers presented their knowledge to others, could be traced by examining these four characteristics. Schrier (1994) stated that *"the role that the foreign language community plays in this process goes beyond providing content knowledge. It is the way professors organize and deliver this knowledge that provides future teachers with the scripts for understanding the structure and process of learning a language"* (p.71). The most important and thorough document known to professionals in the field of teaching English as a foreign/second language was the *Teachers of English to Speakers of Other Languages* (TESOL) *Guidelines*. This document, which was the foundation of the required principles of teacher-preparation programs, came together through the contributions of several TESOL experts. Morain (1990) suggested that we need courses designed to increase oral fluency, such as the art of story-telling, or a course in role-playing and dramatics, which were more suitable for the kindergarten students.

## 2.7.2   Components of English Language Teaching Proficiency

In view of the particularity of preschool English education, I expected to develop such a training module in consideration of the practical situation of course learning in a real setting by combining the proposed training modules (Lin, 2008; Pan, 2012; Wang, 2012; Yang, 2002; Zuo, 2012). Therefore, the expected training module of ELT proficiency should be comprised of the following four components:

(1) Linguistic basic knowledge (such as pronunciation, listening ability and spoken English). Learning pronunciation well in the first place is the most important and basic factor in language acquisition. Gimson (1962, cited in Wang, 2009) stated when a person spoke a language, he/she had to learn almost 100% pronunciation of the language, while he/she just needed to learn 50~90% grammar and 1% vocabulary. Phonetic learning directly affected the ability of oral expression and listening comprehension ability for the children's development (Wang, 2009). Compared with adults, childhood was a key implicit period of learning, and the huge deformability of speech, strong imitative ability and reproductive ability, could easily form good pronunciation and intonation, which had great advantages in second language acquisition (Tian, 2007).

(2) Teaching design (such as the application of syllabus and textbooks, teaching plan). English teaching design was the application of instructional design theory in English subjects. Teaching design was the core of improving teaching quality and teaching efficiency (Harmer, 2000). For the lack of efficient instruction, many English teachers feel very confused about how to teach English, some just conduct the teaching randomly. For the young learners, the main way of English learning was following teacher's direction. So, if teachers knew how to make a good teaching design and teach English well, children would learn it well. However, some studies related to children's English instructional design remain superficial (Zhang, 2007).

(3) Teaching implementation (such as selection of teaching methods and activity organization). The teaching design, organization and implementation of children's English education should follow the characteristics of children's growth and development, seize the children's curiosity, arouse children's emotion and affection, create a relaxed, interesting, vivid and realistic learning environment, adopt intuitive teaching aids and interesting teaching methods, and stimulate children's interest in learning English. Only scientific, reasonable teaching design and implementation might optimize English teaching and learning for children (Li, 2006).

(4) Teaching techniques (such as storytelling, playing games, songs and rhymes, stick figures, English handwriting, tongue twisters, modern educational teaching technologies, etc.). *Teaching Guidelines for Preschool Education* (MOE, 2001a)

stated that language proficiency developed in the process of language application. The key development was to create a language environment which could make them want to say, dare to say, love to say, and can get a positive response. The main purpose of English teaching was to cultivate children's interests in English learning and had a good sense of language. Therefore, an appropriate learning atmosphere with visual and auditory and other educational multimedia technologies could stimulate children to join the classroom efficiently (Zhang, 2007). Li (2012) also claimed the application of multimedia technology in English teaching in kindergartens was the trend of modern educational reform and development. Its appearance remedied the defects of traditional English teaching for young children and it was approved by the parents and children.

*The New Standards of English Curriculum* (MOE, 2001) clearly stipulated that the task of English curriculum among basic education is to inspire and cultivate students' interest in learning English, to enable students to establish self-confidence, to form good learning habits and effective learning strategies, to develop autonomous learning ability and cooperative spirit, to enable students to master certain basic knowledge of English, such as listening, speaking, reading and writing skills, in order to form comprehensive language abilities, to cultivate students' observation, memory, thinking, imagination and innovation spirit; and to help students understand the differences between eastern and western cultures. Thus, understanding the great importance of comprehensive teaching techniques, such as playing games, telling stories, singing songs and so on, could also help improve the overall quality of children's English teaching and learning in the context of world English (Li, 2012).

Various people might assess language teaching proficiency for different reasons. However, as indicated in Rossner (2006), the most important reasons were: (1) as support for professional development (including the professional development of the person doing the assessment); (2) as part of quality assurance, that was to check whether the teaching being assessed was up to the standard agreed within a school and was adequately supporting the learning that students were engaged in.

There is no "best method" for teaching. Teaching proficiency, that is to say a combination of knowledge, skills, values and attitudes, comes about when teachers regard the language teaching and learning process as a joint project for teachers and students, as the result of reflection, supervision and teamwork, and thus see themselves as members of a learning community (Reinmann, 2011).

Language and teaching proficiency cannot be illustrated in catalogues that describes what material has been studied at university or what knowledge a person has demonstrated in an examination. Teacher training at universities focuses primarily on imparting expert knowledge. This gave rise to dissatisfaction that spawned projects outside universities which identified and described educational teaching skills and made these available in training programs. In their educational programmes, the Council of Europe and the European Union had repeatedly emphasized the need for well-trained language teachers and promoted such projects, including the European Portfolio for Student Teachers of Languages (EPOSTL) and the European Profiling Grid for Languages Teachers (EPG) (Newby, et al., 2007). Various descriptions of teaching proficiency and specification of teaching standards had been developed at an international level, for example, Australian Institute for Teaching and School Leadership (AITSL), and Lifelong Learning UK (LLUK). While the European Profiling Grid (EPG), on the other hand, is a tool that was designed to support the assessment and self-assessment of language teaching proficiency among practicing language teachers who have varying degrees of experience ranging from a few weeks as trainees to many years.

### 2.7.3　Linguistic Proficiency

The Australian Second Language Proficiency Rating (ASLPR) described language proficiency in terms of four discrete macro-skills (reading, writing, speaking and listening) (Natalia, 1999). Proficiency was one of the most debated issues in language testing. Bachman (1990) reviewed the most common notions of language proficiency according to different areas of testing, he stated that "...*the term 'language proficiency' has been traditionally used in the context of language testing to refer in general to knowledge, competence, or ability in the use of a language, irrespective of how, where, or under what conditions it has been acquired"* (p.16).

The evolution of language teaching, which implied, among other aspects, different emphases (grammar, knowledge about the language, language as communication, language use as a means and not an end in itself) had certainly changed the conceptualization and definition of language proficiency (Rosalba & Orlando, 2013).

Foreign language teachers' linguistic competence was one of the key factors contributing to the success of instruction as it ensured the provision of a good model for the target language, enabled teachers to address the problems which the learners encountered and made teaching more creative (Banno, 2003). In his discussion of teachers' language ability, Banno (2003) cited several studies (Brown, 1994; Hadley & Yoshioka-Hadley, 1996; Harmer, 2000; Shimizu, 1995) that identified sufficient oral proficiency, standard accent, clear pronunciation, and good grammar knowledge as essential characteristics of a good language teacher. Arguably, the concept of English teachers' proficiency was multifaceted and needed to be defined and contextualized in its relationship with different teaching experiences and teaching approaches. Simply, foreign language teachers should master the language they teach; however, their proficiency level can vary and be specific to their teaching context (Lorena, 2014).

Linguistic proficiency was instrumental in helping teachers develop a positive professional identity which in turn enhanced the quality of instruction (Giacomo, 2016), and the issue of their English language proficiency was gaining significance (Eslami-Rasekh, 2005). Lange (1990) demonstrated that language proficiency constituted the foundational confidence of non-native speakers and English teachers, which were the most basic requirements and most essential characteristics of a good teacher. Similarly, Samimy and Brutt-Griffler (1999) reported that 72% of their nonnative speaking graduate student subjects admitted that their insufficient linguistic proficiency impeded their teaching. Teachers' target language proficiency and their beliefs about language learning were two major factors that determined their classroom teaching practices and their use or non-use of the target language in their classes (Kamhi-Stein & Mahboob, 2005).

The knowledge base of language teaching is typically conceptualized as a highly complex system which included such components as content knowledge, pedagogical content knowledge; general pedagogic knowledge, curricular knowledge, contextual knowledge and process knowledge (Roberts, 1998). Although the first of these, which includes knowledge about and competence in the target language, was of pivotal importance in the sense that it was a prerequisite for language teaching as such, it was often neglected in in-service teacher training which tended to focus on the development of theoretical disciplinary knowledge and specific teaching skills (Kamhi-Stein & Mahboob, 2005).

Although it was clear that linguistic proficiency was the cornerstone of the English Language Teaching (ELT) profession, there were other elements that needed to be taken into consideration. Briguglio and Kirkpatrick (1996) found that the definition of '*language teacher proficiency*' was broad and included attributes of a 'competent' language teacher (p.34). It appeared, however that, with two exceptions, the main area of concern of those interviewed for the report was actually 'linguistic' proficiency (Norris, 1999). This reflection was very valid here and now, because the standards movement in our country had concentrated most of its attention on the language level of teachers, to the exclusion of other aspects that made teachers competent in the exercise of their profession. Language teacher quality was nowadays equated to how well the teacher spoke the target language, leaving aside elements such as pedagogical and methodological preparation, experience, and view of language, philosophy of teaching and social commitment, among others (Rosalba & Orlando, 2013).

Literature on addressing linguistic proficiency issued in ELT, as summarized by Kamhi-Stein (2009), seemed to revolve around four distinct approaches: (1) incorporating a language component in the curriculum and helping NNS trainees develop sociocultural competence (e.g. comparing and contrasting local and western-based pedagogical beliefs) as a stimulus to improve language skills and make instruction relevant to local contexts (Liu, 1999); (2) personalizing language study to encourage trainees to work on individual/self-perceived language needs (Kamhi-Stein, 1999); (3) including an element of familiarization with western based pedagogical principles and, concurrently, working on productive language skills (Carrier, 2003); (4) offering explicit grammar instruction, using real classroom materials, to raise both grammatical and pedagogical awareness (Borg, 2003). However, language proficiency should not only serve a linguistic purpose, but should also help NNESTs develop a sense of professional legitimacy and self-confidence (Kamhi-Stein, 2009). Challenging the notion of the native speaker and questioning the ownership of the English language; preparing teachers to cope with the demands of popular communicative approaches and adapting them to local environments; exposing teachers to concepts like English as an international language and helping them recognize the elusiveness of the notion of language ownership; and addressing culture-specific needs, expectations and limitations would all contribute to the development of a positive professional identity which in turn would 'positively affect teachers' instructional practices and standing in the profession (ibid: 97~98).

### 2.7.4 Teaching Proficiency

Teaching proficiency means the knowledge, skills, abilities, values and attitudes which teachers needed to have in order to promote learning processes and design lessons (Reinmann, 2011; Richards, 2015). It refers to a combination of expert and didactical knowledge, practical teaching experience, skills that have been learned and practiced, insights and attitudes, above all with respect to interaction with students and the teacher's own role. The teaching competencies and professional development were key factors in assuring the quality of education, including language education (Richard, 2015).

Effective quality assurance and professional development imply that teachers, including English language teachers and those employing and training them, have a shared appreciation of their current levels of competence and of teacher development needs. What counts are the attitudes a teacher have towards teaching, the stance he or she adopted towards students, and their willingness to adapt lessons to the conditions, abilities and expectations of the students. In this context, Duxa (2001) talked about "*the ability to act in a way that is appropriate to a specific situation*" (p.66), and Hattie (2009) described this teaching proficiency as follows: "*It is the teachers who are open to experience, learn from errors, seek and learn from feedback from students and who foster effort, clarity and engagement in learning*" (p.35).

Applied in the Chinese educational context, the training of teaching proficiency was a series of systematic practical activities, which was guided by the combination of pedagogy, psychology and discipline education theories. It is the training of basic teaching skills based on professional knowledge, including such skills as teaching design, classroom organization, use of teaching media, organization of extracurricular activities, and teaching research, etc. (MOE, 2001). Therefore, according to *Standard of English Curriculum* (MOE, 2001), Li, Chen and Li (2015) put forward the main training curriculum of English language teaching proficiency for the normal student-teachers that focuses on teaching design skills, classroom teaching abilities and preliminary abilities of teaching research. In this regard, the training program would be designed into four main training modules of English teaching proficiency: (1) linguistic basic knowledge (pronunciation, listening ability and spoken English); (2) teaching design (application of syllabus and textbooks, teaching plan); (3) teaching implementation (selection of teaching methods, activity organization); (4) teaching techniques (storytelling, playing games, songs and rhymes, stick figures, English hand-writing, tongue twister, modern educational teaching technologies, etc.) (Lin, 2007; Wang, 2012; Yang, 2012).

## 2.8    Patterns of Teacher Training and Development

### 2.8.1    Rationale of Teacher Training and Development

Professional development encompasses both teacher training and teacher development and refers to both formal as well as informal activities that seek to promote different dimensions of teacher learning. While a formal programme leading to a qualification might initiate the process of professional development for English teachers, professional development also continued once a teacher commenced his or her career as an English teacher (Richards, 2015). The school and the teacher's classroom have now become the main context for continued professional development (Wu, 2005).

With the development of the new curriculum reform, higher and higher demand was focused on teachers' qualities. As the first element of school development, it was a provoking question about how to use the teachers' professional development to guide students' overall development. However, the traditional teacher training model had gradually highlighted its shortcomings, and it could not keep up with the pace of the new curriculum reform. Therefore, Lan (2012) outlined the three following theories.

**Quality-oriented Education Theory:**

Quality-oriented education should be implemented by penetrating into preschool education, primary and secondary education, occupation education, adult education, higher education and other types of education at all levels, should run through all school education, family education, social education, etc. The implementation of quality-oriented education was to cultivate students' innovative spirit and practical abilities, and to improve teachers' all-round qualities (Zhu, et al., 2006).

**Lifelong Learning Theory:**

Lifelong education was a kind of education of knowledge updating and knowledge innovation. The dominant ideology of lifelong education was to require us to update, deepen and enrich our initial knowledge by using a variety of opportunities in our own lives, in order to adapt ourselves to the rapid development of society. Gong (2005) highlighted that every teacher must have the ability of self-development and self-improvement to constantly improve the self qualities, and continue to accept new knowledge and new technology, and also to update the concepts about education, professional knowledge and structure of ability to keep up with the changing times. The ability of lifelong learning was not only a requirement of the social development, but also a requirement of a educational reform (Lan, 2012).

**Teachers' Professionalization Theory:**

The connotation of teachers' professionalization referred that teachers have their own professional requirements and professional conditions, and special training, training system and management system. More professional teachers were required in the new round of basic education curriculum reform. Consequently, the most effective way of improving the Chinese professional teachers' level was to make teacher training start in the right direction of scientific, standardized and systematic development, and ultimately, in order to build a conducive teacher training model and system (Lan, 2012).

Under the present context of new educational reform, the above-mentioned rationales could provide a systematical frame for developing a better teachers' training model in the research.

## 2.8.2　Overview of English Teacher Training Programs

He (2014) indicated that the pattern of teacher training referred to improve professional knowledge, the level of morality, professional qualities, teaching abilities and independent development level for in-service teachers as the goal of training mechanism, content and method in the field of education. Its basic components were the main body of training, training concept, training object, training objectives, training content, training ways (means and methods) and training management (process, monitoring and assessment), etc. (He, 2014).

Due to the international nature of the English language, English language teacher (ELT) training programs are being implemented all over the world. Considerable attention has been given to the process of training English-as-a-foreign-language (EFL) teachers. Williams (1994) mentioned the diversity of these teacher-training programs (which vary considerably in terms of length and qualifications) and discussed the nature of the ELT training discipline in terms of its uniqueness. Further, he discussed the factors that should be accounted for in a teacher training model, e.g., cultural appropriateness, political influences, teacher background and competence, expectations from students, cost, and accountability. In addition, much concern had been expressed in the literature regarding the content of teacher training and the processes and methodologies of training programs (Berry, 1990).

Generally speaking, most EFL teacher-training programs around the world consist of several components. There is a methodological/pedagogical component, a linguistic component, and a literature component (Cullen, 1994). Strevens (1977) divided the teacher training components into three types: skills, information and theories. The first component consisted of practical skills such as a teacher's command of English, teaching techniques and classroom activities, and classroom management. This component required practical training in performing the skills themselves. The second consisted of information about approaches and methodology, syllabus and materials, and language. This component can be learned from reading, lectures, and other techniques. The last consisted of principles concerning linguistics, psychology, psycho-linguistics, social-linguistics, social theories and education. This component could be learned through discussion, practice in solving problems, and tutorial explanation.

Although in most parts of the world the main emphasis in ELT was on methodology, there had been situations in which emphasis was placed on raising the language level of the future teacher (Diógenes, 2001). Hundleby and Breet (1988) and Berry (1990) reported that, in China, teacher-training programs virtually excluded the methodological aspect and concentrated on the improvement of the language level perse. In such a case, attention was given to linguistic knowledge of the English language rather than the ability to use the English language for real communication. Cullen (1994) stated that only a few teacher training courses were able to achieve the objective of improving the communicative command of the language rather than knowledge of itself. Cullen (1994), however, recognized that in most regions of the world, especially where English was not a medium of instruction, the main interest of English teachers was *"the need to improve their own command of the language so that they can use it more fluently, and above all, more confidently, in the classroom"*(p.164). An in-service teacher training course which failed to take this into account was arguably failing to meet the needs or respond to the wishes of the teachers themselves (Cullen, 1994).

Morain (1990) pointed out that educating a foreign-language teacher was not the responsibility of a single segment of academe, (language proficiency for example) but rather the combination of four components, which were: (1) required language courses; (2) courses in the content area; (3) courses in pedagogy; (4) courses in-school experience. On the other hand, Schrier (1994) outlined four characteristics desirable in future foreign-language teachers. They were: (1) proficiency in the foreign language and its cultures; (2) proficiency in the language and culture of the school's community; (3) expertise in curricular design and its implementation; (4) technological sophistication.

### 2.8.3 Pre-service and In-service Teacher Training Programs

Traditionally, teacher training was split into two types: "pre-service" and "in-service" teacher education, or "teacher preparation" (Eleonora, 2003). The former helped those who had no previous teaching experience enter the class with some degree of confidence in what they were doing by providing them special teaching skills (Freeman, 1982). In contrast, the latter helped the experienced teachers to improve their teaching by enabling them to encourage the learners to become actively involved, to stop being frightened of making mistakes, to take initiative, to progress towards self-management and independence, and to develop social involvement and co-operation in the classroom (Sovichea, 2012). Simply speaking, the goal of the teacher training program, for both pre-service and in-service was to enable trainees to be good teachers.

Great importance has always been attributed to the former, pre-service training program, according to the view which held that the theoretical aspects of a profession were learnt once and for all through intensive instruction (Giorgio, 2009). Antikainen (2005) claimed contemporary teacher education should therefore combine theory and practice in a continuous process which includes lifelong pre-service and in-service education, a well-established trend. The concept of lifelong learning was fundamental and entailed a more important role for the building of in-service learning paths by and for the teachers (Giorgio, 2009). Regardless of the prevailing orientation towards teaching which a society might choose, teacher preparation was usually separated into two very broad categories: pre-service and in-service teacher preparation. As a result of the current transition from 'teacher training' to 'teacher professional development', these two categories were adopting new meanings (Koehnecke, 2001).

Pre-service and in-service teacher training were a complex and culturally situated process (Susan & Joce, 2015). Susan and Joce illustrated that what and how teachers learned about themselves, about curriculum content, and about pedagogical approaches for supporting student learning were philosophically and politically contested territory. "Continuousness" was the basic concept underlying "lifelong education". High-quality education was based on teacher quality, and "continuousness" was one of the most important factors in teacher training. "Continuous Professional Development—CPD" consisted of four similar parts: (1) pre-service or initial teacher education; (2) in-service teacher training; (3) further education; (4) vocational training/education, which was the underlying principle of 'lifelong education' (Ebru, 2016, p.455). Additionally, two models of initial teacher training had been developed worldwide: the *simultaneous* and the *consecutive*. The report (Eurydice, 2002) defined them thus: (1) *Consecutive model*: At the outset, students received general education in order to obtain a degree in a particular subject or branch of study. At or near the end of this period of study, they enrolled in a programme of initial professional training, enabling them to qualify as teachers, which might still contain some general education courses. (2) *Concurrent model:* It involved a programme which, from the outset, combined general education in one or more subjects with theoretical and practical professional teacher training. Each presented advantages and disadvantages, but, in certain conditions, such as an effective interdisciplinary curriculum where the educational and disciplinary subjects were effectively integrated, and a good coordination between academic education and practical apprenticeship, the simultaneous model appeared to carry some advantages (Giorgio, 2009).

The knowledge base of language teaching was typically conceptualized as a highly complex system which included such components as content knowledge, pedagogical content knowledge, general pedagogic knowledge, curricular knowledge, contextual knowledge and process knowledge (cf. Roberts, 1998). Although the first of these, which included knowledge about and competence in the target language, was of pivotal importance in the sense that it was a prerequisite for language teaching as such, it is often neglected in in-service teacher training which tended to focus on the development of theoretical disciplinary knowledge and specific teaching skills (Miroslaw, 2011).

Successful language teaching requires many different types of knowledge and skills related to different areas, there was a consensus that target language proficiency was of primary significance in this respect when it came to non-native teachers, many of whom are in danger of becoming gradually deskilled as a consequence of limited exposure, dealing with low-level students and paying scant attention to self-improvement (Giorgio, 2009). For this reason, in-service training in the domain of language competence was indispensable and it should thus be routinely included in teacher education programs, which did not happen in some instructional contexts (Miroslaw, 2011). As explained in the present paper, courses or course modules aimed at promoting improvement in this area should best be integrated with methodology training, included both a general and an individual component, focused on all the dimensions of communicative competence, drew upon task-based methodology, encouraged a simultaneous focus on form and meaning, and fostered the development of practitioners' autonomy and reflection (Giorgio, 2009). Clearly, specific implementations of these broad guidelines were bound to vary from country to country since the nature of second language teacher education as such was inevitably a function of the specificity of a given educational context (Miroslaw, 2011).

All in all, after pre-service and in-service teacher training, Fu (2007) indicated a qualified kindergarten English teacher should meet the following criteria: (1) must be a qualified kindergarten teacher; (2) have standard English pronunciation, fluent expression and proficient ability; (3) integrate English activities into children's daily life; (4) use children-liked English in accordance with the characteristics of English culture while organizing activities; (5) be good at using non-language symbols to communicate and interact with children. The criteria also indicated that the main emphasis in ELT was on the methodology and language level of the future teacher (Sovichea, 2012). Language competence had, indeed, been rated the most essential characteristic of a good teacher. It had been seen that only a few teacher training courses were capable of achieving the objective of improving the communicative command of the target language (Verma, et al., 2006). Both pre-service and in-service teacher training programs had to take into the need of improving the language command of their trainees into consideration in order to meet their needs and to respond to their wishes (Sovichea, 2012).

### 2.8.4 Foreign Patterns of English Teacher Training Programs

Due to the international nature of the English language, English language teacher (ELT) training programs were being implemented all over the world. Considerable attention had been given to the process of training English-as-a-foreign-language (EFL) teachers (Richards, 2015). Topics such as the nature of teacher-training courses, different approaches to language teacher training and several paradigms of teacher-training methodology had been discussed at conferences throughout the world.

The professionalism of English with professional training and qualifications a recognition of the fact that employers and institutions had come to realize that effective language-teaching programmes depended on teachers with specialized training, knowledge and skills (Richards, 2015). This professionalism was reflected in continuous attempts to develop standards for English language teaching and teachers and in the proliferation of professional journals and teacher magazines, conferences and professional organizations such as TESOL (Teachers of English to Speakers of Other Languages), an international organization based in the US, with over 100 worldwide affiliates; IATEFL (International Association of Teachers of English as a Foreign Language), an international organization based in the UK, and JALT (the Japan Association for Language Teaching) (Richards, 2015). Professionalism was also reflected in requirements for English teachers to demonstrate their level of proficiency in English as a component of certification or as a hiring prerequisite, in line with the demand for professional qualifications for native-speaker teachers and in the greater level of sophisticated knowledge of language teaching required of English teachers.

According to Lan (2012), there were two main types of teacher training in foreign countries. One was the training for trainers-trainees, which was the college-based training mode; the other was the training for trainees-trainees, which was school-based training mode. The trainers-trainees training was based on the colleges or via distance education, while the trainees-trainees training was based at the schools. The traditional teacher training models were of the same essence, although the procedure and process were slightly different. Most trainings took dominance of the different training institutions while subordination of the participants (trainees), the training institutions stood in an active position and the trainees in the passive one (Lan, 2012). Therefore, both were common in spite of the aspects of deficiencies and strengths, three features were summed up in terms of their advantages as follows: (1) unified planning, curriculum and teaching, and convenient management; (2) the knowledge of theories was quickly improved by trainees' efforts because of more systematic, complete training content; (3) the trainees readily got the certificate of completion in a short training time. On the contrary, the prominent weakness of the traditional teacher training pattern was no need for reticence. Both domestic and foreign researchers had recognized the deficiencies of teacher training models, and they began to carry out some active research and exploration from the beginning of the twentieth century, and also made certain effects in practice. However, it was obliged to admit the fact that all these studies characterized scattered and miscellaneous aspects, which were not systematic and not deep, even duplicated or contradictory, still remaining at the theoretical level and lacking of maneuverability and effectiveness (Lan, 2012).

### 2.8.4.1 RPTIM Model in the USA

As indicated in the above-discussed characteristics with unanimous dissatisfaction, a strong consensus that in-service training was critical if school programs and practices were to be improved (Wood & Kleine, 1987). The RPTIM model for staff development, created by Woods, Thompson, and Russell (1981) more than 20 years ago, remains as one of the most comprehensive models for effective staff development. Woods, Thompson and Russell (1981) suggested that Staff Development was the totality of educational and personal experiences that contributed toward an individual's being more competent and satisfied in an assigned professional role. In-service education was but one of the several functions of staff development, which was defined as *"improving skills, implementing curricula, procedures, expanding subject matter knowledge, planning and organizing instruction, and increasing personal effectiveness"* (p.31). Dennis and Susan (1989) defined staff development as those processes that improved the job-related knowledge, skills, or attitudes of school employees. Participants in staff development activities might include school board members, central office administrators, principals, and non-certified staff, while this article focused on staff development for teachers. In particular, it examined what was known about staff development that was intended to improve student learning through enhanced teacher performance.

This model conceptualized staff development into the five stages of the RPTIM model (Woods, Thompson & Russell, 1981), which are: (1) readiness; (2) planning; (3) training; (4) implementation; (5) maintenance (see Figure 2.2). Each stage focused on several practices. Stage I of readiness, emphasized selection and understanding of, and commitment to, new behaviors by a school staff or group of educators. In stage II of planning, the specific planed for an in-service program (to be implemented over three to five years) was developed to achieve the desired changes or professional practice selected in Stage I. In the training stage, the plans were translated into practice. The implementation stage focused on ensuring that the training became part of the ongoing professional behavior of teachers and administrators in their own work setting. Stage of maintenance, began as new behaviors were integrated into daily practice. The aim of this final stage was to ensure that a change in operational performance would continue over time. Furthermore, each stage was defined by a set of practices that identified specific tasks that were to be completed in the stage and the personnel who made key decisions.

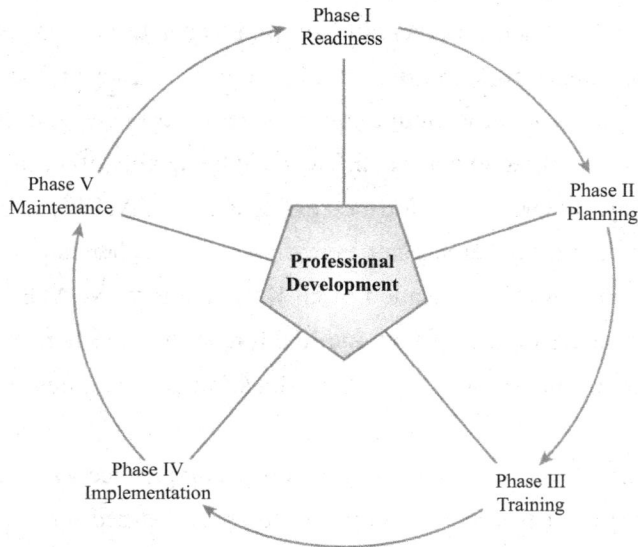

**Figure** 2.2   The RPTIM Model of Professional Development
(*Source:* Wood, Thompson, & Russell, 1981)

Staff development possessed a useful "craft knowledge" that guided the field of education. This craft knowledge included ways to organize, structure, and deliver staff development programs (Caldwell, 1989). As a result, in the past 20 years hundreds of staff development programs have been established in urban, suburban, and rural school districts throughout the United States and Canada. Consequently, staff development both influenced and was influenced by the organizational context in which it took place. The impact of the staff development models that have been discussed depends not only upon their individual or blended use, but upon the features of the organization in which they are used.

### 2.8.4.2 NCATE Program in Hong Kong

Reflective practice was an essential component of pre-service teacher training programs in Hong Kong (Brooke, 2012). It facilitated the linking of theory and practice and empowers trainees to seek reasons behind their practices and their beliefs. Reflection is particularly important today with the emphasis on student outcomes (Ward & McCotter, 2004) which is considered as a performance competency for teachers in CEC (Council for Exceptional Children) and an accreditation standard for teacher education NCATE programs.

The National Council for Accreditation of Teacher Education (NCATE) is the profession's mechanism to help establish high-quality teacher preparation. Through the process of professional accreditation of schools, colleges and departments of education, NCATE worked to make a difference in the quality of teaching and teacher preparation today, tomorrow and for the next century. NCATE's performance-based system of accreditation fostered competent classroom teachers and other educators who worked to improve the education of all K-12 students. NCATE believed every student deserves a caring, competent and highly-qualified teacher. In Hong Kong's education system, university-led teacher education programmes were driven by reflective teaching.

The pre-service teacher training program teaching practice was a very important component for student teachers to put what they have learned into practice. During the process, they might design their own learning tasks either by adopting the tasks in the textbook or by their own creation. There is a lot of self-investigation and reflection on the possibility of better teaching and learning. In general educators and researchers concurred with the argument that reflection was essential. Reflection involved thinking that brought about a better understanding of the complexity of what happened in the classrooms, interpreting assumptions and questions taken-for-granted; and evaluating their own teaching in contextualized situations. It helped teachers make judgments and decisions for appropriate teaching strategies to achieve teaching and learning objectives in the lessons (Calderhead & Gates, 1993; Loughran, 2002; Ward & McCotter, 2004). Therefore, establishing reflective practice was important to both in-service and pre-service teachers of all subjects.

Reflection was widely accepted as important for teachers' professional development. Many studies had been carried out to study teachers' reflections (both experienced and novice in their teaching practice and different frameworks were developed to serve various research agenda. For example: Chipin, Simon and Galipeau (2008) conducted an empirical study for pre-service teachers. They argued that a self-directed reflective approach supported pre-service teachers working with the complex issues during their practicum. In their approach, they promoted among the pre-service teachers the schema of P1 (problem to be solved), TT (tentative theory), EE (error elimination) and P2 (new or reformulated problem) (Ida Ah, 2010).

### 2.8.4.3   INSET and ELTUP in Turkey

Notwithstanding, Turkey's in-service education and training (INSET) programs primarily catered to general classroom teachers and preschool teachers, indeed, English teachers were offered very few opportunities to participate in INSET, and teachers' subject areas were ignored when organizing INSET programs. According to Roberts (1998), the participation of teachers in INSET courses did not necessarily mean that those courses were fully relevant to the teachers' needs. To put it simply, an INSET program which was possibly unrelated to the teachers' needs could be regarded as futile and could be a financial burden for the providing institution and loss of time for the teachers. But this situation could be avoided simply by including teachers' perspectives in the process of planning the program and decision-making. INSET was the type of training and education given specifically to practicing teachers with practical experiences in the classrooms. INSET's improvable and changing nature provided researchers with various concepts to be investigated in the field of English language teaching (ELT). However, in general, the majority of the studies so far about planning INSET for foreign language teacher education in Turkey focused on the needs based on state school settings and courses provided by the Ministry of Education (MEB) (Bulut, Demircioğlu & Yıldırım, 1995; Camuzcu & Duruhan, 2011; Çakıroğlu & Çakıroğlu, 2003; Köyalan, 2011; Gülmez-Dağ, 2012; Uysal, 2012). INSET programs had to take the need into consideration to improve the language command of their trainees in order to meet their needs and to respond to their wishes (Enisa & Melike, 2016).

Specifically, English language teachers in Turkey are usually graduates of English Language Teaching Undergraduate Programs (ELTUP) opened within the Faculties of Education. So, different certificate programs and distance learning opportunities within the Faculty of Open Education were offered in order to meet the teacher deficit. ELTUP in Turkey usually last for 4 years but those with a preparation class last for 5 years. Field courses named Community Service Course served the students in ELTUP in Turkey; surely, both primary and high schools should be organized as two different programs such as "Primary English Language Teaching" and "High School English Language Teaching" (Ayse & Kemal, 2012. p. 85). Courses those were appropriate for the developmental levels and needs of the students with whom the teacher candidates' work should be given in PELTP. The greater importance given to the courses suitable for children such as "Teaching English to Children" (p. 85) which had already been given in the programs would help candidate teachers deal with fewer problems when they started teaching. Similarly, Advanced Reading, Advanced Writing, Advanced Speaking and Advanced Listening Courses should be emphasized in High School English Language Teaching Programs.

Burns and Richards (2009) argued that the speed of worldwide changes in education necessitate them to be knowledgeable about the political status of the current English language, and the new methodology in teaching and learning, besides language competence. In addition, Freeman and Johnson (1998) suggested that teachers must be fully aware of and develop a questioning stance toward the complex social, cultural, and institutional structures that pervaded the professional landscapes where they work.

## 2.8.5　Chinese Application of English Teacher Training Programs

### 2.8.5.1　Exploration of Non-governmental Education Institutions

Teacher professionalism is the main factor restricting the healthy development of children's English education (Lan, 2012; Lin, 2008). Preschool English teachers need not only good English language proficiency and related skills, but also solid basic theoretical knowledge about preschool education, psychology and relevant fields (Shen & Zhao, 2010; Wang & Mi, 2014). Therefore, some non-governmental education institutions had explored the professional development and maintenance of preschool English teachers.

For example, Kunming Children's Foreign Language Institute started to cultivate the professional quality of preschool English teachers in the 90's. Even though they started early, they only limited the content of the training to their own teaching material "Huangbo Children English". With the exposure of internal management, they did not grasp the first advantage; the professional training of preschool English teachers did not develop on the way of specialization and scale (Lan, 2012).

In addition, the committee of Cambridge Children's English examination cooperated with Beijing Language University and aimed at designing projects of teacher training for Cambridge Children's English itself. But this scheme lacked of generalizability of universal promotion because of the limitations of teaching materials (Lin, 2008).

In 2003, Jinghua Haoyang Education Institute of Science and Research and the Foreign Language Department of Qinghua University cooperated to develop "Qinghua University English Teachers Qualification Certificate System", which was the first open examination for the professional qualification of children English teachers for society. The qualification system focused on the training qualification of English professional proficiency and pedagogical and psychological knowledge instead of some certain kind of teaching materials. The system was a continuing education project, trying to make the participant personnel obtain the required competence of engaging in children's English teaching by the formal training or self-study. Except for the above institutions, Beijing New Oriental School, Beijing American English Language Institute, Dezhou Chenlei Bilingual School, and so on, had carried out the professional training development for early childhood English teachers. But unfortunately, there was not a mature and normative professional model for children's English teachers (Wang, 2012).

As a whole, the non-governmental professional development for children's English teachers lack of necessary theoretical guidance, without specific training goals, scientific training methods and systematic operation planning, which was not conducive to the healthy development of children's English education under the present situation of China (Zhang, 2012).

### 2.8.5.2　Government English Teacher Training Programs

So far in China, there were two kinds of teacher training patterns for the urban and rural primary and middle schools: the first kind was short-term training of 10~15 days, all participant teachers assembled in above county-level training organization (including to training center and teacher in-service training school) to attend a face-to-face learning, and then have a final examination, such as modern information application training and linguistic training, and so on. The second kind was a combination model of amateur self-study and face-to-face learning. A normal period of training time spent three or four months to half a year uncertainly, within this period by the weekend or holidays would be participating in training. All in all, scientific and reasonable training models and methods were the necessary conditions to promote and ensure professional development with the new curriculum reform in China (Zhang, 2012).

Accordingly, in order to implement such a massive English teaching and training program, China's central government also launched a series of supporting programs, which included a colossal English language teacher training program— millions of English teachers covered from primary schools to high schools across the nation all took part in the training during 2001~2008. This colossal program aimed at making millions of English teachers in China qualified for English teaching in order to implement the new National English Teaching Guidance and the National English Language Curriculum Standard across the country (Zhang, 2012). But for various reasons, i.e. training program lacked of qualified English language trainers, participants lacked of necessary English teaching knowledge and skills, the results of the program did not reach the expected goals (Dong & Gui 2002; Zhang & Li, 2010). For example, in Yunnan province, although thousands of English teachers whose major was not English, but are now teaching English, passed the so called training, as lack of basic knowledge and skills in English teaching, about 80% of them did not qualify for English teaching in primary schools, secondary schools or high schools, i.e., such English teachers could not either speak English in a correct pronunciation or tone, or explain simplest English grammatical phenomena (Dong & Gui, 2002; Zhang & Li, 2010). So, we could see that a number of Chinese students, although they passed high level English tests, their English language proficiency is not very good (Li, 2010).

## 2.8.6   Teaching and Training Module

English teachers' vocational proficiency is composed of various English teaching skills such as required, stable and systematic professional skills. These can be acquired by practice with integrating didactical theories, utilizing the professional knowledge of English education and completing successful English teaching and learning tasks, which is the basis for student-teachers at the university level (Zuo, 2012).

Consequently, Bloom's taxonomy of the cognitive domain (Bloom, 1956, cited in Huitt, 2011) deemed the teaching objectives were divided into three areas: cognitive learning field, psychomotor learning field and affective learning field. Each field consisted of a number of sub-categories, and there was a hierarchy among the sub-classes. In view of a hierarchical framework of educational objectives, different discipline-centered systems would be formed by integrating into corresponding training content. Zuo (2012) divided the training content of English language and teaching proficiencies in the context of the new curriculum standard for English teachers into three training modules: (1) general English teaching skills, including English language knowledge and English language proficiency, correlative teaching skills or techniques, such as Mandarin, blackboard writing and drawing design, computer-aided instruction (CAI); (2) basic English classroom teaching skills, including task-based teaching, teaching implementation, teaching design, materials processing, using modern educational teaching technology and teaching micro-skills, such as leading-in, presentation, display, practice, consolidation, questions and feedbacks; (3) comprehensive teaching skills, including teaching supervision, teaching strategy, teaching evaluation, teaching reflection, teaching experimental design, teaching report analysis and so on.

Each specific skill was an independent and interrelated factor in a certain system of English teaching proficiency. The English language teaching proficiency highlighted its characteristics of diversity, comprehensiveness, variability, situationalization and practicality, etc. (Zuo, 2012). The hierarchical system of language teaching and training modules could embody in training objectives, training content, training time, training methods, training strategy, training environment, and training evaluation. Conforming to the hierarchical system, Liu (2012) discussed "multimodality" (Gibbon, Mertins & Moore, 2000) in his study, he claimed that the multimodal discourse could provide an authentic context of English learning and teaching environment (Zhou & Ni, 2016), a more flexible space of English teaching model, and a pluralistic procedure of English teaching evaluation.

Aiming at cultivating effectively qualified English teachers at the university level, it was of great necessity to plan as a whole to implement course teaching and module training for preschool education majors (Jin, 2016). This teaching module was just consistent with the ultimate goal of preschool English education in order to cultivate suitable talents for the development of the society, furthermore, for the current reform of the teaching model of English curriculum in professional preschool education field. This teaching and training module could combine the vocational pre-service training course and English course organically, which was also in line with the trend of bilingual education and teaching (Wang, 2014).

## 2.9　Instructional Design

Instructional design (sometimes called instructional systems design) is defined as a systematic and scientific approach to designing instruction and creating instructional materials (Clare & Natalie, 2014). It is the framework in which teachers would carry out the planned teaching and learning steps in a lesson (Richards & Lockart, 1994). Instructional design could be said to be a system of procedures specifying the planning, design, development, implementation and evaluation of effective and efficient instruction in a variety of educational environments. The specifications of the instructional design process were both functional and attractive to learners. Moreover, Gustafson and Branch (2002) also believed that the procedures within the instructional design could lead to a clear approach that was more effective, efficient, and relevant to instruction.

Instructional design approaches emerged as efforts were made to apply scientific principles and discoveries to promote learning. The instructional design process, which operationalized the instructional design approach, involved the five following phases: (1) design; (2) development; (3) implementation; (4) evaluation; (5) management. During the instructional design process, an instructional designer or design team worked through each of these phases systematically. Each phase involved using specialized processes, structures, and tools. The instructional design process used both a systematic way of thinking about the world and instructional outcomes and a methodical one (Clare & Natalie, 2014).

Using instructional design approaches will empower teachers to work as educational designers as they decide how and when to use the instructional models. Instructional designers use different instructional design models to work through the five basic phases of the instructional design process. All instructional design model process through these same five phases, but each model uses different processes, structures, and tools to complete them. Instructional models (i.e. models of teaching), however, are frameworks for implementing instruction in a classroom setting. Like instructional design models, each instructional model has a unique theoretical basis (Joyce, Weil & Calhoun, 2009, cited in Clare & Natalie, 2014) that informs its specialized structure and dictates the particular activities that occur during each of its steps. An instructional model is a procedure for implementing a lesson or learning sequence; however, it is not a process for systematically developing learning experiences and materials. Instructional models work in limited settings, while instructional design models facilitate learning across most, if not all, educational contexts. Whereas models of teaching are the blueprints used to build a particular lesson, instructional design models are the processes used by those who develop such blueprints.

## 2.10   The ADDIE Model

A number of instructional design models have been designed to guide users in the instructional design process (Martin, 2011). According to Gagne et al. (2005), most systematic models of design have similar components, but can vary greatly in the specific number of phrases and their graphic representation. The ADDIE model contains five phases, or five components (analysis, design, development, implementation, and evaluation) as in Figure 2.3, which illustrates how each major component is linked to the others. The solid lines indicate that the process flows from analysis to evaluation and the dotted lines feedback pathways. Evaluation activities can reveal where revisions are required in each of the other four components. Each ADDIE phase was purposeful and focused on the specific outcomes, and use of ADDIE model represents a dynamic, flexible guideline for building effective instructional material, it could provide a well-organized, strategic plan for training and instructional design that ensured quality through consideration of all of the elements (Gagne et al., 2005; Martin, 2011; Clare & Natalie, 2014).

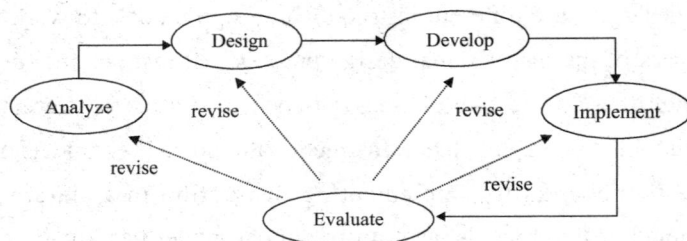

**Figure** 2.3   The ADDIE Model
(*Source*: Gagne et al., 2005, p.21)

Figure 2.3 illustrates the connection of each component. The following details describe the components and subcomponents of the ADDIE model (Gagne et al., 2005, p.23-28).

The ADDIE Model was considered the most widely used methodology of systematic training model and one of the most applicable used systematic instructional systems design models (Allen, 2006; Gagne et al., 2005; Reiser & Dempsey, 2007). ADDIE is simple and works flexibly in many different contexts to support the creation of instructional plans, experiences, and materials. Its memorable acronym describes the major activities in each of its phases-Analysis, Design, Development, Implementation, and Evaluation.

## 2.10.1　The Analysis Phase

The first phase of ADDIE is the analysis phase. The four major goals in this phase are to: (1) determine the instructional goals and objectives; (2) examine current and desired learner needs and characteristics; (3) identify contextual factors that might promote or hinder instruction (e.g., social and physical learning environment, available time, and so on); (4) locate available resources. This clarifies the who, what, when, where, and how of instruction. During this phase, the designer engages in activities that challenge him or her to understand important dimensions of the learning context. The designer carefully considers the content and learning goals as they relate to the characteristics of the specified audience. Typically, the analysis phase involves conducting a needs assessment (also called a needs analysis).

A needs assessment is a formal process implemented by a designer to identify information about the learning goals, the audience, the learning contest, and available resources that will influence the design of instruction. A needs assessment requires a designer to: (1) determine the desired status of the audience that will be achieved through interaction with the instruction to be designed; (2) determine the actual status of the audience before interaction with the instruction to be designed; (3) analyze the gap between the two. This gap, or difference, between the desired and actual status represents the "need". All in all, the analysis phase is foundational for the rest of the design process. What is learned during this phase forms the basis for all activities that follow.

According to Brown (1995), a need analysis (NA) was understood as "*gathering information that will serve as the basis for developing a curriculum that will meet the learning needs of a particular group of students* (p.35)".

Furthermore, Brown (1995) defined an NA as follows: "*The systematic collection and analysis of all subjective and objective information necessary to define and validate defensible curriculum purposes that satisfy the language learning requirements of students within the context of particular institutions that influence the learning and teaching situation* (p.36)".

He further maintained that a list of goals and objectives should be established "*as a basis for developing tests, materials, teaching activities, and evaluation strategies*" (p.35). Goals were "*general statements of the program's purposes*" (p.71) while objectives were "*specific statements that describe the particular knowledge, behaviors, and/or skills that the learner will be expected to know or perform at the end of a course or program*" (p.73). Given this, based on the results of the NA, the goals and objectives were provided for teacher training in the design phase.

### 2.10.2　The Design Phase

The second phase in the ADDIE model is the design phase. This phase involves creating the actual plan for addressing the need or needs identified in the analysis phase. The goal in this phase is to develop the best plan for meeting these needs. The best plan is the one that most closely and appropriately uses the information gained in the analysis phase. During this phase, plans for evaluating the quality of the instruction in development are also made. Because ADDIE is used by instructional designers, the products created often include high-budget items intended to be used in a permanent for. Therefore, extensive evaluation during development (i.e., formative evaluation) is conducted. Plans for testing the product—sometimes called "best testing"—with the intended audience are devised during this phase.

### 2.10.3　The Development Phase

The third phase in the ADDIE model is the development, or "create" phase. In this phase, the instructional designer creates the instructional materials, sometimes called the "product", needed to support the goals identified in the analysis phase (through a needs assessment) and planned for in the design phase. If new information is discovered during the development phase, it may be necessary to loop back and rework some of the previous phases of ADDIE. The develop phase is the "messy and applied" phase when abstract ideas are brought to life. Illustrations leave the designer's mind and appear on paper in the form of assignments, assessments, or other instructional materials to foster learning. During the development phase, instructional designers frequently work collaboratively with subject matter experts, graphic designers, and media technology experts.

### 2.10.4　The Implementation Phase

The fourth phase of the ADDIE model is the Implementation, or "teaching/ delivery of instruction" phase. This phase involves testing the product that has been created. It might involve testing the materials and implementing the instruction, unit, or lessons mapped out in the design phase. Implementation is often considered the teaching phase of the instructional design process. During this phase, designers have the opportunity to learn by applying their theoretical constructs in practical situations. For example, they might examine the question: "Does the product work in practice?" The implementation phase is when designers find out. Formative evaluation is usually conducted as a part of this phase, merging the implementation and the next phase, evaluation.

## 2.10.5   The Evaluation Phase

The final phase in ADDIE is the evaluation phase. During this phase, instructional designers implement the plan for the evaluation of the instruction they have created. Even though the evaluation plan is typically created during the design phase, instructional designers can proceed with the full plan only after the instruction has been produced, created, and delivered. During this phase, designers implement their evaluation and then use the information gained from it—such as anecdotal data and student feedback and questions—and from their own observation and judgment to modify the instruction as needed.

Each of the five phases in the ADDIE model is unique and important. Each involves activities that contribute to making the instructional design process more efficient and the product resulting from it more effective. Table 2.1 provides a listing of the ADDIE phases and a short description of the important activities performed within each phase.

**Table 2.1   Major Activities within Each ADDIE Model Phase**

| ADDIE Model Phase | Major Activities |
|---|---|
| Analysis | -Analyze academic standards and break into learning goals<br>-Identify and examine learner needs<br>-Consider important characteristics of the learning context<br>-Conduct needs assessment<br>-Inventory available materials and resources<br>-Select appropriate instructional models of teaching |
| Design | -Review types of knowledge addressed in learning goals<br>-Configure other instructional tools<br>-Formulate plans for development of instructional plans and materials<br>-Conceive an evaluation plan<br>-Devise, sequence and plan the pacing of the unit |

| ADDIE Model Phase | Major Activities |
|---|---|
| Development | -Create lesson plans<br>-Develop an evaluation plan<br>-Produce instructional materials |
| Implementation | -Teach the unit<br>-Implement the use of instructional materials developed<br>-Implement evaluation plan |
| Evaluation | -Analyze data generated from the evaluation plan<br>-Determine levels of student growth, effort, and achievement<br>-Examine the quality of the instructional plan and materials and make modifications as needed |

(*Source*: Clare & Natalie, 2014, p.35)

## 2.11 Related Research

Li (2005) investigated the problems of English education in Jinghua Haoyang kindergartens in Xingtai City of China. He found that different kindergartens had different educational contents by arising from the use of various teaching materials; more importantly, it was difficult to set up an effective language learning environment, even though the leaders of kindergartens and teachers realized its importance, and lastly, the professional quality of English teachers needs to be improved. Aiming at solving these problems, some practical measures like working out teaching aims, choosing teaching content, and determining the way to train qualified teachers, were carried out in the setting. Specifically, the teaching aims in his study are to build children's interest of English learning, to set up self-confidence and to develop a sense of language and form good personalities; and the teaching contents and materials chosen are extensive, connecting with children's daily life and local custom closely, such as mixed-age class, music, games, drama, story and outside classroom environment set up by parents and teachers together. All in all, Li (2005) indicated that the training plan for professional English teachers was put forward as a guiding ideology about the unity of large scale, rapid speed and high quality.

Wang (2012) observed that, as higher vocational colleges for cultivating kindergarten teachers should further understand the basic direction of the preschool teachers' professional level and development, and should conduct more in-depth research on preschool English teaching and training. Therefore, she developed a training model of English teaching proficiency for preschool education majors in the context of higher vocational colleges. The training model consisted of ways of mastering English basic knowledge, combining the English knowledge and preschool professional theories and basic abilities, and strengthening the training of children English teaching proficiency. She illustrated that a qualified children's English teacher should master normative English pronunciation, better listening ability and spoken English, and some English cultural background knowledge. She also highlighted that the main training content should conclude such abilities over games teaching, stories teaching, songs and rhythms teaching, pronunciation teaching, spoken and listening teaching.

After investigating the present situation of English student-teachers' teaching proficiency in a local college, Pan (2012) pointed out there were three problems with the training program. First, unreasonable courses offered a lack of cross connection of multidisciplinary; second, less teaching practice, a lack of rich teaching experiences; third, low quality of instruction, lack of flexibility and pluralism. Thus, their teaching reform mainly focused on student-teachers' practical ability in order to provide more chances for teaching practice, such as developing a second classroom and organizing more extracurricular activities, carrying more special topics training and constructing more bases for teaching practice.

Han (2014) highlighted that possessing English language knowledge could make a qualified English teacher, but teaching English with artistic means would create an excellent English teacher. Specifically, children's English teachers must have solid basic skills, including mastering the art of teaching language, the use of writing art on the blackboard, the use of various visual aids, also must have some artistic talents, such as painting, calligraphy, singing, commanding and director, and so on. On one side, the proper use of visual aids and visual means, classroom stick figures and children's handwork could fully mobilize children's enthusiasm to participate in the classroom. On the other hand, preschool English teaching emphasized children's participation, arranging a large amount of classroom activities which were closely related to their own life and experiences, all the activities could not complete without ingenious teaching design and careful organization. The English teachers should act as not only good directors but also good actors to deal with timely guidance and simultaneous participation.

Han (2014) created her special compound innovative training model for preschool English talents. Specifically, the creative training model was main compound of the English Education + Preschool Education model. Han emphasized the premise of the compound talent training model would not sacrifice the quality of English teaching to strengthen the professional knowledge teaching of preschool education. The curriculum included three models, namely English curriculum, preschool education curriculum and professional skills courses. The model of English curriculum set up English listening and speaking, English reading, and preschool English education; the model of core curriculum of preschool education curriculum set up preschool pedagogy, preschool psychology, kindergarten organization and management, classroom activities and design, and teaching methodology; while the model of professional skills curriculum set up teacher spoken language, basic music, piano, dance and art. All in all, it should pay special attention to the organic and balanced integration among the three models in order to cultivate real compound-type and applied-type English talents for children's education.

Çakır and Güngör (2017) investigated the 3rd year and 4th year pre-service teachers' evaluations of the practices in teaching English to young learners in terms of 21st century teacher qualifications. Employing a mixed methods design, the study included the qualitative data that came from semi-structured interviewed questions administered to pre-service teachers in five different English language teaching programmes. The quantitative data came from the content analysis of the course "*Teaching English to Young Learners*" syllabus in the universities. The findings indicated that pre-service teachers had individual learning needs mainly on organizational skills, the use of technology, and characteristics of young learners. The current syllabus for the courses was found to be ineffective in preparing pre-service teachers for 21st century teacher qualifications.

## 2.12   Summary

This chapter reviews the related literature of the multi-ethnic context of multilingual education and bilingual education in Yunnan province in China, the general requirements or detailed dimensions of teachers' quality and professionalism of the initial English teachers are discussed by different researchers, and the importance and components of ELT proficiency are also successfully identified. Then, the various descriptions of different training models are compared, it seems that there are both strengths and weaknesses in terms of different training tendencies, subjects, goals, objectives, contents and other practical aspects. In terms of the instructional design models, the ADDIE Model containing Analysis, Design, Development, Implementation and Evaluation was considered the most widely used and systematic training model and one of the most applicable systematic instructional design models. The ADDIE is simple and works flexibly in many different contexts to support the creation of instructional plans, experiences and materials, which are applied for the present study in order to better understand the research problems of developing a feasible training module for the ELT proficiency in such a context of Yunnan multi-ethnic minority community. I preferred mixed methods research according to the nature of the study, so the next chapter presents the research paradigm, design, methodology, data collection and data analysis.

# CHAPTER 3
# RESEARCH METHODOLOGY

The purposes of the study aimed at investigating the student-teachers' English language teaching (ELT) proficiency, developing a training module to improve ELT proficiency, and determining its effectiveness. Thus, mixed methods research was selected to answer the research questions and as a guide to collect and analyze the data simultaneously. This chapter is structured according to the following sections:

3.1  Research Paradigm and Rationale

3.2  Research Design

3.3  Research Process and Training Phases

3.4  Research Methods

3.5  Ethical Considerations

3.6  Summary

## 3.1  Research Paradigm and Rationale

This section presents the rationale for the research paradigm chosen for this study. In terms of paradigm, it might be viewed as a basic set of beliefs, assumptions or a worldview, and a way of breaking down the complexity of the real world (Denzin & Lincoln, 2000). Schwandt (2007) described that the term paradigm played a significant role in the argument about the rationality of scientific inquiry. It was particularly fashionable to talk about the qualitative versus quantitative "paradigm debate" in the research methodology of social sciences.

Creswell (2003) proposed three elements of inquiry to establish the groundwork for the framework and to form different approaches to the research; they are alternative knowledge claims, strategies of inquiry and methods. With these perspectives, I addressed three questions central to the design of research: (1) what knowledge claims were being made (including a theoretical perspective); (2) what strategies of inquiry would describe the procedures; (3) what methods of data collection and analysis would be used? By using these three elements of inquiry, I then identified the mixed methods approach to inquiry (Creswell, 2003).

Stating a knowledge claim meant that I would start a certain project about how I learnt and what I hoped to learn during the inquiry. There are four positions for knowledge claims, post-positivism, constructivism, advocacy/participatory and pragmatism. I preferred the pragmatism paradigm which allows the freedom to choose many possible approaches, especially conducive to mixed-methods research. Additionally, it was also "free" to choose the methods, techniques, and procedures of the research to collect and analyze data rather than subscribing to only one way, and which was the best to meet the purpose of investigating the student-teacher's professional qualities, especially their English language teaching (ELT) proficiency. There was also a concern with applications "*what works*" and solutions to the problems of the study (Patton, 1990). Instead of methods being important themselves, I expected to use the strategy of multi-methods to derive knowledge about the problem of developing a feasible training module of EFL proficiency in the study.

## 3.2 Research Design

In this section, the research design of mixed methods research is presented. This process of research design would turn the research questions into a project (Robson, 2002). Knowing the research design of the study gave me a sense of the overall procedure, as well as showing me a relationship between variables and conceptualized thoughts (Springer, 2010). The mixed methods research design is a procedure for collecting, analyzing, and integrating or "mixing" both quantitative and qualitative research methods in a single study to understand the research problems (Creswell & Plano Clark, 2011). In other words, the basic assumptions are to use both quantitative and qualitative methods in combination to provide a better understanding of the research problems and questions than either one method by itself (Creswell, 2012). Specifically, the present study allowed for the triangulation of not only analysis but also methods, instruments, sources and theories to present a detailed and balanced picture of the given situation. The triangulation design of the mixed methods is illustrated in the following section.

Based on the problems of the study, the knowledge claims of a pragmatism paradigm were chosen for the research design. The purposes of the study aimed at investigating the student-teachers' needs for professional development, especially their English language teaching (ELT) proficiency, developing a training module to improve the proficiency among student-teachers in multi-ethnic communities of Yunnan province and then examining its effectiveness; and the specific research questions, which are:

(1) What are the challenges facing the current student-teachers in teaching English to beginning learners in multi-ethnic community schools in Yunnan Province?

(2) What are the specific components of training activities for student-teachers in teaching English effectively in multi-ethnic community schools in Yunnan Province?

(3) How does the training process develop and to what extent does the training module improve student-teachers' ELT proficiency?

Therefore, the mixed methods research was selected to answer the research questions of the study for the following reasons. Firstly, it needed both quantitative and qualitative data to conduct the present study in order to provide a better understanding of the research problem than either one type by itself. Secondly, it was a good design to use if it sought to build on the strengths of both quantitative and qualitative data. Thirdly, one type of research (qualitative or quantitative) was not enough to address the research problems or answer the research questions of the study, as more data was needed to extend, elaborate on, or explain. Fourthly, an alternative perspective of the student-teachers was expected to provide and develop a more in-depth understanding of their ELT proficiency (Creswell, 2012).

The strengths of combining quantitative and qualitative research methods have been emphasized by many scholars (Creswell, 2009; Dörnyei, 2007; Greene, 2007; Mason, 2006), and has been gaining increasing popularity (Dörnyei, 2007). Furthermore, mixed methods research could enable to investigate of the phenomenon as a whole rather than just a part of it; using the mixed methods to gather and evaluate data might also assist to increase the validity and reliability of the study (Creswell, 2003).

To sum up, this mixed methods design was judged to be best suited to this study with its *"great potential to promote a shared responsibility in the quest for attaining accountability for educational quality"* (Johnson & Onwuegbuzie, 2004. p.24). I would like to gain a deep and broad description of the training module in order to develop ELT proficiency among student teachers in multi-ethnic communities in Yunnan Province. Once the mixed methods research design was selected for the study, the next step was to decide on the specific design that best addressed the research problems (Creswell, 2009). To develop the adequacy of the research strategy, I needed first to ask whether this research design could be conducted without harming people or significantly disrupting the setting (Marshall & Rossman, 2010). Some ethical rules of behavior must be followed to prevent me from doing harm to others and to protect myself at the same time (Marshall & Rossman, 2010).

Applied to the present research, it meant that I could improve my inquiry by collecting and converging (or integrating) different kinds of data bearing on the same phenomenon (Creswell, 2012). To converge the two sources of quantitative and qualitative results, and the phenomenon in a single study would continue to be an attractive approach to mixed methods research (Creswell, 2012). That was, I collected quantitative and qualitative data separately in two phases so that the complete data from one source could enhance, elaborate, or complement the data from the other source (Greene & Caracelli, 1997).

To identify the specific types of strategy designs according to Creswell (2012), the following questions were examined:

1. What priority or weight to give the quantitative and qualitative data collection?

2. What is the sequence of collecting the quantitative and qualitative data?

3. How to actually analyze the data?

4. Where to mix the data in the study?

Greene (2007) also indicated that a good researcher needs to use a combination of both raw data and individual impressions in order to get a full picture of the topic. Hence, based on the purposes and research questions of this study, I conducted the study with a convergent mixed methods design which matched with my study well because I expected this convergence to supply the strengths of one form to the weaknesses of the other form so that a complete understanding resulted from collecting both quantitative and qualitative data (Creswell, 2012). Thus, I believed the rationale of this cross-validating combination that the quantitative data and results would provide a general picture of student-teachers' performances on ELT proficiency; and more specific analysis through qualitative data collection was also required to interpret a deeper insight into student-teachers' ELT proficiency.

Generally speaking, the mixed methods research is best suited to an "umbrella" paradigm of pragmatism (Creswell, 2012). The purpose of this design was to better understand or develop a more complete understanding of the research problems by obtaining different but complementary data, and another purpose of validation (Creswell, 2012). Given the research rationale and identification of the mixed methods research, I gave equal priority to both quantitative and qualitative data, and collected both quantitative and qualitative data in a simultaneous sequence during the study.

Comparing the strengths and weaknesses of this research design, one of the most advantageous characteristics of conducting this mixed methods research was the possibility of triangulation, such as the use of multiple means (instruments, data sources, participants and methods of analysis, and so on) to examine the same phenomenon. Triangulation allowed me to identify different aspects of a phenomenon more accurately by approaching it from different vantage points using different methods and techniques, that was, achieving triangulation by gathering multiple sources of data could increase the validity of the results (Titus, 2015). Creswell (2012) pointed out that successful triangulation requires careful analysis of the type of information provided by each method, including its strengths and weaknesses.

Every coin has two sides, I could claim it would be labor intensive in terms of the weakness of the research design, because it required both expertise and time to collect both quantitative and qualitative data at the same time (Creswell, 2012). Additionally, based on the present situation, it was a challenge for me to compare and integrate the results from two different forms of analysis without enough experience even though the data collection was conducted concurrently.

## 3.3 Research Process and Training Phases

Once the research design of the study was identified, I also developed a merging framework of the research and training processes in order to show how I conducted the mixed methods research study in the action and practice during the course of the whole training. The main purpose of the study was to develop a feasible training module to improve ELT proficiency among student-teachers in such a setting, so according to the ADDIE process of training and development (Richard & Elwood, 2009), six different but related phases among the ADDIEM training process were involved in the central research problems of ELT proficiency, it included: Phase one: Needs analysis; Phase two: Training Design; Phase three: Training Development; Phase four: Training Implementation; Phase five: Training Evaluation, and Phase six: Training Modification. These ADDIEM training phases constituting the complete research process of the study represented a clear consistency with the research design. Specifically, the results of RQ1 could be extracted from the Phase I and Phase II, the results of RQ2 could be extracted from Phase III and Phase IV, and the results of RQ3 could be extracted from Phase V and Phase VI, see Figure 3.1.

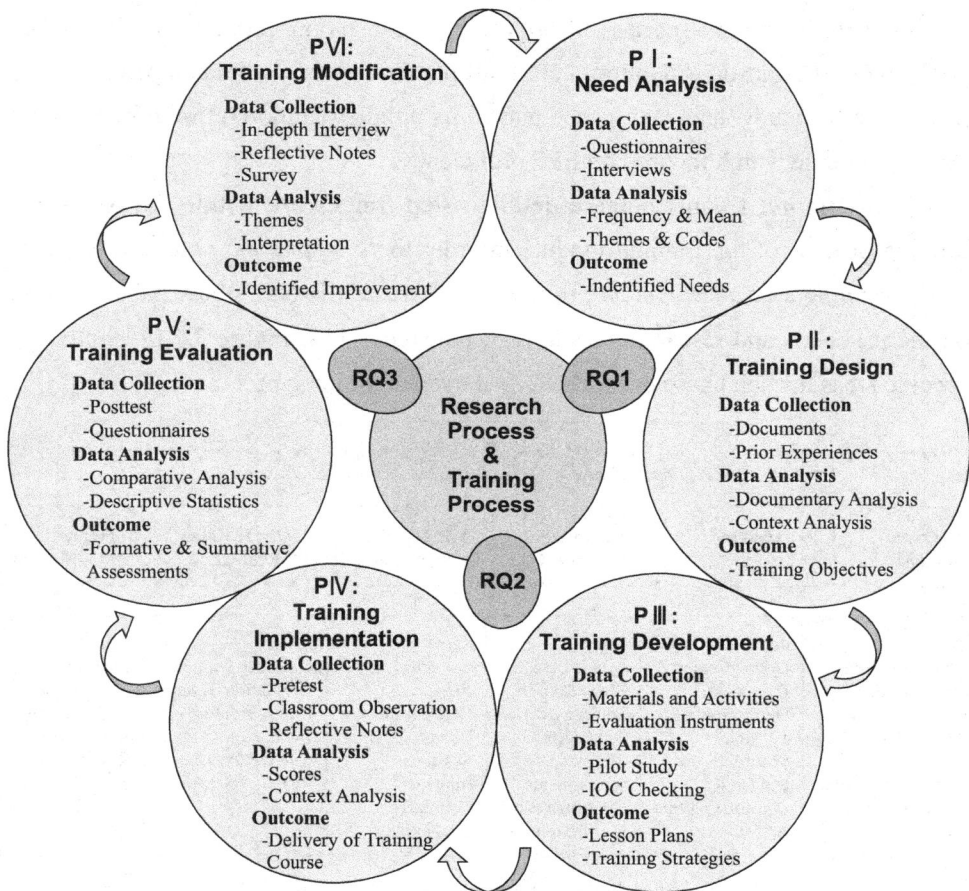

**Figure** 3.1   Research Process and Training Phases
(*Source*: Adapted from Creswell, 2012; Johnson, 2014)

In terms of the origins of the ADDIEM process, it is rooted in a five-phase process (analyze, design, develop, implement, and evaluate). It is probably the most widely used methodology of systematic training (Allen, 2006). Allen (2006) offered the following reflections on the ADDIE training model: *"The ADDIE process is an adaptation of the systems engineering process to problems of workplace training and instruction. The process assumes that alternative solutions to instructional problems will be more or less cost efficient depending on the instructional need and environmental constraints, and that a systems approach intelligently choosing among alternative solutions will produce the most effective results"* (p.431). Combined with another process of Training for Performance System (TPS) for developing human expertise for the purpose of improving organization, process, and individual performance (Swanson & Holton, 2009), all phases consisted of a complete training process of the study, and each phase played its uniquely important role for the final training module which focused on ELT proficiency.

Furthermore, I constructed a detailed step framework within the ADDIEM training process of the training module in order to *"lead and maintain the integrity of the training and development process"* (Richard & Elwood, 2009, p.244). Based on the problems and research questions of the study, thus, Figure 3.2 illustrates the specific steps in each phase of the ADDIEM cyclical training process.

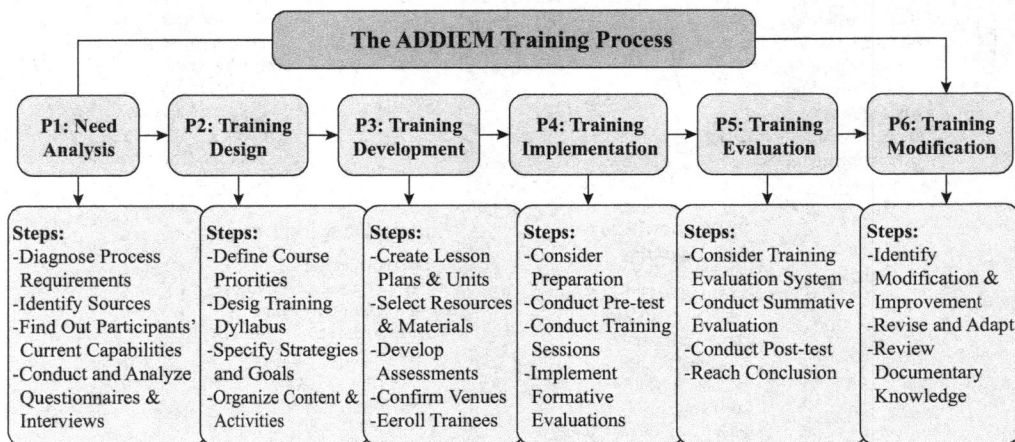

**Figure** 3.2    Specific Steps within the ADDIEM Training Process
(*Source*: Adapted from Richard & Elwood, 2009)

All in all, each phase of the ADDIEM training process consisted of several steps or activities which helped lead me to develop the course training and conduct all activities systematically. Similarly, the ADDIEM training process also helped me make decisions on how to gather the necessary information so as to propose a feasible training module for the study. Given the detailed steps in each process phase, I got familiar with the instruments mentioned above and procedures to focus on the term "ELT proficiency". It deserves to be mentioned here that the ADDIEM training process is cyclical to cater to the nature of training. As a mixed methods research design, aspects that should be paid attention to in order to gain a comprehensive understanding of the problems were discussed and interpreted during the course of data collection and analysis (Creswell, 2012).

## 3.4   Research Methods

The present study was mixed in its design, combining both quantitative with qualitative approaches during the data collection and analysis phases of the study, and complex as it employed the process of training and development in the research process as the overall instrument. Thus, the combination of research methods was likely to recur in each step of the training and development cycle. Particularly, the study incorporated the convergent (or concurrent) parallel design (Creswell, 2012). Primarily aiming to explore the student-teachers' professional needs, especially their ELT proficiency in multi-ethnic schools in Yunnan Province, both the quantitative method and qualitative method, with equally priority balanced, were conducted simultaneously during the first phase of the study. Quantitatively, I employed a survey to assess the student-teachers' English language and teaching proficiency practices in the classroom, and at the same time, practices in a natural teaching environment during the course of their teaching practicum were observed. By comparing the two types of data, I expected to see if there was a good match between what student-teachers thought they processed lacked and what they were actually doing in terms of English language teaching proficiency practices.

### 3.4.1   Context of the Study

Under the present context of lacking qualified bilingual teachers in preschool education, and the lack of an effective professional training system for English teachers, it was urgent to cultivate qualified kindergarten and primary teachers, and explore an effective training model for Chinese bilingual teachers (Zhu, 2007). As a vocational department specializing in kindergarten and primary teachers training in multi-ethnic areas, Dali University, as a provincial comprehensive university, is located in the centre of the Dali Bai autonomous prefecture out of 8 other municipalities and 7 minority autonomous prefectures in the north-west of the frontier Yunnan Province of China. It was also my own working place, holding its special geographical location and unique cultural environments in all of Yunnan Province. It should take the underlying responsibility to develop in-depth research about ELT proficiency training for the professional development of kindergarten and primary school teachers (Wang, 2012).

Dali University is located in the centre of Dali Bai autonomous prefecture in the north-west of the frontier Yunnan Province of China.

More attention is being paid to preschool education in recent years because of its promising employment opportunities in Yunnan Province and even in other minority areas (Lv, 2016). The enrollment of the past 5 years for the undergraduate majors of preschool education and primary education in Dali University is at a relatively higher proportion, each year, as it enrolls on average 150 undergraduates (Enrollment Network of Dali University, 2017), and Dali University has offered a graduate-level major of preschool education and primary education since 2016. With regard to the 4-year undergraduate program, its cultivating objective is to produce high-quality graduates with preschool and primary teaching, and scientific research and management competencies, who can master basic theoretical and professional knowledge of preschool education, possess observation ability and skills in analyzing children's physical and mental characteristics and carry out care and education for them. Moreover, they are expected to be familiar with the national educational policy, related laws and regulations, to know the developing dynamics related to theories and practices, to have the organizational and operational skills of subjects, and to have a higher professional quality of teaching in preschool and primary education, and scientific research and management (Cultivating Program of Preschool Education Major of Dali University, 2014). As one of the selective courses, *English Pedagogy for Preschoolers* is open for preschool education majors in the second semester of the third academic year, while other English courses, such as *College English*, are arranged for all non-English majors in the first and second academic years. The required teaching practicum in kindergartens and primary schools with a length of 5~6 weeks, then, is arranged in the 1st or 2nd semester of the fourth academic year.

Additionally, I had been fulfilling the responsibility in the Faculty of Education of Dali University with several years of teaching experience in the implementation of these curricula for the preschool education majors and primary education majors, such as, *English Pedagogy for Pre-schoolers*, *English Teaching in Primary School*, and *College English* for non-English majors. Therefore, I was fairly familiar with the research site and had convenient access to the setting. This indeed saved me time, effort and funding, which were the main reasons behind the choice of the research site, because such a setting helped me gain a high level of insight about the actual situation (Creswell & Clark, 2007).

### 3.4.2  Quantitative Research Design

#### 3.4.2.1  Population and Respondents

The population of the study was mainly student-teachers (including both bachelors and masters), majoring in preschool education and primary school education, who were studying at the current campus of Dali University; and some English teachers who had some English teaching experience in different schools were also involved. Due to the number of trainees being very large, the purposive sampling procedure was selected by using a gatekeeper technique to provide valuable information related to the research questions (Teddlie & Tashakkori, 2009). The sample was divided into 5 groups. Group A consisted of 155 3rd year students in the academic year of 2015, they were distributed into 3 classes and they took part in a learning course named *Preschool English Education* for a semester (32 periods). Group B consisted of 75 4th year students in the academic year of 2014, and they had taken a required teaching practicum in some kindergartens for about 5~6 weeks. Group C consisted of 30 Master's degree students majoring in preschool education on campus. Group D consisted of 20 teachers with some English teaching experience, and they were mainly from two different primary schools, four different kindergartens, four different middle schools and one training school. All these samples were involved in answering different survey questionnaires based on the conceptual framework set forth in Chapter One.

In fact, 152 (90.48%) student-teachers responded to the first set of questionnaires while 16 (9.52%) English teachers answered the second set of questionnaires. Out of 152 student-teachers in the first cohort, 126 (75%) were bachelor's and 26 (15.48%) were master's degree students, both were majoring in preschool education and were on the campus of Dali University. In the second cohort, out of 16 English teachers, 11 (6.55%) were kindergarten English teachers, 2 (1.19%) were primary English teachers, and 3 (1.78%) were middle school English teachers. The actual number of respondents to the questionnaires is shown with their demographic analysis in Table 3.1.

Table 3.1 Number and Percentage of Respondents (N = 168)

| Cohort | | Number | Percentage |
|---|---|---|---|
| Student-teachers | Bachelors | 126 | 75.00% |
| | Masters | 26 | 15.48% |
| English teachers | Kindergarten | 11 | 6.55% |
| | Primary school | 2 | 1.19% |
| | Middle school | 3 | 1.78% |

### 3.4.2.2 Quantitative Instruments

For the quantitative phase of the mixed methods research, a questionnaire, pre-test and post-test were employed.

According to Robson (2002), the questionnaire is the most widely used instrument for gathering research data in quantitative research. Most of what was studied about human behavior stems from questionnaires. Two sets of self-administered questionnaires, aimed at identifying the possible challenges for the phase of training needs analysis and specific components in developing ELT proficiency training module, were employed for the two groups of student-teachers (2014 and 2015 academic years); Moreover, pre-test and post-test designs were the preferred method to compare different participant groups and measure the degree of change occurring as a result of treatments or interventions for many true experimental designs (Kumari, 2013). Pre-test and post-test procedures were conducted during the training process for both training implementation and training evaluation. The pre-test and post-test were administered to measure the trainees' ELT proficiency before and after the implementation of the training.

Validity and reliability were two factors that I was concerned about while designing the research, analyzing the results, and judging the quality of the study. Frankel and Wallen (2000) defined validity as the ability of a process of collecting evidence to support inference; it was a process of determining whether the instrument measured what it was supposed to measure. They further argued that reliability referred to how consistent a research procedure or instrument is. The degree of consistency was demonstrated in the study. Thus, a pilot study was used first to test the consistency of internal data, the reliability of the measurement scales for the variables used in the questionnaire and to test the goodness of the data (Sekaran, 2000). In short, a pilot study allowed a time period to complete the questionnaires, which ensured clarity of the questions and instructions, whether the questionnaires had covered all important topics and whether the layout was clear and attractive; and it also identified sensitive questions that respondents might be reluctant to answer, and facilitate consideration of the comments and suggestions by the respondents (Bryman & Bell, 2007). It implied stability and dependability of the instruments or procedures in order to obtain information. Yin (2003) identified four tests for judging the quality of case study designs: construct validity, internal validity, external validity, and reliability.

Furthermore, Best and Kahn (2003) emphasized that validity and reliability are essential to the effectiveness of the data collecting procedure. Based on the theoretical framework of the research design, the data collection instruments were chosen after considering the validity and reliability upon their appropriateness (Creswell, 2003).

Therefore, to enhance the study rigor and increase internal validity, the following measures were employed. Firstly, I designed the items according to the conceptual framework in advance based on the literature about research-based instructional practices and my own experiences in classroom management. I divided all the questionnaires into five aspects: Linguistic Basis, Teaching Design, Teaching Implementation, Teaching Techniques and Comprehensive Aspects. Based on the reviewed literature, my own experiences with ELT proficiency and teacher training, and comments and recommendations from my advisors, Dr. Janpanit and Dr. Denchai, the 5th version of questionnaires was developed and finalized. After being checked and examined by the proposed experts in the EFL field of teacher training, the Item-Objective Congruence (IOC) was used to evaluate and determine its validity and reliability, it was 0.906. Surely, to ensure a high degree of validity, a pilot study was tested for content validity and clarity of the items with a sample group of experts who had professional development training experience. Content validity was established when the items or questions in the survey accurately represented the characteristics of attitudes they were intended to measure (Creswell, 2003). To further promote trustworthiness, two colleagues who had research skills and experience in this field were invited to examine the structure and items of the questionnaires before conducting them. Secondly, the original diagnostic pretest was administered at the very beginning of the need analysis phase to assess the trainees' prior knowledge/ skills of the first training topic: Comprehensive Pronunciation of Linguistic Basis for placement purposes. It was expected that the trainees could write out certain phonetic symbols, and then were graded by the trainer for later comparison with the posttest after the training implementation.

### 3.4.2.3 Quantitative Data Collection

Two cohorts of respondents were respectively given two different self-administered questionnaires after the pilot test and experts' check (reflective notes: July 2, 2018 ~ August 6, 2018), which were developed and employed by selecting carefully according to the Conceptual Framework (reflective notes: December 10, 2017~July 1, 2018). A paper-based questionnaire was administered to two cohorts in the study. The questionnaire aimed at identifying the possible problems occurring in the English teaching classroom in kindergartens or primary schools. The specific procedures included distribution of the questionnaires to all of the student-teachers and English teachers, including consent forms and instructions for completing each section. And I collected the questionnaires right after completion by the respondents.

In terms of the pretest and posttest, a paper test was designed and provided for the trainees on the particular training unit of Module I: Topic 1: Comprehensive Pronunciation (reflective notes: October 23, 2018). The trainees were asked to write out the phonetic symbols in brackets based on the underlined sounds, and list the letter or monogram in the blanks within 20 minutes, and then, all the test papers were collected with their code numbers.

### 3.4.2.4  Quantitative Data Analysis

In quantitative research, the demographic variables were analyzed for descriptive and analytical statistics. The purpose of the survey was to determine the range and type of student-teachers' self-reported perceptions, experiences and attitudes. Frequencies, percentages, and mean scores were reported for every item and every scale. I used a descriptive statistics technique to tabulate the frequency counts, percentages, means, and standard deviations for individual items to address these problems by SPSS, version 19. Thus, most of the results are presented in the tables and described in narrative forms.

## 3.4.3  Qualitative Research Design

### 3.4.3.1  Informants and Participants

Informants chosen purposively were invited to participate in an interview. The number of informants was determined by the completeness or saturation of the information provided by a given number of participants. Saturation was used to indicate when to stop gathering data (Rubin & Rubin, 1995). Thus, five English teachers working in kindergartens around Dali city, two administrators in the Faculty of Education of Dali University, three stakeholders in bilingual kindergartens, and eight parents involved in bilingual kindergartens, which were close to my proximity, were interviewed with different interview guides in the Need Analysis Phase and training Development Phase. Another additional group of participants was enrolled from the target student-teachers as the real trainees in the training Development Phase. The estimated number of additional participants were conducted by statistical tests with sufficient power result of 45, calculated by using the Power Software (Erdfelder, Faul, & Buchner, 1996). Finally, 58 participants were identified by using a volunteer sampling technique. More active volunteers still applied for enrolling in the training group but were refused because of consideration for the training effectiveness. The 58 participants were engaged in the practical training and were expected to provide useful feedback and suggestions about the effectiveness of the training.

### 3.4.3.2 Qualitative Instruments

Many techniques were used in the qualitative fieldwork. The major clusters of data gathering techniques were interviews, classroom observations, documents, personal experiences, and reflective notes about the qualitative data collection, as follows.

Three different sets of semi-structured and open-ended interviews were used to gather their perspectives and values about English teaching proficiency from the involved English kindergarten teachers, administrators, stakeholders and parents to encourage the participants. Additionally, a focus group interview, which was efficient and time saving, was used as the primary technique of data collection. This small group interview on some specific topics was employed for some trainees after training development (Patton, 2002).

The main purpose of classroom observation was to help understand how the student-teachers interpreted and implemented the impact of the training in their classroom teaching and learning. The first hand and authentic phenomena that existed in the classrooms, such as daily reports, classroom performance, volunteer response, feelings and opinions were investigated to facilitate interpreting the trainees' attainment of achievement, performance, their facial expressions and emotions, and to make adaptable interactions, improvements for the possible modification of the training. In terms of observation techniques, I recorded unstructured or semi-structured field notes about their behavior, performance and activities including the classroom environment at the research site by field notes, research diaries and document sheets, etc. (Sarma, 2012).

The related documents included some teaching logs, syllabus of the curriculum, assignments, worksheets, checkouts, and so on, combined with my own personal experiences about the uncertainties and queries, were used to extract instrumental verifications, opinions or conclusions to be used as a necessary supplement for the interview and classroom observations as well.

Last but not least, Creswell (2003) stated that in qualitative research, the investigator was also one of the instruments. The investigator's conceptualization, background, psychology and emotions could respond to the problems which contributed to the final outcomes of the study. Thus, to assure the credibility of the study, I kept detailed reflective notes throughout the study because Brookfield (1995) underlined that writing reflective notes enabled clarification and exploration of the complexities of teaching and gain insights into professional practices (p.190, cited in Hue & Li, 2008). Williams, Woolliams and Spiro (2012) also highlighted that it was not sufficient to have an experience in order to learn. Without reflecting on the experience, it might quickly be forgotten, or its learning potential lost. In terms of planning data collection and recording mode, I also acted as an instrument, the initial design ought to display an awareness of these facts and to make provision for the kinds of data collection activities (Lincoln & Guba, 1985).

### 3.4.3.3 Qualitative Data Collection

Growing out of the central research questions, interview items must be designed open-ended to encourage the participants to voice their perspectives and share their values and beliefs about the topic (Creswell & Plano Clark, 2011). Namely, the interview aimed at analyzing the training needs and investigating the problems by open-ended questions. The interview guidelines were developed and then were checked, corrected, adjusted and finalized by the advisory committee in order to improve its quality. Afterwards, the interviews were also examined by the proposed experts in the relative EFL field of teacher training. The interviews were simultaneous and lasted 30~45 minutes for the five kindergarten English teachers, two administrators, three stakeholders and eight parents that were invited to participate from July 12, 2018~August 14, 2018.

With regard to the qualitative research, it was intended to take place in a natural setting. I conducted the interviews in a convenient setting for the participants, such as time and place, which helped me develop a level of detail about the individual or place, and to be highly involved in the actual experience of the participants (Creswell,

2003). Because the data collection took place in China, where the participants found difficulty in speaking English, which was also a barrier for conducting the interview, I used the Chinese language as the media for interviewing the participants in order to ensure the quality of each interview in terms of the richness of the data. Lastly, the whole course of the interviews was tape-recorded to assure its completeness of data, because it reduced the tendency of interviewers to make an unconscious selection of data favoring their biases and it was also possible to reanalyze the taped interview data to test possible hypotheses not considered in the original study survey (Creswell, 2003).

Observational data are another valuable source of data in qualitative research, as it *"represents first hand encounter with the phenomenon of interest rather than a second hand account of the world obtained in an interview"* (Merriam, 1998, p.94). Therefore, participant observation in the classroom allowed me to be part of the natural setting and become part of it (Coleman & Briggs, 2005). This type of observation involved writing field notes and recording events using audiovisual means in a relatively unstructured way. The classroom observations were mainly conducted in the training implementation phase, which included a series of sub-sections, such as daily reports, classroom performance, volunteer responses, feelings and emotions, and so on. The trainees who were drawn from purposive sampling were observed during their classroom performances with an observational checklist, matrix and protocol which involved the student-teachers interaction, the use of comprehensive inputs background knowledge, and strategies (Briggs & Coleman, Morrison, 2012). Furthermore, their impromptu actions and performances in the classroom were compared against the actual teaching experience as observed by myself and the learning experiences as acquired from the questionnaires by the participants.

Documents, as an umbrella term, refers to *"a wide range of written, visual, digital, and physical materials relevant to the study at hand"* (Merriam, 2009, p.139). Such integrated documents included daily teaching logs, hand-works or teaching aids, syllabus of courses, referenced textbooks, teaching videos and pictures, literature reviews, analysis of findings and discussion via the internet, libraries, and other relevant dissertations, theses and journals, and so on, which were related to the

English teaching proficiency in the training program, were used to further elicit these student-teachers' learning and teaching experiences during the process of training implementation. I compiled these documents and reviewed them to make clarification and confirmation to understand the participant's perspective and behavior (Maxwell, 2005).

In terms of reflective notes, the student-teachers were also asked to record any reflections about their learning during the entire training process except my own reflection. I believed that the reflective notes could allow student-teachers to reflect on new knowledge learned in class, solidify their learning experience by recording their evolving thought processes as they progressed further in the training, learned new materials, and formed new conclusions (Stevens & Cooper, 2009, p.3). Therefore, I purposively provided the student-teachers with some opportunities in 5~8 minutes reports/conclusions at the end of each class to share their new opinions or perspectives, giving them a risk free venue to explore, think, and practice skills acquired in class in order to identify their improvement, uncertainties and disadvantages. To myself, I took reflective notes as immediately as possible before, during or after each training unit to make sense of and learn from both the trainees' and my experiences, which allowed me to demonstrate that I could think critically about my own skills or practice in order to improve further (Stevens & Cooper, 2009, p.33).

### 3.4.3.4 Qualitative Data Analysis

The goal of data analysis is to make sense of the qualitative data from the study. Analysis consisted of three concurrent flows of activity: data reduction, data display, and conclusion drawing/verification (Miles & Huberman, 1994). Data analysis began right away after data collection in order to facilitate later data collection phases (Lincoln & Guba, 1985). Qualitative research techniques were used to analyze complex subjects like the student-teachers' interaction and changes in practice, because it allowed for their behavior to be observed and for individuals to respond with descriptions of personal feelings, perceptions, beliefs and emotions (Patton, 2003), which stressed the importance of people, places and situations.

Creswell (2003) provided six steps, they are: (1) to organize and prepare the data for analysis; (2) to read through all the data; (3) to begin detailed analysis with a coding process; (4) to use the coding process to generate a description of the setting or people as well as categories or themes for analysis; (5) to advance how the description and themes were represented in the qualitative narrative; (6) a final step in data analysis involves making an interpretation of meaning of the data.

Therefore, an automatic switch from sounds to words functioned in WeChat was mainly transcribed verbatim and checked by myself for maximization of accuracy. Transcribed interviews were broken down into units and themes that were more easily analyzed (Creswell, 2003). Also, field notes during classroom observations were analyzed and feedbacks were given after the research was complete and the final draft approved. Interpretive commentaries related to the data were included in the analysis. Charting the interview responses by questions allowed me to graphically view patterns and themes. Initial reflections of apparent themes and patterns were discussed and recorded at that time as a narrative description or summary of preliminary impressions (Creswell, 2003).

To reduce the risk of bias and misrepresentation of the data, I triangulated the data in different ways, which enhanced the use of multiple methods, as well as member checking, peer debriefing, thick description, and addressing plausible hypotheses (Creswell, 2012). There were several general data collection methods available such as interviews, training observation, and documents employed in the study, and the domain of data collection procedures generally included records of interviews, the decision of themes and categories for analysis, transcription convention and procedures, coding, sorting, and so on. Nevertheless, collecting data in such a mixed methods study followed rigorous quantitative procedures and persuasive qualitative procedures (Creswell, 2012).

### 3.4.4 Linkage between Data Collection and Data Analysis

The present study was congruent with Creswell (2009) in ELT proficiency to collect all the data from the questionnaires, pre-post tests, interviews, class observations, reflective notes and documents. In this convergent design, after collecting both quantitative and qualitative data concurrently, I used parallel construction for both types of data to assess information; separately analyzing both types of data; and then merging the two databases, comparing results through procedures such as a side-by-side comparison in a discussion, transforming the qualitative dataset into quantitative scores, or jointly displaying both forms of data (Creswell, 2012). The merging approach had also been called simultaneous integration (Morse & Niehaus, 2009), so I made an illustration of the need analysis to merge the results to answer the research questions by comparing the two datasets or by transforming one of the datasets and conducting further analyses.

The purposes of the study aimed at seeking different perspectives from student-teachers and tried to construct the training module to develop their ELT proficiency in such case of context. To sum up, I illustrated a close relationship between the research questions, data collection and analysis to show how these three aspects were combined. There are three research questions in the first column; the second column is about how the data were collected by multiple methods; in terms of the third column, it presents how the data were analyzed by different procedures. Simply speaking, each research question can be interpreted in corresponding linkage of data collection and analysis (see Table 3.2).

**Table 3.2 Relationship among the Research Questions, Data Collection and Data Analysis**

| Research Questions | Data Collection | Data Analysis |
|---|---|---|
| What are the challenges facing the current student-teachers in teaching English to beginning learners in multi-ethnic community schools in Yunnan Province? | -Questionnaires<br>-Interviews<br>-Personal Experiences<br>-Documents | -Descriptive Statistice<br>-Transcription & Interpretation<br>-Comparison & Examination<br>-Documentary Analysis |
| What are specific components of training activities for student-teachers in teaching English effectively in multi-ethnic community schools in Yunnan Province? | -Interviews<br>-Questionnaires<br>-Class Observations<br>-Artifacts/Documents | -Transcription & lnterpretatin<br>-Descriptive Statistics<br>-Videotaped Observations<br>-Artifacts/Documentary Analysis |
| How does the training process develop and to what extent does the training module improve student-teachers ELT proficiency? | -Surveys<br>-In-depth lnterviews<br>-Pretest & Posttest<br>-Class Observations<br>-Reflective Notes | -Descriptive Statistics<br>-Transcriptions & Interpretation<br>-Comparative Analysis<br>-Videotaped Observations<br>-Interpretation |

Therefore, both quantifying qualitative data and qualifying quantitative data were adopted according to Creswell (2012). On one side, qualitative data were coded, and codes were assigned numbers, and the number of times codes were recorded as numeric data. Quantitative data were descriptively analyzed for frequency of occurrence; lastly, the two datasets were compared. On the other hand, quantitative data from questionnaires were factor analyzed. These factors then became themes that were compared with themes analyzed from qualitative data. Specifically, I proposed frequency/descriptive statistics, one sample t-tests to interpret quantitative results, and qualitative data analysis utilized a three-step coding process consisting of thematic coding, pattern coding, and triangulation. This dual data analysis procedure in the mixed methods was utilising to capture multiple perspectives to develop a more complete training module for ELT proficiency in such a context.

The goal here was to triangulate the findings from the two forms of data. Triangulation of the two sets of findings served to validate both the qualitative and quantitative findings. Data were collected through multiple sources that included questionnaires, interviews, classroom observations, documents and my notes, so the techniques of triangulation strengthened the design by integrating the data collected from all sources. Thus, the results were corroborated with interview data, and the use of interviews and observations to validate through questionnaires (Creswell, 2003).

## 3.5 Ethical Considerations

Ethical considerations guided me in planning, data collection, data analysis and findings, which were considered in the whole of the research because it involved collecting information from people and about people (Sovichea, 2012). Before participating in the qualitative part and completing the survey of the study, I ensured that ethical issues were the priority and discussed this issue with each participant in advance. Since mixed methods research combines quantitative and qualitative research, ethical considerations need to attend to typical ethical issues that surface in both forms of inquiry (Creswell, 2012). Specifically, quantitative issues related to obtaining permission, protecting the anonymity of respondents, and not disrupting sites of the study. In qualitative research, these issues are related to conveying the purpose of the study, avoiding deceptive practices, respecting vulnerable populations, being aware of potential power issues in data collection, respecting indigenous cultures, not disclosing sensitive information, and masking the identities of participants. For this convergent design, the quantitative and qualitative sample sizes were different; therefore, care needed to be taken to not minimize the importance of the sample because of its size (Creswell, 2012). Punch (2009) suggested that the main ethical issues in social research are harm, consent, privacy, and confidentiality of the data. This study involved mainly with humans in assessing and collecting the data from pre-service trainees' perspectives; therefore, I considered the research rationale, methods, procedures, and steps in a systematic way in response to the ethical considerations.

### 3.5.1 Harmfulness

Richards and Morse (2007) stated that a researcher must ensure that no participants' anonymity is violated indirectly, through the linking of their demographic characteristics. In a similar discussion, Stake (2010) asserted that, in social research, the dangers are rarely physical but mental. They are dangers of exposure, humiliation, embarrassment, loss of respect and self-respect, and loss of standing at work or in the group. Berg (1998, cited in Sakulkoo, 2009, p.76) also noted that *"by carefully considering possible harm to subjects in advance, researchers can sometimes avoid personal embarrassment and breaches of confidentiality"*. Furthermore, Marshall and Roseman (1999, cited in Sakulkoo, 2009) concluded that I could not anticipate everything, but he or she must reveal an awareness of, and an appreciation for and commitment to, ethical principles.

### 3.5.2 Informed Consent

Berg (1998, cited in Sakulkoo, 2009, p.75) described the meaning of informed consent as *"the knowing consent of individuals to participate as an exercise of their choice, free from any element of fraud, deceit, duress or similar unfair inducement or manipulation"*. Informed consent is an important way to respect individual differences. Denzin and Lincoln (2005) explained that consistent with the commitment to individual autonomy, social science insists that research subjects have the right to be informed about the nature of the consequences of the study. Creswell (2003) suggested that researchers should ask the participants to sign an informed consent form before they are engaged in the study and give each participant an opportunity to ask questions. Richards and Morse (2007) advised that participant consent forms should clarify the uses of research materials, such as photographs, videos, and other documents. Moreover, they needed to include the rights of participants as follows: (1) the right to be fully informed about the study's purpose; (2) the right to confidentiality and anonymity; (3) the right to refuse to participate in the research; (4) the right to withdraw from the study at anytime; (5) the right to ask questions. Thus, I designed the consent form and gave it to the participants for agreement before conducting the questionnaires, interviews and observations.

### 3.5.3　Privacy and Confidentiality

I protected the privacy of each participant and confidentiality of data to the maximum extent possible, and communicated how this was done in the consent statement. Teddle and Tashakkori (2009) suggested that there are two aspects of the privacy issue: anonymity and confidentiality. Anonymity refers to the process of protecting the identity of specific individuals. On the other hand, confidentiality means that the research participants are protected by remaining unidentifiable. Thus, I used code numbers rather than names, collected only necessary information, reported group rather than individual results, and secured research materials in ways to maintain confidentiality (John, Werner, Randy & Simone, 2006). Last but not least, any materials from questionnaires, interviews or observations must be stored in a safe place (Hesse-Biber & Leavy, 2006).

## 3.6　Summary

In this chapter, the specific procedures for the convergent mixed methods research study, such as the research paradigm and rationale, research design, research process and phases, research methods, and ethical considerations are displayed. To highlight the convergence of the research and focus on the research questions all the while, I divided and presented the process of data collection and data analysis into two branches, quantitative and qualitative, aiming at displaying a much clearer and complete structure for each step.

# CHAPTER 4
# FINDINGS

This chapter presents the findings obtained from the qualitative and quantitative research methods by acquiring knowledge of developing a training module to improve the ELT proficiency at the beginning level. This chapter is divided into the following sections based on the ADDIEM Training Framework.

4.1    Context of the Present Study

4.2    Findings of Research Question 1

4.3    Findings of Research Question 2

4.4    Findings of Research Question 3

4.5    Summary

## 4.1    Context of the Present Study

This section presents a general description of developing and implementing the ADDIEM Training Framework, which was developed for the entire training process. Specifically, six different phases constituted this complete training process, also the research process of the study, which were kept very consistent with the research design by using the mixed quantitative and qualitative research and data, such as questionnaires, pre-test and post-test, interviews, class observations, reflective notes, audio-visual materials, and training-related documents were consequently employed as the data collection instruments of the study.

Based on the problems and research questions of the study, I constructed a detailed framework within the training process in order to lead and maintain the integrity of the training and development process (Richard & Elwood, 2009). Each training phase consisted of several steps and activities which led me to develop the training and conduct all activities systematically. It was informed that the outcomes of the current student-teachers' challenges were identified in the Needs Analysis Phase, the training objectives and its syllabus were specified in the Training Design Phase, the lesson plans, instructional strategies and assessment criteria was prepared and determined in the Training Development Phase, the training candidates and location, and the delivery of the training were confirmed and conducted in the Training Implementation Phase, the formative and summative assessments were conducted and the training effectiveness was interpreted in the Training Evaluation Phase, and lastly, the acquired improvements and modification were identified in the Modification Phase. Thus, the training process was formed during the entire research process.

As a whole, the six training phases were systematically and logically sequenced in the long training process from October 2017 to March 2019 in Dali University. The training program gained multi-support and assistance from the staff especially two directors of teaching and research sections of the faculty; more importantly, the intended student-teachers involved in the stage of voluntary enrollment with particularly higher enthusiasm in despite of a limited number of trainees. Getting rid of a few unexpected absences and two special dropouts, the identified 58 trainees (actually only 45 were sufficient by using the Power Software) maintained certain ongoing positivity and interactivity based on the practical classroom observations and my reflective notes. Ultimately, it was not only highly accepted by the effectiveness of great benefit and satisfactory from the current student-teacher feedback, but also obtained a high appraisal from the current colleagues who highlighted the general proposed instructional designs.

## 4.2  Findings of Research Question 1

*Research Q 1: What are the challenges facing the current student-teachers in teaching English to beginning learners in multi-ethnic community schools in Yunnan Province?*

In order to answer this question, two sets of questionnaires were conducted by both student-teachers and English teachers based on their general perceptions, beliefs, current capacity towards the English language and teaching proficiency. Meanwhile, three groups of interviews were conducted with regards to parents, English teachers, and principals and stakeholders' general bilingual teaching practices, viewpoints, attitudes, professional development and social requirements. In the following section, the Needs Analysis Phase from the ADDIEM training process presents how to identify the "challenges" that occurred in the current situation.

## Results of the Needs Analysis Phase

### Quantitative Results

Based on the conceptual framework of the relationship between the training module and desired ELT proficiency, a total of 168 respondents were involved in the questionnaires in order to elicit their general perceptions and beliefs of their current capacities towards English language and teaching proficiency. Four aspects (Linguistic Basis, Teaching Design, Teaching Techniques and Teaching Implementation) totalling 64 items were posted in the student-teachers' questionnaire for 152 respondents, and 58 other ELT related questions on the item questionnaire were for 16 English teachers. Descriptive statistics were used to determine the frequencies from the student-teachers' self-assessment about their current ELT proficiency.

The 5-point Likert-type scale (1 = strongly disagree, 2 = disagree, 3 = neutral, 4 = agree, and 5 = strongly agree) was applied to rating the highest percentage of each item from the 168 informants' self-evaluation. It clearly indicated that their self-perceived needs about the current proficiencies voiced by both student-teachers and English teachers should be improved based on the rating range of Agree or Strongly Agree. The following Table 4.1 presents the Percentages of the proposed needs extracted from the two sets of questionnaires.

Table 4.1　Percentages of the Proposed Needs Extracted from the Two Sets of Questionnaires (N = 168)

| Aspects | Proposed Needs | 152 Student-teachers | 16 English teachers |
|---|---|---|---|
| Linguistic Basis | (1) to improve English pronunciation | 83.55% | 93.75% |
| | (2) to increase vocabulary | 92.76% | 75.00% |

Continued Table

| Aspects | Proposed Needs | 152 Student-teachers | 16 English teachers |
|---|---|---|---|
| **Linguistic Basis** | (3) to improve grammar | 84.87% | 81.25% |
| | (4) to improve British and American cultural knowledge | 70.39% | 62.50% |
| | (5) to improve cross-cultural communication knowledge | 75.66% | 75.00% |
| | (6) to improve listening ability | 84.21% | 87.50% |
| | (7) to improve speaking ability | 84.21% | 75.00% |
| | (8) to improve reading ability | 86.84% | 81.25% |
| | (9) to improve writing ability | 82.89% | 68.75% |
| **Teaching Design** | (1) to get more knowledge of preschool teaching syllabus | 85.53% | 56.25% |
| | (2) to get more knowledge of English teaching methodology | 86.18% | 56.25% |
| | (3) to learn how to analyze textbooks and contents | 88.82% | 81.25% |
| | (4) to learn how to analyze the young learners | 90.13% | 62.50% |
| | (5) to improve how to set teaching objectives and strategy | 88.16% | 62.50% |
| | (6) to improve how to select and utilize media and materials | 83.55% | 50.00% |
| | (7) to improve how to encourage young learners' participation | 88.82% | 75.00% |
| | (8) to improve how to design teaching plan | 84.87% | 87.50% |
| **Teaching Techniques** | (1) to improve telling stories techniques | 85.53% | 87.50% |
| | (2) to improve game playing techniques | 86.18% | 62.50% |
| | (3) to improve singing songs and rhymes techniques | 82.24% | 75.00% |
| | (4) to improve drawing stick figure techniques | 81.58% | 68.75% |
| | (5) to improve English handwriting | 76.32% | 68.75% |
| | (6) to improve playing tongue twister techniques | 55.92% | 75.00% |
| | (7) to improve the use of modern educational teaching technologies | 78.29% | 75.00% |

Continued Table

| Aspects | Proposed Needs | 152 Student-teachers | 16 English teachers |
|---|---|---|---|
| **Teaching Implementation** | (1) to improve how to select the appropriate teaching methods | 88.16% | 81.25% |
| | (2) to improve how to organize classrooms and teaching activities | 87.50% | 68.75% |
| | (3) to improve how to arrange teaching process | 88.82% | 87.50% |
| | (4) to improve how to evaluate teaching performance | 92.76% | 50.00% |

For example, when considering 1st item separately, it was found that 83.55% of the 152 student-teachers approved "*a qualified kindergarten English teacher should have standard and comprehensible English pronunciation*", and that was, they agreed or strongly agreed to improve their English pronunciation. In correspondence with student-teachers' cognitions, the results from other data indicated that 93.75% of the 16 English teachers also agreed or strongly agreed "*need to improve comprehensible pronunciation of English*". And so forth, the other themes from the Field of Linguistic Basis, such as Vocabulary, Grammar, British and American Cultural Background Knowledge, Cross-cultural Communication Knowledge, Listening Ability, Spoken English, Reading Ability, and Writing Ability could also be extracted by the highest rate of "agree and strongly agree". It indicated that the highest percentage of the preferential item from the 4 different aspects rated by the student-teachers and the English teachers varied totally. Such as, in the aspect of Linguistic Basis, 92.76% of student-teachers felt the need to improve their vocabulary, while 93.75% of English teachers chose to improve their English pronunciation; Teaching Design, 90.13% of student-teachers felt the need to improve how to analyze younger learners, while 87.50% of English teachers felt the need to improve how to design lesson plans; in the aspect of Teaching Techniques, 86.18% of student-teachers felt need to improve their game playing techniques, while 87.50% of English teachers felt need to improve story-telling techniques; and for Teaching Implementation, 92.76% of student-teachers felt need to improve how to evaluate teaching performance, while 87.50% of

English teachers felt need to improve how to arrange the teaching process. According to the parallel design of the study, all above descriptive analytical statistics were merged and analyzed with the following qualitative results to triangulate identifying the ultimate challenges.

**Qualitative Results**

In the process of need analysis, three different groups of interviews were also simultaneously conducted with parents, English teachers and principals, and stakeholders regarding their attitudes and viewpoints on bilingual teaching practices, professional development and social requirements. The coding method was used to organize the data. All the expectations from the parents, English teachers, stakeholders and principles were categorized and classified into eight categories of codes in the following Table 4.2 from most to least relevant according to the proposed themes.

**Table 4.2  Categories of Codes and the Classifications of Expectations Extracted from the Three Groups of Interviews**

| Categories of Codes | Classifications of Expectations | | |
| --- | --- | --- | --- |
| | Parents | Principals & English Teachers | Stakeholders |
| **Necessity/ Importance of Developing English Education at the Beginner Level** | -very necessary/ important<br>-as an international language<br>-language sensitive period<br>-to be helpful and beneficial to children's language development | -the younger, the better<br>-English as a global language<br>-to build a good language environment<br>-can foster interest, enrich knowledge<br>-every kindergarten should pay more attention to English education | -depends on social needs and adaptability<br>-governmental kindergartens are forbidden to develop English teaching in a Chinese situation |
| **Necessity of Developing Professional Training** | -proper training is of great necessity | -take more and further training<br>-to merge English into early education<br>-staff training is particularly important | -need professional training<br>-should not be neglected |

Continued Table

| Categories of Codes | Classifications of Expectations | | |
| --- | --- | --- | --- |
| | Parents | Principals & English Teachers | Stakeholders |
| Preference of Teaching Styles/ Methods | -game-centered activities<br>-to learn with playing<br>-to encourage more<br>-picture teaching<br>-assistant teaching tools | -real materials and body language<br>-role playing, story-telling, game-playing<br>-watch cartoons | - game-oriented<br>- life-oriented<br>- simplified |
| Content/ Purposes of Training | -professional English knowledge<br>-methodology about kindergarten education | -standard and comprehensive pronunciation, spoken English<br>-teaching methodologies, skills, techniques, strategies | -social communicative language<br>-natural spelling rules<br>-expand horizons and skills |
| Focusing on Teacher's Qualities | -have fluent and accurate spoken English pronunciation, professional proficiency and knowledge<br>-have morality, warm heart and accomplishments<br>-have high teaching management and organizational ability<br>-have good handwriting<br>-be fully immersed in teaching | -have comprehensive pronunciation, listening and speaking abilities, fluent communicative ability<br>-to be imaginative, passionate, creative, patient, active, energetic<br>-have a good personality<br>-have abilities to organize activities and games<br>-can build a pleasant environment<br>-can teach through lively activities<br>- know how to treat children | -standard English pronunciation<br>-organizational ability<br>-spoken English<br>-classroom languages<br>-daily organizational words |

Continued Table

| Categories of Codes | Classifications of Expectations | | |
|---|---|---|---|
| | Parents | Principals & English Teachers | Stakeholders |
| **Expectations/ Attitudes of Learning English for Young Learners** | -motivate interest, build a good language environment<br>-helpful for future learning, necessary enlightenment<br>-learn by themselves<br>-dislike teaching the rote way<br>-learn English songs<br>-learn oral expressions<br>-learn standard pronunciation | -be good for language development<br>-to provide more chances<br>-to let open mouths, speak more<br>-to adapt effective teaching models<br>-to attract children's attention | -to arouse interest<br>-to take language critical period<br>-to build a good language environment |
| **Problems/ Suggestions about English Education and Training** | -low professionalization<br>-rigid teaching activities<br>-passive and immature teaching<br>-not professional, not qualified, not competent<br>- undergraduates' poor pronunciation | -lack of interesting languages, effective classroom management and content, good language proficiency, more professional training, qualified professional teachers, and enough educational resources<br>-hope to be more systematic<br>-to neglect the nature of language teaching<br>-to take exams for the single purpose<br>-to be paid less attention | -low professionalization<br>-unbalanced development in different areas<br>-combine training into language courses<br>-to avoid formism<br>-to elaborate on training plans<br>-change training model/objectives |

These seven interrelated categories of codes were listed as follows: (1) Necessity/ Importance of Developing English Education at the Beginner Level; (2) Necessity of Developing Professional Training; (3) Preference of Teaching Styles/Methods; (4) Content/Purposes of Training; (5) Focusing on Teacher's Qualities; (6) Expectations/

Attitudes of Learning English for Young Learners; (7) Problems/Suggestions about English Education and Training. All these categories were revised, induced and summarized repeatedly from the beginning to the end of data analysis of the interviews, and finalized in order to excavate the intrinsic essence of the problems of the study. Briefly, the *italic phrases* shown in Table 4.2 represent the original quotations of data extracted from the three different groups of interviews, which were synthesized properly in order to avoid the repetitiveness of data.

Taking the category of the Focusing on Teacher's Qualities as an example, Parent A stated that she hoped that the English teacher would *"have fluent and accurate spoken English pronunciation..."* English teacher B mentioned that as a qualified English teacher, he/she should *"have comprehensive pronunciation..., good listening and speaking abilities..., fluent communicative ability"*, and Stakeholder C thought highly of *"standard English pronunciation"* as English teacher's prior quality. Based on the analysis of coding data, the theme *"English pronunciation"* was considered as an intended challenge which had certain necessities to be improved during the training. Similarly, the other themes, such as vocabulary, grammar, knowledge of British and American cultural backgrounds, knowledge of cross-cultural communication, listening ability, speaking ability, reading ability and writing ability, which have been extracted by the highest rate from the questionnaires before, were also inferred and identified by the different categories of codes and the specific themes which could be used to verify the proposed needs from quantitative data.

In sum, the Needs Analysis Phase provided the findings resulting from the analysis of both the survey data which used two sets of close-ended questionnaires to investigate student-teachers' current needs and the three groups of interviews towards the parents, kindergarten principals and English teachers, and stakeholders' expectations about the bilingual practice of teaching and training.

Merging the quantitative findings and the qualitative findings together, I concluded the interrelations between the proposed aspects which were highly rated with the percentages by all participants and the intended challenges extracted from all the data which were properly synthesized based on the three following regards: (1) the conclusive categories of themes extracted from the questionnaires and interviews; (2) the researcher's personal experiences and present understanding about the topic;

(3) the relevant research reviews and references.

**Table 4.3   Interrelations between the Proposed Aspects and the Identified Challenges**

| Proposed Aspects | Identified Challenges |
|---|---|
| Linguistic Basis | (1) Comprehensive Pronunciation<br>(2) Comprehensive Listening Techniques<br>(3) Practical Spoken English |
| Lesson Design | (4) Application of English Curriculum and Syllabus<br>(5) Application of Textbooks<br>(6) Design of Lesson Plans |
| Teaching Techniques | (7) Story Telling<br>(8) Playing Games<br>(9) Singing Songs and Rhymes<br>(10) Stick Figures<br>(11) English Handwriting<br>(12) Modern Educational Teaching Technologies |
| Teaching Demonstration | (13) Demonstration of Lessons<br>(14) Feedback and Reflection |

In conclusion, Table 4.3 shows the interrelations between the proposed aspects and the identified challenges based on the above-mentioned quantitative and qualitative analysis. The four aspects were revised, sorted, recombined, and finalized; and then, the fourteen areas which constituted the identified challenges facing the current student-teachers about their ELT proficiencies were simplified and refined. Namely, the four revised aspects (1. *Linguistic Basis*; 2. *Lesson Design*; 3. *Teaching Techniques* and 4. *Teaching Demonstration*) would be correspondingly transformed into the specific training components, and the final fourteen areas (1. *Comprehensive pronunciation*; 2. *Comprehensive Listening Technique*s; 3. *Practical Spoken English*; 4. *Application of English Curriculum and Syllabus*; 5. *Application of Textbooks*; 6. *Design of Lesson Plan*; 7. *Story Telling*; 8. *Playing Games*; 9. *Singing Songs and Rhymes*; 10. *Stick Figures*; 11. *English Handwriting*; 12. *Modern Educational Teaching Technologies*; 13. *Demonstration of Lessons*; and 14. *Feedback and Reflection*) needed to be improved as the identified challenges, which were employed in the training design phase as the identified priorities of training objectives for the next training phases.

## 4.3　Findings of Research Question 2

*Research Question 2:* *What are specific components of training activities for student-teachers in teaching English effectively?*

As the activities in the Need Analysis phase have identified areas of ELT proficiencies, the student-teachers, English teachers, parents, stakeholders and principles viewed as challenges facing initial ELT of student-teachers in multi-ethnic schools in the current context. A systematic training blueprint was developed throughout the ADDIEM Training Process. The different outcomes from the training Design phase, the training Development phase, the training Implementation phase, the training Evaluation phase, and the training Modification phase are presented sequentially to answer research question 2 as follows.

### 4.3.1　Results of the Training Design Phase

I constructed the training design based on the integrated results from both quantitative and qualitative data analysis in the need analysis phase. Working through the analysis phase focused my attention on: (1) identifying instructional goals; (2) identifying learners' needs; (3) selecting the teaching context; (4) locating available resources (Clare & Natalie, 2014). Therefore, the identified challenges (areas in this phase) mainly led to construct a feasible training blueprint for meeting the proposed needs conversely. It seemed likely to be called a Course Design during the phase of training design. Training design was essentially the process by which the needs analysis of the target group was interpreted to produce an integrated series of teaching and learning experiences that eventually resulted in the realization of the set objectives (Hutchinson & Waters, 1987). The identified challenges (areas) extracted from the need analysis phase were focused on as the indentified priorities which facilitated framing the blueprint in the training design and using strategic efforts to address them (Clare & Natalie, 2014).

**Table 4.4　Steps and Activities within the Training Design Phase**

| Phase | Steps | Activities |
|---|---|---|
| Training Design | (1) to define training priorities<br>(2) to design the training syllabus<br>(3) to specify strategies and goals<br>(4) to organize the content and objectives | (a) to distribute the training components<br>(b) to construct the instructional framework<br>(c) to set training criteria of assessment<br>(d) to define detailed content and activities<br>(e) to employ instructional techniques<br>(f) to draw a tentative schedule |

Based closely on the ADDIEM training process of the study, Table 4.4 presents the major steps and activities within the Training Design Phase. In light of the proposed blueprint, 4 major steps and 6 activities were organized to guide the whole training design. Specifically speaking, the 14 identified areas were firstly defined as the training priorities, and then, defining the training syllabus, specifying strategies and goals, and organizing objectives were sequentially arranged in the training design phase.

Determining goals was an essential part of the instructional design and development, and defining specific instructional objectives was also more often than not a critically important consideration (Abbie & Timonthy, 2016). In order to illustrate how the goals were translated into the objectives and how the intended training outcomes of objective specifications were determined to apply to the blueprint of the training design systematically, the 14 identified areas which highly voiced the necessity of training were addressed again as the desirable outcomes of specific objectives. Table 4.5 shows how these desirable outcomes were employed and classified into the different training components and areas in the whole desirable training.

**Table 4.5　Outcomes of the Specific Objectives Classified into the Training Components and Areas**

| Components | Areas | Outcomes of Specific Objectives (Trainees will be able to) |
|---|---|---|
| Linguistic Basis | Comprehensive Pronunciation | -pronounce English phonemes correctly<br>-correct problematic sounds (e.g., [θ]-[ð]-[s],[d]-[t], [ʃ]-[tʃ]...)<br>-apply rules about accents, stress and intonation in communication correctly<br>-sing the Alphabet Song |

Continued Table

| Components | Areas | Outcomes of Specific Objectives (Trainees will be able to) |
|---|---|---|
| Linguistic Basis | Comprehensive Listening Techniques | -follow frequent classroom instructions in daily activities<br>-demonstrate an explanation of audio-visual materials<br>-use listening techniques correctly (recognizing, pointing, coloring, drawing, doing, asking, guessing, predicting, etc.) |
| | Practical Spoken English | -describe pictures or scenes appropriately<br>-communicate personal information and express emotion and feeling<br>-apply frequent classroom terminologies (greeting, apology, acknowledgement, etc.) in daily life |
| Lesson Design | Application of Curriculum and Syllabus | -explain the nature of the *English Curriculum Standard*<br>-present lesson design according to the Syllabus |
| | Application of Textbooks | -explain general theoretical bases, features, objectives, content, approaches, strategies, principles and evaluations<br>-use textbooks appropriately for units, areas, targets, key and difficult points, etc.<br>-explain characteristics of different levels textbooks |
| | Design of Lesson Plans | -apply a standard instructional framework to different lessons<br>-state specific teaching objectives and strategies explicitly<br>-arrange appropriate and reasonable teaching processes or steps<br>-analyze beginning learners' abilities and levels<br>-review other lesson plans in peers or groups |
| Teaching Techniques | Story-telling | -explain the significance and principles of story-telling techniques<br>-select proper English stories according to teaching areas and targets appropriately<br>-narrate a story with standard pronunciation<br>-select or create the appropriate teaching aids for story-telling<br>-apply different story-telling techniques (doing, reacting, identifying, acting, coloring, drawing, making, repeating, imitating, asking, music, facial expression, gesture, etc.) |

Continued Table

| Components | Areas | Outcomes of Specific Objectives (Trainees will be able to) |
|---|---|---|
| Teaching Techniques | Playing Games | -explain the significance and principles of game-playing techniques<br>-select proper English games according to teaching areas and targets appropriately<br>-select or create appropriate teaching aids for game-playing<br>-apply different game-playing techniques |
| | Singing Songs and Rhymes | -explain the significance of songs and rhymes techniques<br>-select proper English songs and rhymes according to teaching areas and targets appropriately<br>-apply different songs and rhymes techniques (role playing, competing, acting, imaging, music, dance, etc.) |
| | Stick Figures | -explain the significance of stick figure techniques<br>-apply different stick figure techniques (utensils, plants, animals, sceneries, people, synthesis, etc.) |
| | English Handwriting | -explain the importance of English hand-writing<br>-write the 26 English letters (both capital and small letters) correctly and normatively<br>-apply the basic skills of English handwriting (italics, print, and cursive for both capital and small letters) |
| | Modern Educational Teaching Technologies | -explain the importance of modern educational teaching technologies<br>-use basic teaching aid software and multimedia equipment (PPT, flash, CAI, courseware, network resources, computer, projector, CD player, etc.)<br>-select the proper modern educational teaching technologies according to teaching areas and targets appropriately |
| Teaching Demonstration | Demonstration of Lessons | -state clear objectives for each lesson<br>-explain proper key teaching points and difficult points<br>-describe teaching procedures systematically and logically<br>-design effective teaching strategies and methodologies<br>-describe expectations, activities and evaluation procedures |
| | Feedback & Reflection | -explain the importance of classroom management, feedback and reflection<br>-select proper reflection strategies for classroom activities<br>-design effective and multi-assessments of performance<br>-create an exciting learning environment |

This training program was comprised of four operational training components identified in the phase of need analysis as: (1) Linguistic Basics; (2) Lesson Design; (3) Teaching Techniques; (4) Teaching Demonstration, and was covered by a total of 14 areas. The general goals of the training program aimed to improve basic professional qualities and practical teaching skills which were based on ELT proficiency at the beginning level for the current student-teachers to optimize their pre-service professional development towards the specific objectives.

Making reference to Bloom's Taxonomy of cognitive domains (Bloom et al., 1956), the specific training objectives for each training component were developed, revised and finalized in order to reflect realistically the necessity of the training. On one side, each specific objective was derived from and identified by the quantitative and qualitative data during the phase of need analysis instead of listing randomly; on the other side, the suitability of the objectives was also based on the levels of current student-teachers' expertise that it expected them to achieve under the parallel analysis of context in the present study. Therefore, corresponding instruction and assessment criteria were determined for 1~3 levels of Knowledge, Comprehension and Application, which were deemed to be adequate and appropriate for them. That is, all the items of outcomes were determined as the specific objectives serving each area of the training components, and the degree of difficulty, and the relationships between objectives also were reflected overall.

After reviewing the outcomes of the specific objectives, the training syllabus was processed and finalized as another component of the training design, which included the trainer's information, training name, trainees' grade, majors and levels, general training information, training description, training limitations, general training objectives, training strategies, instructional framework, training assessment, references and a tentative schedule finally were presented in Table 4.6. For all the details of the complete training syllabus can be seen in the Appendices.

**Table 4.6  Elements and Descriptions of the Proposed Training Syllabus**

| Elements | Descriptions |
| --- | --- |
| Trainer's Information | Basic information: \ <br> Contact information: \ |

Continued Table

| Elements | Descriptions |
|---|---|
| Training Name | English: ELT Proficiency Training for Pre-service Teachers<br>Chinese: 职前教师英语教学技能培训 |
| Majors and Levels | Majors: Preschool Education, Primary Education<br>Levels: Bachelor and master |
| Training Information | Semester: 2nd semester of the 2018~2019 academic year<br>Weeks: 12 weeks<br>Periods: 36 (3 periods/week)<br>Time: 10:00-12:10 a.m. (40 minutes/period)<br>Classroom: Room 201, the 1st Teaching Building<br>Campus: Ancient Town Campus, Dali University, Dali District |
| Training Description | This training is comprised of four components: (1) Linguistic Basics; (2) Lesson Design; (3) Teaching Techniques; (4) Teaching Demonstration. Each component consists of different areas and there are total 14 areas. The training aims to improve basic professional qualities and practical teaching skills which are based on ELT proficiency at the beginning level for the student-teachers to optimize their pre-service professional development, especially to strengthen the instructional demonstration before they do the teaching practicum. |
| Training Limitations | All the results extracted from both questionnaires and interviews from the Conceptual Framework of the present study were combined, some areas related with language teaching competences such as vocabulary, grammar, reading and writing ability, British & American cultural background knowledge, and cross-cultural communication knowledge, were not covered in the training design because of the applicability and practicality for the need of the trainees at the beginning level, but it doesn't imply that they are not important and necessary for trainees. |
| General Training Objectives | This training provides four operational training components and 14 areas that promoted trainees' professional development towards the following objectives. Upon successful completion of this training, trainees were expected to be able to improve such capabilities in terms of the four components. |
| Training Strategies | Problem-based Learning Model was adopted as the main instructional model according to the training characteristics and objectives. Problem-Based Learning Model is an active and effective learning model that helps learners present or identify their problems, allows them to learn and hone authentic problem-solving skills, develop the cooperative competence and apply their knowledge and experiences for practical purposes in the present study (Clare & Natalie, 2014, pp.284-288). |

| Elements | Descriptions |
|---|---|
| Training Instructional Framework | During the stage of teaching procedures, a "3Ps+2Ds Instructional Model" was designed to present the steps and activities according to the ultimate training objectives. 3Ps refers to Preparation, Presentation and Practice while 2Ds refers to Demonstration and Discussion. |
| Requirements of Attendance | Trainees recruited from the purposed sample were required to participant in the training from beginning to end according to the agreement statement. Trainees could be excused due to an illness or other special reasons, and they must attend the final training test or assessment in principle. If there were some circumstances that may interfere with the trainees' ability to attend class, it was discussed with the trainer. |
| Training Assessment | Standard evaluation: \ <br> Assignments: \ <br> Training survey evaluation forms: \ <br> Additional encouragement, rewards and penalties: \ |
| References | — |
| Tentative Teaching Schedule | Section: \     Week:\     Date: \     Duration: \ <br> Areas: \     Assignments:\ |

Nation and Macalister (2010) stated: "*A negotiated syllabus involves the steps of: (1) negotiating the goals, content, format and assessment of the training; (2) implementing these negotiated decisions; (3) evaluating the effect of the implementation in terms of outcomes and the way the implementation was done* (p.150)", the following elements were "negotiated" in order to make the syllabus workable and effective, they were: negotiation procedures, training planning (for participation, procedures, and goals), training evaluation, and training resources and materials (Nation & Macalister, 2010). That was just as the rationale of the training syllabus design of the training process, and the above-shown training syllabus was negotiated to provide a changeable instructional model for the following phase of training development.

Additionally, with the higher emphasis on constantly increasing flexibility and accountability for students' learning, the most successful instruction was that which resulted in growth and achievement for all the students. "*It would seem that using systematic processes to ensure that the identified needs of students direct all instructional decisions would be the most productive approach*"(Clare & Natalie, 2014, p.28). However, there was no prepared training pattern which was applied for such a context of the study; consequently, the proposed instructional model "3Ps + 2Ds" was designed by the researcher as a referential instructional design framework by maximizing the identified challenges for all the students in such a context. The "3Ps + 2Ds" instructional model refers to the following 5 abbreviations: preparation, presentation, practice, demonstration and discussion, which were emplaced sequentially as the main body of each lesson plan. The proposed "3Ps + 2Ds" instructional model was expected to help: (1) clarify the goals for training; (2) identify training decisions on known trainees' needs; (3) locate and choose appropriate training resources; (4) understand the effect of the training materials or methods (Clare & Natalie, 2014).

### 4.3.2  Results of the Training Development Phase

The objectives' specification and syllabus negotiation were designed in the training design phase to form the main specific components of training activities. The following findings that resulted from the training development phase were also indispensable elements. Similarly, the major steps and activities within the training development phase, as shown in Table 4.7, indicate how the researcher creatively connected student-teachers' needs with the appropriate training resources and materials, and how the researcher systematically used the modular approach to design the interrelated lesson plans, developed evaluation instruments, and so on.

Table 4.7  Steps and Activities within the Training Development Phase

| Phase | Steps | Activities |
|---|---|---|
| Training Development | (1) to create lesson plans or units<br>(2) to select training resources and materials<br>(3) to develop assessments<br>(4) to confirm venues<br>(5) to enroll the trainees | (a) to design 14 different lesson plans<br>(b) to select appropriate materials and tools<br>(c) to determine a proper criteria of evaluation<br>(d) to develop assessment instruments<br>(e) to select trainees and provide training guides<br>(f) to make schedules and locate a classroom |

*"Good lesson plans are the foundation of successful student learning, accurate assessment, and effective classroom management"* (Serdyukov & Ryan, 2008, p.1). The development of a lesson plan is a critical stage in the design of a training program, it helps set the sound phase for implementation of the training program and displays a signal that such training is to be conducted professionally. Therefore, once the specific training objectives and training syllabus have been designed in the preceding phase, the modular lesson plans are organized and prepared to outline the training program in terms of the sequence of activities and events, and to guide the trainer that provided a step-by-step breakdown for conducting the sound training program (Serdyukov & Ryan, 2008).

Table 4.8 presents a sample lesson plan with the necessary descriptions for terms revised and referenced under the current practical context to cover the main elements included in a lesson plan. The left column lists the main required and interrelated terms of a lesson plan, while the right column states the necessary descriptions of the reason why I chose them.

**Table 4.8   A Sample Lesson Plan of the Training**

| Lesson Plan<br>Component (I. II. III. IV):        Topic:              Date: | |
| --- | --- |
| **Main Terms** | **Descriptions of Reasons** |
| Backgrounds & Principles | -to show the importance of the certain teaching topics<br>-to present the relative theories & principles about the topics |
| Context Analysis | -to analyze the student-teachers' current levels or experience, prior knowledge, and problematic situations of ELT proficiency |
| Subject Contents | -to redefine the sub-subjects or sub-units |
| Objectives | -to specify the defined purposes from the outcomes |
| Key Points & Difficult Points | -to differentiate the key and difficult points<br>-to guide the final evaluation of the objective attainments |
| Strategies & Methods | -to illustrate reasonable teaching approaches and methods |
| Materials & Tools | -to show concrete access to enhance the training processes, such as PowerPoint, Multi-medias, videos, handouts, worksheets, etc. |

Continued Table

| Main Terms | Descriptions of Reasons |
|---|---|
| Procedures | -to show the major instructional model (or structure) step by step |
| "3Ps + 2Ds Instructional Model"<br>I. Preparation (min)<br>　Activity 1, 2…<br>　Designing Instruction:<br>II. Presentation (min)<br>Activity 1, 2…<br>　Designing Instruction:<br>III. Practice (min)<br>Activity 1, 2…<br>　Designing Instruction:<br>IV. Demonstration (min)<br>Activity 1, 2…<br>　Designing Instruction:<br>V. Discussion (min)<br>Activity 1, 2…<br>　Designing Instruction: | -to demonstrate 3Ps + 2Ds Instructional Model in a real context (Preparation + Presentation + Practice + Demonstration + Discussion)<br>-to introduce the complete details of conducting the teaching process systematically and logically in each stage<br>-to give a reasonable time-reminder on each stage<br>-to explicate how the teaching activities are organized and interacted in each stage thoroughly<br>-to interpret the instruction/purposes/reasons for designing/conducting/organizing the activities<br>-to provide the necessary literal additional remarks |
| Reflective Evaluation | -to design a proper criteria and instruments of evaluation (formative/summative assessment, checking, testing, quiz, etc.) |
| Assignments | -to leave students some assignments for consolidation |
| Relative References | -to list all mentioned citations of reference |
| Learning Resources | -to provide the learning resources, such as websites, apps, and linkages |
| Feedback & Reflection | -to record class observations and take reflective notes |

The model of the lesson plan here might vary from other situations, but it shared a number of common elements. *"Three essential features of a complete, well-organized lesson plan are the objectives, procedures, and evaluation"* (Eby, Herrell & Hicks, 2002. p.145). The lesson objectives specified the training purposes, the lesson procedures described both *"what training experiences can be provided"* and the way which could be *"effectively organized"*, while the lesson evaluation described the way I had planned in advance to determine *"whether these purposes are being attained*" (Eby et al., 2002. p.145). An available computer was employed as a medium to ensure that the products (all drafts of lesson plans) were responsive to the needs of the trainees and effective in achieving the desired training outcomes (Dick, et al,, 2001, p.10). That is, using a computer-based delivery provided more normative and regular administration of daily files and materials to be available on hand at any time/place. Furthermore, the complete development process of the lesson plans was not only a computer-based instruction but also an individualized instruction, which just characterized the unique features of the training process of the study.

The fourteen areas were identified from the need analysis phase, so the 14 pieces of corresponding lesson plans were organized and developed based on such an adjustable and flexible model of lesson plan according to the different areas and objectives. During the training of selecting and identifying instructional activities for all areas of lesson plans, such instructional strategies/models/techniques were consulted and developed to work best based on the trainees' needs and the training goals and objectives. They were mainly about, Problem-based Learning, Open-ended Learning, Directed Learning, Cooperative Learning, Concept-Attainment Model, Inductive Learning, Authentic Teaching, Simulations and Games, Individualized Instruction, and so on, and all of them were discussed and embedded in different lesson plans.

Furthermore, taking the current and practical context of the venue into consideration, and consulting with the Department of Educational and Teaching Administration of Dali University, a classroom equipped with multi-media and a maximum of 120 persons was available as the training place for the next training implementation. The training place (Room 202) located in the 1st teaching building of Ancient Town Campus in Dali University, provided a goodish and suitable place for the trainees.

Simultaneously, a notice of training volunteers' enrollment was issued to 9 classes of the Faculty of Education after getting permission from the dean of the faculty, and finally 58 participants (Statistical tests with sufficient power is only 45 by using the Power Software) from the target population were recruited for participating in the training by using volunteer sampling. The necessary training requirements, criteria and guides were disclosed to each participant and attached on the agreements of consent at the same time.

In sum, the whole process of development consisted of the preparation of lesson plans, the selection of instructional strategies, the location of the training place and the recruitment of training volunteers, and the indispensable sub-sections for the components of the training processes and activities.

### 4.3.3　Results of the Training Implementation Phase

The preparation of the lesson plans, development of basic assessment instruments, management of training spots, participants applied into a real training process, and the delivery method of the training model were implied thought the training program, and implemented according to the following steps and activities as shown in Table 4.9.

**Table 4.9　Steps and Activities for the Training Implementation Phase**

| Phase | Steps | Activities |
| --- | --- | --- |
| Training Implementation | (1) to consider preparation<br>(2) to conduct a pre-test<br>(3) to conduct training sessions<br>(4) to implement formative evaluations | (a) to state current teaching and learning experiences<br>(b) to make complete preparation of content, medias, environment, classroom, trainees' lists, etc.<br>(c) to carry out the real training activities<br>(d) to observe the classroom<br>(e) to conduct a survey questionnaire<br>(f) to collect participants' feedback |

The preparation stage of delivering the training program was started by inviting two professional consultants to act as the instructional coaches for the training program. These two people worked in the current faculty of education of Dali University as directors of the teaching and research section of preschool education and primary education, respectively, and were assigned to facilitate the training activities in the program. At the same time, the researcher asked for permission from both the dean of Faculty of Education and the director of Educational and Teaching Administrative Department in Dali University to ensure getting the environmental identification of the setting. Then, the next implementation stage of the training program began with an orientation activity for ice breaking. The researcher organized all the participants enrolled from the volunteers for first meeting with them. The training purposes, major procedures, possible tasks, training manuals, training structure, teaching and learning approaches, encouragement and punishment, including the researcher's background and experience were also covered to announce to the trainees during the signing of the training consent agreement. Moreover, two appointed groups of QQ and WeChat were built to facilitate the training process for sharing training materials (such as learning resources, linkages, websites, pictures, videos, speech, etc.), temporary management or assignments, and seasonable notices, even free opinions, and so on. All the trainees were given numeral codes according to their practical class and major information. Lastly, 58 trainees (actually only 45 were sufficient by using the Power Software) were confirmed to enroll in the training by classifying their basic information in Table 4.10. Ten more volunteers still applied for enrolling in the group but were refused with consideration of the training effectiveness. Among the trainees, there were two males and 56 females, 11 ethnic minorities, but the majority were of Han nationality. They were derived from 8 different classes from 2 grades with 2 majors, and from both bachelor and master programs which were running promisingly in the Faculty of Education of Dali University.

**Table 4.10    Basic Classification Information of the Trainees**

| Codes of Range | Number | Grades & Classes | Majors | Levels |
|---|---|---|---|---|
| 1~10 | 10 | Grade 2016, class 1 | Preschool education | Bachelor |
| 11~13 | 3 | Grade 2016, class 2 | Preschool education | Bachelor |
| 14~21 | 8 | Grade 2016, class 3 | Preschool education | Bachelor |
| 22~29 | 8 | Grade 2016, class 4 | Primary school education | Bachelor |
| 30~35 | 6 | Grade 2018, class 1 | Preschool education | Bachelor |
| 36~44 | 9 | Grade 2018, class 2 | Primary school education | Bachelor |
| 45~50 | 6 | Grade 2018, class 3 | Preschool education | Master |
| 51~58 | 8 | Grade 2018, class 4 | Primary school education | Master |
| Total | 58 | 2 grades, 8 classes | 2 majors | 2 levels |

With regard to the implementation of the whole training process, the training program had a total of 36 periods and was conducted in the 2nd semester of 2018 academic year at Dali University, lasting a total of twelve weeks (3 periods per week) from October 23, 2018 to January 15, 2019. Table 4.11 shows the schedule of the training implementation in terms of practical training duration. It was originally expected that each topic would be delivered in 3 periods once a week, however, just as mentioned before in the training syllabus, the partial training areas were adjusted according to the practical situation. The 1st topic of Pronunciation was separated into 2 parts and took another period because it contained so much content and activities in the lesson plan so that it could not be handled in only 3 periods. Additionally, the 6th topic of the Lesson Plan was also taken apart into 2 periods while the 7th~9th areas, the 10th~11th areas, and the 13th~14th areas were combined into one certain duration respectively, for the possible reasons are discussed in the next chapter. There was a proposed training date on January 1, 2019 in the training schedule, but the exact day was postponed because of the New Year holiday.

**Table 4.11    Schedule of the Practical Training Implementation**

| Sections | Weeks | Dates | Periods | Areas | Results |
|---|---|---|---|---|---|
| | | Oct. 23, 2018 | | Conducting Pre-test | |
| Component I | 1 | Oct. 23, 2018 | 3 | 1. Pronunciation (a) | -Topic 1 was separated into two parts |
| | 2 | Oct. 30, 2018 | 3 | Pronunciation (b) | |
| | 3 | Nov. 6, 2018 | 3 | 2. Listening Ability | -normally |
| | 4 | Nov. 13, 2018 | 3 | 3. Spoken English | -normally |
| Component II | 5 | Nov. 20, 2018 | 3 | 4. Application of Syllabus | -normally |
| | 6 | Nov. 27, 2018 | 3 | 5. Application of Textbooks | -normally |
| | 7 | Dec. 4, 2018 | 3 | 6. Lesson Plan (a) | -Topic 6 was separated into two parts |
| | 8 | Dec. 11, 2018 | 3 | Lesson Plan (b) | |

Continued Table

| Sections | Weeks | Dates | Periods | Areas | Results |
|---|---|---|---|---|---|
| Component III | 9 | Dec. 18, 2018 | 3 | 7. Story-telling<br>8. Playing Games<br>9. Songs and Rhymes | -Topics 7, 8 and 9 were combined into one part |
| | 10 | Dec. 25, 2018 | 3 | 10. Stick Figures<br>11. English Hand-writing | -Topics 10 and 11 were combined into one part |
| | | *Dec. 25, 2018* | | *Conduct Post-test* | |
| *January 1, 2019 was postponed because of the New Year holiday* | | | | | |
| Component IV | 11 | Jan. 8, 2019 | 3 | 12. Modern Educational Teaching Technology | -normally |
| | 12 | Jan. 15, 2019 | 3 | 13. Demonstration of a Lesson<br>14. Feedback & Reflection | -Topic 13 and 14 were combined into one part |
| | | *Jan. 15, 2019* | | *Conduct survey questionnaires, evaluation forms* | |

In terms of the implementation of the pre-test, post-test, and the final evaluation, the pre-test was conducted in the very beginning of the training, and the post-test was implemented as soon as the 11th topic of English Hand-writing was delivered, and the survey questionnaires and evaluation forms of satisfaction were finally conducted at the end of training.

### 4.3.4 Results of the Training Evaluation Phase

Evaluation of the entire training program was successively conducted after all the training phases were completed. As Moore (2015) stated, "*evaluation serves many roles in the teaching-learning process*" (p.250), "*it should not be limited to only* the *'desired outcomes' but must also be sensitive to all factors potentially associated with the training of instruction*" (p.251). So, when progressing to the training evaluation phase, I went back to the very first step of the ADDIEM training process of the study, in which I completed a training needs analysis. During the preceding phases, all the components were presented before including the identified needs, the specific objectives, the negotiated syllabus, the selected instructional strategies, the designed materials, the prepared lesson plans, the enrolled trainees, and even the confirmed classroom, etc. were addressed again to illustrate how I measured those improvements (see Table 4.12).

**Table 4.12   Steps and Activities within the Training Evaluation Phase**

| Phase | Steps | Activities |
|-------|-------|-----------|
| Training Evaluation | (1) to construct a training evaluation system (2) to conduct a formative and summative evaluation (3) to conduct a post-test (4) to reach a conclusion | (a) to review the whole training process to select the appropriate techniques of measurement (b) to conduct the formative evaluation (identified needs, specific objectives, negotiated syllabus, selected instructional strategies, existing materials, prepared lesson plans, enrolled trainees, confirmed classroom, etc.) (c) to conduct the summative evaluation (overall achievement of needs, participant satisfaction, etc.) (d) to conduct a final post-test evaluation (e) to reference document theories and interpret training effectiveness |

Standing upon another point of view, all those improvements were examined by considering both separately and in connection with each other to attempt to understand the whole training process completely. Accordingly, the continuous feedback was obtained throughout the needs analysis, design, development, and implementation of the training process which constituted a dynamic and flexible evaluation system as follows in Table 4.13. Moore (2015) emphasized to be sensitive on all the potential or possible instruments of measurements associated with the whole training process, and these three primary evaluation types: pretest, formative and posttest (summative) differed in terms of their special characteristics and purposes; hence, the evaluation itself played a continuous and systematical role which applied into different phases of the training process by its natural and chronological position. Taking such distinct characteristics and purposes of three evaluation types into consideration, the results of training evaluation were induced from three different types of pre-assessment, formative assessment and summative assessment respectively.

**Table 4.13    The Evaluation Systems for the Training Process**

| Evaluation Types | Applied Phases | Proposed Instruments | Description of Measurements | Description of Purposes/Results |
|---|---|---|---|---|
| Pre-Assessment | At Beginning of Need Analysis | 1. Original Pretest 2. Additional Pretest | 1. to test phonetic symbols about English vowels and consonants 2. to grade manuscripts of English handwriting left by the Trainees | 1. self-evaluated by trainees (incomplete, difficult) 2. graded by trainer (written record, representative) |
| Formative Assessment | Need Analysis | 1. Questionnaires 2. Interviews 3. Pilot Study 4. Personal Experiences 5. Documents | 1&2. to develop and finalize questionnaire and interview guidelines with 5 versions 3. to conduct the first pilot study in a middle school 4. to list the trainer's uncertainties and queries 5. to extract instrumental verifications and opinions from literature reviews | 1&2. revised and checked by 4 experts with IOC of 0.906 3. both questionnaire and interview were piloted with a consistent feasibility by some English teachers randomly 4&5. expected to be compared and proved in an accessible context |

Continued Table

| Evaluation Types | Applied Phases | Proposed Instruments | Description of Measurements | Description of Purposes/Results |
|---|---|---|---|---|
| Formative Assessment | Training Design | 1. Reference Materials 2. Context Analysis 3. Peer Reviews | 1.To consult and extract persistent references via all kinds of literature 2. To analyze trainees' prior knowledge, problematic experiences and under the current context of the study 3. To obtain professional advice and experiences from 2 excellent colleagues | 1. To attain more authentic arguments to support desired outcomes 2. Double check the trainees' required competencies 3. To increase feasibility and practicability of training from a vocational and professional stance |
| | Training Development | 1. Criteria of Developing Lesson Plans 2. Regulations of School 3. Pilot Study 4. Electronic Files of Classification 5. Text Materials 6. Contextual Permission 7. Volunteer Enrollment | 1&2. To consider mainly applicability and operability based on the instructional regulations and criteria of the school 3. To conduct a second pilot study 4. To form normative management of electronic files of classification and keep in a U disk 5. To carry workable reference textbooks and relevant paper materials all the time 6. To get the contextual permission from the concerned Dean and Director 7. To enroll publicly for trainees | 1&2. Four samples of lesson plans were examined by 3 experts with IOC of 1.00 3. The lesson plan of Topic 10 was tried out with consistent feasibility in a similar training (Stick Figure) 4&5. To keep normative administration of daily files and materials to be available on hand at any time/place 6. To avoid ethical issues 7. 58 participants were recruited (actually 45 were sufficient measured by Power Software) |

Continued Table

| Evaluation Types | Applied Phases | Proposed Instruments | Description of Measurements | Description of Purposes/Results |
|---|---|---|---|---|
| Formative Assessment | Training Implementa-tion | 1. Peer Coaching<br><br>2. Class Observation<br><br><br>3. Assignment/ Worksheet/ Checklist<br>4. Videotaped Records<br>5. Informal Conversation<br>6. Reflective Reports<br>7. Necessary Stimulants<br>8. Evaluation Form (a) | 1. To provide professional recommendations and coaching from two excellent colleagues in a same faculty<br>2. To investigate the first hand and authentic phenomenon existed in each classroom, such as Daily Report, Classroom Performance, Volunteer response, Feeling and Opinion Sharing<br>3&4. To record and reflect trainees' natural and real classroom performances by written form or video<br>5. To gain constructive suggestions or advices from certain trainees after class<br>6. To record impromptu ideas or actions<br>7. To use proper stimulants, such as games, competitions, pair, group, etc.<br>8. To evaluate training formatively | 1. To increase feasibility and practicability of training<br>2,3&4. To facilitate to interpret trainees' attainment of achievement, performance, trainer's feelings and emotions, and to make adaptable interaction, improvements for modification (Starting with both advantages and disadvantages)<br>5&6. To record the reminders to check validity of observation<br>7. To arouse trainees' learning interests, passion, awareness, etc by using games, competitions, partnership, and intervention, etc.<br>8. To evaluate trainees' achievement, suggestions and improvement upon Component I by open-ended questions with IOC of 1.00 |

Continued Table

| Evaluation Types | Applied Phases | Proposed Instruments | Description of Measurements | Description of Purposes/Results |
|---|---|---|---|---|
| Summative Assessment | Training Evaluation | 1. Evaluation Form(b) 2. Survey 3. Posttest | 1. To evaluate the training summatively 2. To examine trainees' satisfaction of training with 5-level rating scale and 2 open-ended questions for more suggestion 3. To re-conduct the same test in pre-assessment about manuscripts of English handwriting | 1. To evaluate trainees' achievement, feelings and suggestions upon Component II,III,IV by open-ended questions with IOC of 1.00 2&3. To analyze and compare the results statistically and descriptively with high frequency, percentage and level of suitability |

**Pre-assessment:**

As shown in Table 4.13, the original diagnostic pretest evaluation was administered at the very beginning of the need analysis phase to assess the trainees' prior knowledge/skills upon the first topic of Comprehensive Pronunciation in Component I of Linguistic Basis for placement purposes. It was expected that the trainees could write out the phonetic symbols based on the underlined sounds correctly, and then graded by the trainer for later comparison with the proposed posttest. However, it was revealed that all the trainees faced serious existing problems of how to distinguish and write, especially how to pronounce the English phonetic symbols correctly and comprehensively instead of only writing them out simply. Everyone might know there were 26 English letters, but might not know all 48 English phonetic symbols. I purposely set a question *"Do you know how many English phonetic symbols there are in English?"* It seemed quite embarrassing for the trainees' different answers of less than 50 percent of accuracy; some trainees wrote 26 and 108 without any ground thinking, not to mention their written situation. Although, I had given the order number of both 20 Vowels and 28 Consonants in the obvious front leading of each item on the test sheet. Trainee 34 (code of participant) showed his feedback *"I never learned the English phonetic symbols well when I was in primary school.... So, I cannot pronounce them correctly."* And the majority of the trainees had the same idea. It was doubtful to imply that the trainees did not pay more focus on the written form of English phonetic symbols at all, but only on the verbal form "pronunciation", which was coordinative with the indentified needs extracted from the phase of need analysis.

The original pretest gave me invaluable information regarding the appropriateness of the training. It might be workable per se that this pretest about English phonetic symbols was implemented to identify the trainees' foundational knowledge and skills required for training, but it seemed to be difficult for further design of a specific posttest in summative assessment in terms of the trainees' practical competencies in beginning level of ELT. After all, English pronunciation was one of the most difficult skills to acquire and trainees should spend lots of time to improve their pronunciation (Pourhosein, 2016). Therefore, an additional pretest about English handwriting replaced the original one in order to facilitate the final comparison of training achievement easier about such certain basic skills in written form. The results of the additional pretest are discussed in summative assessment.

**Formative Assessment**

With regard to the formative assessment, it was alternated to apply to the major phases of needs analysis, training design, training development and training implementation all the time. The results from the formative assessment are presented as below.

**In the Needs Analysis Phase**

Questionnaires and interviews were designed as the main instruments to identify the required needs from the student-teachers in the current setting. Two sets of questionnaires (revised from October 8, 2017 to July 9, 2018) with a five-point scale, and three sets of interview guidelines (revised from December 10, 2017 to August 12, 2018) were developed and finalized, and both of these two instruments were checked by four experts with an IOC score of 0.906. After that, the first pilot study was conducted with my prior convenience to be piloted by five English teachers working in a local middle school, all of them thought highly of its consistence in view of the general teaching competences of an English teacher. Simultaneously, the accuracy of English-Chinese translation for both questionnaires and interviews was checked by asking about the design purposes, examining grammar, adjusting word order, refining expressions and finalizing the manuscript by two experts working in the current faculty of foreign languages in Dali University. Certainly, the study was expected to compare my uncertainties and queries with the instrumental verifications and opinions from literature reviews in such an accessible contest, my personal experiences about English teaching and learning and some necessary documents were also employed to be considered in order to identify the challenges which needed to be improved for the current student-teachers.

**In the Training Design Phase**

The training design was constructed based on the integrated results of both quantitative and qualitative data analysis in the preceding phase. The training goals, trainees' needs, training context and instructional resources were focused on framing a feasible training blueprint, especially on specifying the training objectives, negotiating the training syllabus; therefore, as much as possible materials were consulted and extracted persistently via all kinds of reference literature reviews in order to attain more authentic arguments to support the desired outcomes. To analyze the trainees' prior knowledge and problematic experiences, the context analysis was also conducted to double check the trainees' required competencies. At the end of the training design, two excellent colleagues working in the current faculty in Dali University were invited as peep reviewers to give instrumental recommendations and professional experiences to increase feasibility and practicability of training upon a vocational and professional stance.

**In the Training Development Phase**

The development of lesson plans was a critical stage in this training development phase. It was of great significance to develop a modular framework of lesson plans which must closely connect the trainees' requirements with appropriate training resources, materials and activities. There was not a fixed instructional criterion which might be taken, but applicability and operability based on the instructional regulation in the current context were taken into consideration firstly in terms of the sequence of activities and trainees' present learning levels. Secondly, four samples from the organized lesson plans were examined by three experts who were holding profound teaching and training experiences with the IOC score of 1.0. One of the lesson plans, the 10th topic of Stick Figures was tried out with high consistency in a completed course taught by myself in the same semester. During the whole development of the lesson plan, I continued using my own familiar delivery method to build a normative management of electronic files and materials at the time, such as folder classification according to real sequence, revised drafts, advisors' feedbacks, reference reviews, possible activities, and so on; and still kept all the files duplicated in a mobile hard disk once a week in case of any accidents. This normative administration of daily electronic files and text materials brought great convenience for me to be available on hand at any time and place.

The developed training named *"ELT Proficiency Training for Pre-service Teachers"* was neither a required course nor a selective one for the proposed trainees, which meant it was not compulsory for them. Therefore, the enrollment notice was issued to the target population with a defined criterion I created in terms of the maximum number, grades and majors, levels, training requirements and guides, encouragements and punishment, final evaluations, and assignments. Finally, fifty-eight participants (actually 45 was sufficient measured by Power Software) were recruited for participating in the training by using volunteer sampling after getting the contextual permission from the dean and the concerned director in the real setting. This just constituted the prerequisites for next phase of training implementation.

### In the Training Implementation Phase

At the beginning of formal training implementation, two professional consultants were employed as the instructional coaches who were expected to provide instrumental recommendations and guidance during the training implementation to increase the feasibility and practicability of the training program.

Class observation was the major instrument covered the whole phase of training implementation, in which included a series of sub-sections, such as Daily Report, Classroom Performance, Volunteer Response, and Feelings and Opinion Sharing. All of these sub-sections aimed to investigate first hand and authentic phenomenon that existed in each classroom in order to facilitate interpreting the trainees' attainment of achievement, actual performance, including both I and the trainees' feelings and emotions, and to make adaptable interaction and improvements for modification. Generally speaking, the classroom observation held both advantages and limitations during the whole training implementation. With regard to advantages, many objective and authentic details existing in the classroom were easily found to facilitate the performance-based and outcome-based measurements, such as, positive and enthusiasm interacting, out-of-expectation and satisfaction attaining, etc. While in terms of limitations, higher careful-order thinking, more time-consuming, higher difficulty in making comparison, worse emotion affected by someone's intended absence, silence-keeping or facial expression, and so on.

Certainly, assignments, worksheets, checklists and videotaped records implemented in the classroom also played beneficial roles by recording and reflecting trainees' natural and real classroom performances in written and video forms, I extracted the instrumental data by reviewing and looking back for the final interpretation. Additionally, some informal conversations in and after class that happened between some trainees and me. It seemed as much like chatting and prattling that inadvertently happened among close friends while some impromptu ideas or actions had been recorded for better implementation in the next class. Lastly, necessary stimulants, such as proper games, temporary competitions, collaborative partnerships, appropriate intervention, etc. were adopted as one of the instructional strategies I prepared to arouse trainees' learning interests, passion, awareness, and so on.

Last but not least, a formative evaluation form was conducted after the delivery of first 3 lesson plans covered in Component I (Linguistic Basis). Twelve items of open-ended questions which involved the trainees' percentage of expectation on the areas, training activities, participation, training arrangement, training model of "3Ps+2Ds", trainer's instructional competences, training materials and resources, achievements, favorite activities (stage, materials), improvements and general suggestions were designed together, and also got a peer review and were checked by 3 experts with an IOC score of 1.00.

## Summative Assessment

In order to inform the trainees of their end-of-training achievement, future improvement and practice, three authentic kinds of summative assessments were conducted in the training evaluation phase. Another evaluation form examined by the three experts with an IOC score of 1.00 was designed to synthetically evaluate Component II (Lesson Design), Component III (Teaching Techniques), and Component IV (Teaching Demonstration). Twelve open-ended questions involved successively in trainees' expectations, activities, participation, arrangement, training model, trainer's instructional competences, materials and resources, obtained achievements, favorite activities (stage, materials), further contents, improvements and general suggestions. The general conclusions from the evaluation form indicated that the whole training was in a high coherence with some practicability and feasibility as expected, and most of the trainees expressed their heartfelt acknowledgements for the trainer, and also showed their eager desire for future training activities.

If we thought the pretest as an "*entry point*", then the posttest would be an "*exit point*" (Eby, Herrell & Hicks, 2002). The posttest was used to assess the trainees' learning outcomes in a performance-based way. The posttest in this stage of summative assessment was highlighted in the specific topic of English Handwriting skills. It was used to compare and analyze what improvements had been attained within a similar topic about the trainees' manuscripts of English. The posttest was

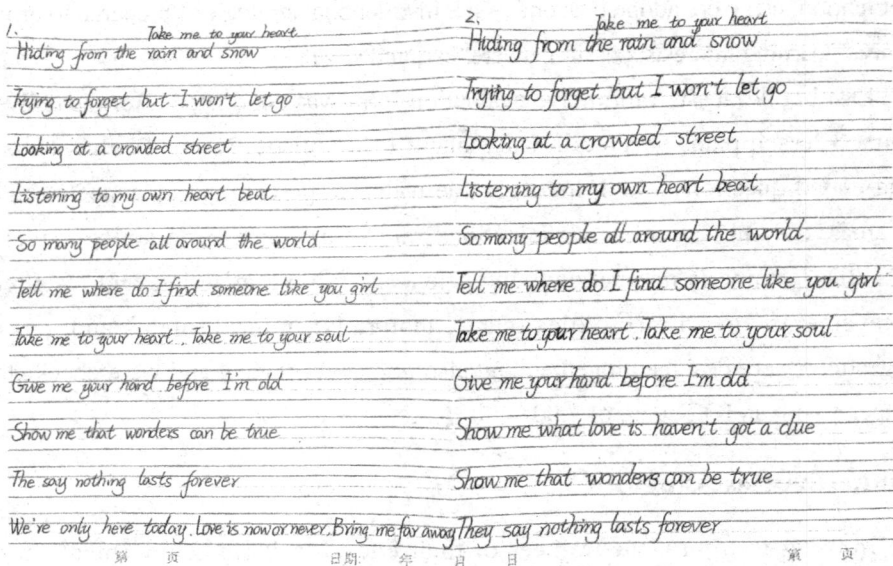

**Figure 4.1**  A Sample of a Trainee's English Manuscript for the Pretest and Posttest

not graded but it showed us the great progresses obviously by a glance at the tests. In other words, based on the practical training under the special top of English handwriting, the majority of the trainees basically framed the identified objectives of writing English letters more legibly and fluently by applying the basic writing techniques. The Figure 4.1 shows a copy of one trainee's scanned English manuscript for both the pretest and posttest.

Retracing the last section of the summative assessment, a survey was adopted to investigate the trainees' satisfaction of training with a 5-level rating scale (5. very satisfied, 4. satisfied, 3. basically satisfied, 2. just so so, and 1. not satisfied) and two more open-ended questions. The survey involved the training contents, the trainer's performance and the trainees' feelings, two more open-ended questions were expected to interpret what benefits and what perfections in terms of the trainees' general viewpoint. The following Table 4.14 shows the Percentages and Means of the results of the survey.

**Table 4.14    Percentages and Means of the Results of the Survey (N = 47)**

| Items | Key Points | Very Satisfied | Satisfied | Basically Satisfied | Just So So | Not Satisfied |
|---|---|---|---|---|---|---|
| Training Contents | (a) Training Pertinence | 36.17% | 55.32% | 6.38% | 2.23% | 0 |
| | (b) Training Practicability | 72.34% | 25.53% | 6.38% | 0 | 0 |
| | (c) Training Flexibility | 40.43% | 51.06% | 6.38% | 2.23% | 0 |
| | (d) Training Objectives | 31.91% | 40.43% | 23.4% | 4.26% | 0 |
| | (e) Training Content Selection | 48.94% | 38.3% | 12.76% | 0% | 0 |
| | (f) Training Time Arrangement | 23.4% | 29.79% | 36.17% | 10.64% | 0 |
| | **Means** | **42.20%** | **40.07 %** | **15.25 %** | **3.23%** | **0** |
| Trainer's Performance | (a) Training Courseware Design | 48.94% | 42.55% | 8.51% | 0 | 0 |
| | (b) Basic Teaching Abilities of the Subject | 65.96% | 31.91% | 2.23% | 0 | 0 |
| | (c) Training Clarity of Difficult & Key Points | 59.57% | 34.04% | 4.26% | 2.23% | 0 |

Continued Table

| | | | | | | |
|---|---|---|---|---|---|---|
| Trainer's Performance | (d) Classroom Instruction and Linguistic Expression Ability | 61.7% | 29.79% | 8.51% | 0 | 0 |
| | (e) Training Interactive Controlling Ability | 59.57% | 34.04% | 6.38% | 0 | 0 |
| | (f) Training Materials Preparation | 57.45% | 36.17% | 6.38% | 0 | 0 |
| | (g) Training Progress and Steps | 21.28% | 51.06% | 23.4% | 6.38% | 0 |
| | (h) Training Attitude and Responsibility | 80.85% | 12.76% | 6.38% | 0 | 0 |
| | *Means* | **56.92%** | **34.04%** | **8.26%** | **1.08%** | **0** |
| Trainees' Feelings | (a) Your Whole Learning Attitudes (Concentration, Attendance) | 14.89% | 44.68% | 34.04% | 6.38% | 0 |
| | (b) Your Proficiency before Training | 8.5% | 8.51% | 8.51% | 46.8% | 27.66% |
| | (c) Your Proficiency after Training | 4.26% | 25.53% | 48.93% | 19.15% | 2.23% |
| | (d) Your Whole Learning Satisfaction | 8.51% | 40.42% | 31.91% | 19.15% | 0 |
| | *Means* | **9.04%** | **29.79%** | **30.85%** | **22.87%** | **7.47%** |

In terms of the training contents (including training pertinence, training practicability, training flexibility, training objectives, training materials and activities selection, and training time arrangement.), 42.20% of the trainees felt very satisfied, 40.07 % felt satisfied, 15.25 % felt basically satisfied, 3.23% thought it was just so so, and no one felt not satisfied, among which 72.34% of *Training Practicability* displayed the highest suitability of being very satisfied.

In terms of the trainer's performances (including training courseware design, basic teaching abilities of the subject, teaching clarity of difficult & key points, classroom instruction and linguistic expression ability, teaching interactive controlling ability, training materials preparation, training progress and steps, and training attitudes and responsibility), 56.92% of the trainees were very satisfied,

34.04 % were satisfied, 8.26 % were basically satisfied, 1.08% thought it was just so so, and no one felt not satisfied, among which 80.85% of *the Trainer's Training Attitude and Responsibility* displayed the highest suitability of being very satisfied.

While entirely different with regard to the trainees' feelings (including their learning attitudes, such as concentration, attendance, their proficiency before and after training, and their general learning satisfaction), 9.04% of the trainees felt very satisfied, 29.79 % felt satisfied, 30.85 % felt basically satisfied, 22.87% felt it was just so so, and 7.47% felt not satisfied, among which 48. 93% of *the Trainees' Proficiency after Training* displayed the highest suitability of being basically satisfied.

Two more open-ended questions added at the bottom of the survey mainly involved the benefits, feelings and the perfections from the trainees. The coding themes by a sequence of existing frequency extracted from the two questions focused on *"having great achievability of attainment" "feeling beneficial" "being satisfied with both the trainer's performance and training activities" "expressing personal appreciation and acknowledgement" "self-awareness of the importance of professional development" "self-consciousness of lower basic knowledge" "showing eager desires for future and further training program" "limited training duration and adding accordingly"* and so on.

Altogether, performing the important roles throughout each phase of the whole training process, the continuous feedbacks obtained from the training evaluation phase also revealed a higher suitability and an effective tendency of the training program.

## 4.3.5　Results of the Training Modification Phase

The findings resulting from the training evaluation phase throughout the complete training process, accordingly modifications and improvements were identified under the combination of the trainees' practical performances, real feelings and constructive suggestions, the trainer's original intention, my own reflective notes, with the experts' constructional recommendations, and the contextual documents and orientation.

The feedback from the student-teachers was frequently concerned with the insufficiency of training duration, which was critically required as the primary aspect of modification. For the training design, some sub-areas such as comprehensive pronunciation, design of lesson plan and demonstration of lessons, these three areas might be afforded more time because most of the trainees reported *"it's of great significance as the basic skills especially as a normal university student"* (p.14), while such as some training areas (game-playing, songs and rhythms, story-telling, and modern educational teaching technologies) might be reduced or synthesized because they were actually embedded in the process of delivery with other training areas at all times. Specifically, the trainees frequently underlined the necessity of extending or increasing the training time for the following prioritized areas: English pronunciation, comprehensive spoken English and listening ability, lesson design, teaching techniques, and presentation and evaluation of lessons. In brief, such possible influencing factors should be taken into consideration and an appropriate alternative scheme should be set to ensure sufficient and adjustable training time regarding the different training components in order to serve the trainees' needs and gain more effectiveness and satisfaction.

In addition, with regard to other important factors, such as proposed participants' ethnic backgrounds (their different groups, homes, languages, etc.) should be taken into account when enrolling. Correspondingly, some necessary questions of both questionnaire and interview in the Need Analysis phase of training also focused mainly on their original educational situations of learning English at the very beginning in their ethnic communities. One more factor was the number of trainees, it might be seriously limited (normally it is better to have no more than 45 students) to ensure the effectiveness of training in terms of training activities, interactions and management based on the completion of this practical implementation of training. Lastly, the selection of the training environment (here refers to multi-functions equipped classroom, high-quality projector) played a critical role, which could provide positive facilitations for the effective presentation and demonstration of training as well.

In conclusion, the whole systematic training process and the immediately identified outcomes were merged to constitute the specific four components of the training activities, which were: I. Linguistic Basis; II. Lesson Design; III. Teaching Techniques; IV. Teaching Demonstration. All the above-mentioned results from each phase of the training process were practical training procedures and detailed training activities, and at the same time, they were the specific outcomes of the training as well, such as different activities but in common during the complete training process: specifying the training objectives, defining the training syllabus, preparing the lesson plans, selecting instructional strategies, organizing the training resources and materials, locating the training place, recruiting the training volunteers, delivering the real training, evaluating the training phases and modifying further training practice.

## 4.4 Findings of Research Question 3

*Research Question 3: How does the training process develop and to what extent does the training module improve student-teachers' ELT proficiency?*

### 4.4.1 The Development of the Training Process

As aforementioned, the results from the whole training process were not only the specific outcomes of the training program, but also the practical training procedures as well. Therefore, in order to answer this question, combining the specific training process with the identified components of training activities again could illustrate how the training process was developed effectively and systematically. That is, the results from research questions 1 and 2 were also used to identify and provide reasonable elaborations for the present one.

One of the main purposes of the study was to develop a feasible training module to improve ELT proficiency among student-teachers in such a setting. So, I developed

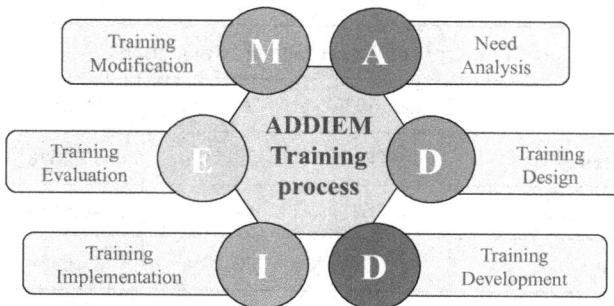

**Figure 4.2** The ADDIEM Training Process
(Source: Adapted from Richard & Elwood, 2009)

the interrelated ADDIEM Training Framework which evolved into the core research problem of ELT proficiency as shown in Figure 4.2; it was applied to *"lead and maintain the integrity of the training and development process"* (Richard & Elwood, 2009, p.244). The systematic framework was exhibited as a training blueprint throughout the whole training process.

The ADDIEM Training Process included: need Analysis, Training Design, Training Development, Training Implementation, Training Evaluation, and additional Training Modification. All phases consisted of a complete training process of the study, and each played its unique role for the final training module which focused on the student-teachers' ELT proficiency.

### 4.4.2   The Improvements of the Student-teachers' ELT Proficiency

#### Overall Aspects of Improvements in the Quantitative Data

In terms of the overall improvement for the trainees' ELT proficiency upon the analyses of completing the training process, the results indicated a high and positive consistency based on the two evaluation forms for training components I, II, III & IV, respectively. The total trainees held the affirmative 100% of feeling beneficial from the training, and the following Table 4.15 shows the mean and percentage of their satisfaction from the survey after the training. Generally speaking, based on the whole training process, 7.03% of the trainees had the satisfaction of 60~69%, 20.28% of the trainees thought their satisfaction was 70~79%, 42.03% trainees graded 80~89% satisfaction, and 30.66% trainees deemed higher satisfaction of 90~100%.

**Table 4.15   Percentage and Mean of the Trainees' Satisfaction**

| The Scale of Percentage of Satisfaction | | | | |
|---|---|---|---|---|
|  | 60~69% | 70~79% | 80~89% | 90~100% |
| Component I | 9.80% | 23.53% | 37.26% | 29.41% |
| Component II. III & IV | 4.26% | 17.02% | 46.81% | 31.91% |
| Mean | 7.03% | 20.28% | 42.03% | 30.66% |

#### Specific Aspects of Improvements in the Qualitative Data

With regard to the specific improvements for the trainees' ELT proficiency upon the various training components, Table 4.16 displays the detailed aspects of improvement coded from the data in an existing high-low frequency; at the same time, these conclusive categories were justified correspondingly by original italics quotation extracted from the trainees' responses and feelings. P#17 in brackets represents the practical coding number of participant #17, et cetera.

**Table 4.16   Categories and Specific Improvement of the Trainees' ELT Proficiency**

| Main Categories | Specific Aspects of Improvement |
|---|---|
| Enhanced Learning Interests and Confidence | ...learning English like this is so unexpectedly interesting (P#17) ...feel relaxed. (P#20)<br>...I improved some skills from three training components with the teacher's help... makes me love English more. (P#13)<br>...dare to communicate with others...be more confident. (P#28)<br>...lets me know more about English study, not afraid of using it,...have a strong desire to learn English well. (P#31)<br>...have no previous fear on English, instead of wanting to learn further English,...it is interesting and practical. (P#36)<br>...is a long-term process, I will try to find a shortcut by using the teacher's methods of demonstration. (P#20)<br>...improved my learning interest in English, letting me feel the charm of English classrooms again and again. (P#42)<br>...there is no clear effect, but it has a silent transforming influence for me. (P#14)<br>...I made a breakthrough in many aspects, such as I dare to communicate in English. (P#28)<br>...let me learn so much knowledge which cannot learn in daily life, let me understand English and is so originally interesting, no more reciting boring English words, no more writing dull English sentences, everything is useful and practical, is good for our professional development, I hope to participate more in similar training. (P#15)<br>...learning English is a long process, but I learned so many teaching techniques and methods, more importantly, I feel that learning English is such a relaxing activity. (P#20) |
| Improved Comprehensive English Pronunciation | ...I corrected my pronunciation of words. (P#2, P#35, P#51); can pronounce better comprehensive pronunciation after reviewing the phonetic symbols; can pay more attention to English pronunciation. (P#3, P#6, P#9, P#13, P#16, P#34, P#49, P#52, P#57) |

Continued Table

| Main Categories | Specific Aspects of Improvement |
|---|---|
| Improved Comprehensive English Pronunciation | ...I realized my incorrect way to pronounce, can pronounce the correct sound of words only having comprehensive pronunciation. (P#17)<br>...I feared learning English pronunciation all the time, I forget all the phonetic symbols, but now I can learn them actively and gained a lot. (P#44)<br>...mainly benefited from English pronunciation, I am weak at pronouncing English sounds, teaching resources about how to pronounce helped a lot, my personal learning targets were achieved. (P#24)<br>...we just pay more attention to written scores but neglected learning the most basic English pronunciation, now I can focus emphasis on it. (P#50) |
| Improved Spoken English and Listening Ability | ...I dare to open my mouth to speak English instead of being afraid of making mistakes. (P#36)<br>...mainly benefited from spoken English. I am not afraid to speak. (P#57)<br>...I made so much progress; I can communicate in English. (P#28)<br>...I can focus some key information instead of every aspect while listening. (P#44)<br>...I improved my listening techniques after review. (P#17) |
| Acquired Skills and Techniques in Instructional Design | ...I know clearly the framework and key and difficult points in designing lesson plans, I understand how to transfer the requirements into practical classroom content by applying instructional syllabus. (P#2)<br>...different and fruitful teaching resources and materials gave me various feelings and I benefited from them. (P#26)<br>...previous English courses just were to only study, while this game-based teaching and learning doesn't feel insipid and tiring but attractive and happy, it helped a lot, and my personal learning target was achieved as expected. (P#57)<br>...my main obtainments are to know more about instructional design and made progress, still need to know more excellent instructional design and techniques. (P#39)<br>...I feel it is practical that I learned so many techniques in terms of instructional design especially in the stage of practice.(P#19)<br>...lesson design is a required course as a normal college student. The techniques taught in the classroom may clearly lead me on how to design an instructional activity.(P#14)<br>...I learned how to combine the games and interactions into practical teaching, especially I know more about the teaching techniques and skills in our future practice of primary school. In a word, I improved personally and prepared for |

Continued Table

| Main Categories | Specific Aspects of Improvement |
|---|---|
| Acquired Skills and Techniques in Instructional Design | my future employment. (P#28)<br>...the stage of games can focus all the attention of a classroom, which can break the embarrassment between strangers. (P#54)<br>...what I expected to learn are all involved in the training, I learned much that I could not get in ordinary courses, my practical ability and oral skill improved a lot, I learned many creative teaching methods and techniques. (P#32)<br>...I know how to select teaching materials to organize teaching content according to the teaching syllabus in future practice. (P#29)<br>...I benefited in terms of teaching techniques but still need further improvement because I need more practical operation and exercises. (P#25)<br>...I benefited a lot with regard to teaching methods and techniques; more importantly, I felt it was relaxed training to learning English. (P#20)<br>...I benefited most from how to make PPT, it helped me a lot. (P#5)<br>...learned many interactive methods and how to make the classroom effective. (P#26)<br>...all the teaching resources and materials shared in the groups are good for strengthening and improving our learning. (P#36)<br>...teaching recourses, materials and videos are so close to our daily life, they are so practical for our professional development. (P#35)<br>...we should consider all-over the factors in lesson design based on the teaching syllabus, and  the teaching method should not be simple, should arouse students' learning interests by using game techniques. I will keep on doing more practice. (P#27)<br>...learned some techniques of how to sing English songs. (P#41)<br>...I know that lesson design, presentation and evaluation are so important for a normal college student. I learned much practical knowledge during the training demonstration of teaching procedures and methods. (P#16)<br>...I can distinguish the difference between presenting and giving a lecture clearly now. (P#14)<br>...I can grasp teaching objectives and classroom management to some extent. (P#36)<br>...all the teaching recourses and materials provided in and out of the classroom and are very valuable. (P#58) |
| Positive Self-reflected Awareness | ...let me know my own shortcomings and weakness. (P#1, P#2)<br>...realized my weak basic knowledge and need double effort. (P#41)<br>...the training let me know my weaknesses and how to improve. Making full |

Continued Table

| Main Categories | Specific Aspects of Improvement |
|---|---|
| Positive Self-reflected Awareness | preparation is of great importance to teach. (P#35)<br>... I feel I should make improvement on presentation and evaluation; I should overcome my hurried and nervous moods. (P#14)<br>...my personal learning targets were achieved, but still need more practice in real situations. (P#27)<br>...I could not attend all classes because of personal reasons, every aspect should be improved in the future, and I lack a strong basis and insufficient knowledge. (P#31)<br>...I cannot apply flexibly because I am not familiar with primary English textbooks and know less about English teaching. (P#26) |

Coding from the original data, I displayed the main following categories in terms of enhanced trainees' learning interests, confidence and desires, improvement of comprehensive English pronunciation, spoken English and listening ability, the trainees' acquirements about applying skills and techniques on general instructional design, and their self-reflected awareness of disadvantages and shortcomings as the specific aspects of improvements upon the student-teachers' ELT proficiency which is discussed in the next chapter. Overall, the majority of the student-teachers felt *"beneficial from the whole training to a great extent"* (P#58). Some trainees said that they joined the training for their personal purposes, and they expressed to have gained what was expected and have reached their learning targets by chatting with some trainees randomly after class. Certainly, other trainees reported the training did not meet their personal learning targets with a factual but understandable problem of the limited training period.

Starting from my personal point of view as the trainer, on one hand, I could draw a conclusion that the whole implementation of the training was positively beneficial for the student-teachers' overall professional development based mainly on their practical performances and classroom observations. On the other hand, it also indicated that there was an obvious improvement on the feedbacks based on the two practical assignments. Firstly, it could be found that certain improvements attained from viewing the trainees' manuscripts of English handwriting by comparing their formative progress. The majority of the trainees basically framed the identified objectives of writing English letters more legible and more fluently by applying the basic writing skills and techniques of English Handwriting in terms of the five following visual features as legibility components: letter form, alignment, size, spacing and slant (Spinelli, 2011). Another daily assignment was the lesson plan named *We Love Animals* designed by the trainees after delivering the 6th training area of the Lesson Plan. My general and objective feeling of evaluation about the trainees' submitted tasks was that the majority of the trainees understood how to place the framework of a lesson plan clearly, how to set the key and difficult points properly, and how to transfer the requirements into practical classroom content appropriately by applying instructional syllabus and textbooks. Specifically, their language and instructional descriptions were relatively simple but clear, and their teaching objectives were basically within reason and accordance with their teaching targets, especially, the majority of the trainees added a certain procedure of *Teaching Reflective Notes* by following a referenced sample lesson plan, in which they could make a beginning to end self-checking to compare both proposing steps and performing achievements together. Therefore, it implied that they acquired more or less about the requirements from the teaching pattern or standard based on the present educational situation and context.

Additionally, some training activities or training areas were highlighted frequently by the trainees as the most favorite during the training process such as the game-oriented area, Simon Says, ABC songs, English letter matching, tongue twisters, listening English songs and filling in lyrics, phonetic symbols clicking and reading cards, finger games, listening and drawing, storytelling, and English writing, and so on. Simultaneously, the trainees provided plenty of constructive suggestions about the training as well, which facilitated some evidence for the general improvement and modification in further practice, and all of these are discussed in the next chapter.

To sum up, the ADDIEM training framework (need Analysis, Training Design, Training Development, Training Implementation, Training Evaluation and additional Training Modification) was applied to lead and maintain the integrity of the training and development process, and was exhibited as the training blueprint throughout the whole training process. Thus, all the training activities were conducted sequentially and the whole training process was developed systematically as a whole. With regard to the improvement of the student-teachers' ELT proficiencies, both of the overall quantitative results and the specific qualitative categories were demonstrated together to interpret the participants' feedbacks and the trainer's perspectives. More specifically, a 100% feeling beneficial from the training and a positive higher satisfaction of their proficiencies from 25.53% before training to 78.72% after training. The detailed aspects of the student-teachers' improvement of ELT proficiency are categorized by the following themes based on their feedbacks: (1) Advanced learning interests and confidence; (2) Improved comprehensive English pronunciation; (3) Improved spoken English and listening ability; (4) Acquired skills and techniques applying on the instructional design; (5) Self-reflected awareness. Based on the practical evidences from the two daily assignments, it could also be identified that the student-teachers acquired more legibility & fluency of English handwriting by comparing their formative progress, and they well fulfilled the standards of lesson design under the present educational situation and context based on the summative assessment.

## 4.5　Summary

This chapter presents the results from the student-teachers, English teachers, parents, school principals and stakeholders' general perceptions, beliefs, current capacities and expectations towards English language teaching proficiency at beginning level through questionnaires, interviews, classroom observations, reflective notes, pretest and posttest, surveys and related documents.

The systematic framework of the ADDIEM Training was exhibited all the while as a blueprint which covered the whole training process to answer the three research questions of the study. The identified challenges facing the current student-teachers, the detailed components of training activities, and the systematic development of the training process and the visible and beneficial improvements of the student-teachers resulting from the research questions in multiple perspectives can corroborate positively to develop a more complete and effective training module of the ELT proficiency in such a context of the study.

# CHAPTER 5
# CONCLUSION, DISCUSSION
# AND RECOMMENDATIONS

This final chapter reviews the methodology applied in the study, summarizes the results from the research questions, and discusses the implications and recommendations in the following sections:

5.1 Summary of the Results

5.2 Discussion of the Findings

5.3 Implications of the Study

5.4 Recommendations of the Study

5.5 Summary

## 5.1  Summary of the Results

(1) With regard to the findings of RQ 1 *"What are the challenges facing the current student-teachers in teaching English to beginning learners in multi-ethnic community schools in Yunnan Province?"* Two sets of questionnaires were applied for the student-teachers and English teachers' general perceptions, beliefs, current capacity towards English language and teaching proficiency. Three groups of interviews were conducted with regard to parents, English teachers, kindergarten principals and stakeholders' general bilingual teaching practices, viewpoints, attitudes, professional development and social requirements. The quantitative data was merged with the qualitative data that resulted from the Needs Analysis Phase, all fourteen training areas were attached in the main four components of the training, respectively,

and were included in the training design phase as the identified challenges facing the current student-teachers about their ELT proficiencies by revising, sorting, recombining, and finalizing. The fourteen training areas were covered in the four training components as Linguistic Basis including ① Comprehensive pronunciation; ② Comprehensive Listening Techniques; and ③ Practical Spoken English, Lesson Design including ④ Application of English Curriculum and Syllabus; ⑤ Application of Textbook; and ⑥ Design of Lesson Plan, Teaching Techniques including; ⑦ Story-telling; ⑧ Game playing; ⑨ Singing English Songs and Rhymes; ⑩ Stick Figures; ⑪ English Handwriting; and ⑫ Modern Educational Teaching Technologies and Teaching Demonstration including; ⑬ Demonstration of Lessons; ⑭ Feedback and Reflection. Only a few student-teachers that enrolled in the present study were real ethnic minorities while the majority were Han student-teachers from ethnic communities, so the questionnaires and interviews only focused on the general perspectives of ELT proficiency which was required in multi-ethnic communities instead of discussing the specific bilingualism or multilingualism. These fourteen areas of challenges were identified by a general standpoint which applied the same accordance to the majority of multi-ethnic communities in Yunnan Province as well.

(2) With regard to the findings of RQ 2 *"What are the specific components of training activities for student-teachers in teaching English effectively?"* It was considered as the biggest part because each finding generated from each training phase might be an indispensable sub-section for the specific components of the training processes and activities. Therefore, based on the elaborations of identified challenges provided in the needs Analysis Phase, the immediately identified outcomes from the training Design phase, the training Development phase, the training Implementation phase, the training Evaluation phase, and the training Modification phase were merged sequentially to answer the research question.

Firstly, the fourteen training areas which highly voiced the necessity of training from the identified challenges were defined as the priorities of the training objectives, and then, the defined training syllabus, specified strategies and goals, and organized objectives were used sequentially in the training Design phase. Secondly, the preparation of lesson plans, the selection of instructional strategies, the training location and the recruitment of training volunteers were accomplished successively in the whole training Development phase. Thirdly, 12 weeks of training named *ELT Proficiency Training for Pre-service Teachers* was delivered with a total of 36 periods in the 2nd semester of the 2018 academic year in Dali University from October 23, 2018 to January 15, 2019 in the training Implementation phase. Fourthly, a developed evaluation system induced from three different types of pre-assessment, formative assessment and summative assessment was conducted successively during all the training phases were completed respectively in the training Evaluation phase. The continuous feedback obtained from the training evaluation phase revealed ultimately a higher suitability and an effective tendency of the training. Lastly, based on the findings resulting from the training evaluation phase throughout the complete training process, accordingly modifications and improvements were identified by a combination of the trainees' practical performances, real feelings and constructive suggestions, my original intention and reflective notes, with the experts' feasible recommendations and the contextual documents and orientation in the training Modification phase. All results as aforementioned from each phase of the training process constituted the specific components of the training activities for student-teachers in teaching English effectively.

(3) According to the findings of the RQ 3 *"How does the training process develop and to what extent does the training module improve student-teachers' ELT proficiencies?"* The ADDIEM training process from beginning to end helped not only lead to develop the training systematically and to conduct all training activities sequentially, but also helped make decisions of how to gather necessary information to answer what liked to be learned so as to develop a feasible training module for the study. In terms of how the training module improved the student-teachers' ELT proficiencies, both of the overall quantitative aspects and the specific qualitative aspects were demonstrated together. A total of 100% of affirmative certainty of being beneficial from the training and a positive higher frequency about the trainees' original expectations to a great extent were evidently indicated from the survey. More specifically, the detailed aspects of improvement by the student-teachers' ELT proficiency extracted from the main conclusive categories in terms of the trainees' learning interests, confidence and desires, improvement of comprehensive English pronunciation, spoken English and listening ability, the trainees' acquirements about

applying skills and techniques on general instructional design, and their self-reflective cognitions of disadvantages and shortcomings which were coded from the original data were identified and justified correspondingly by the original quotations extracted from the trainees' responses and feelings in the survey and evaluation forms. Some trainees expressed to have gained what to expect and have achieved their learning targets pleasantly from the training. Additionally, it also indicated that an obvious improvement based on the completion of two practical assignments submitted by the trainees. One was that the trainees' more proper and relatively normative English hand-writing on a test basically fulfilled the identified objectives by applying the basic writing skills and techniques, the other was that the trainees acquired more or less about the requirements from the training patterns in designing lesson plans based on the present educational situation and context. Moreover, the trainees also highlighted their favorite activites during the training process, such as game-oriented, singing English songs, tongue twisters, English letter matching, finger games, storytelling, and so on.

## 5.2    Discussion of the Findings

In this section, the findings of the research questions are discussed and compared respectively with the literature reviews.

**Research Question 1**: *"What are the challenges facing the current student-teachers in teaching English to beginning learners in multi-ethnic community schools in Yunnan Province?"*

The intended needs from the questionnaires for the student-teachers were investigated and the possible expectations were summarized from the parents, English teachers, kindergarten principals and stakeholders based on both quantitative and qualitative analysis. The findings of the study revealed a number of challenges. Teaching the English language in a multi-ethnic context was an enormous challenge for the English teachers due to their different educational backgrounds and their current English proficiency performed in the classroom (Wang, 2015). That was, the student-teachers who were majority Han or ethnic minorities involved in the training lacked the confidence, obviously and seriously, to use English because they did not want to make mistakes (Feng, 2005).

Li and Zhou (2005) regarded that the linguistic, cultural, and socioeconomic gaps between the majority at Han and minority ethnic groups placed the latter at a great disadvantage due to the requirement of multilingual proficiency, active discrimination policy, and highly demanding curriculum. English is a compulsory course for all undergraduates at university. At the tertiary level, ethnic minority students were expected to master not only generic skills, but also multilingual proficiency at least in the national language—Chinese—and at times in English. Mandarin Chinese is the dominant medium of instruction for most curricula from secondary school onwards, all the student-teachers had to pass the Standard Mandarin Test before they applied for the Teacher Certification in the current context of China; at the same time, they also must pass at least the CET-4 (College English Test-4 Level) which is the compulsory national English testing system for all university non-English major students in China. Therefore, the minority students might face more challenges and difficulties than their Han cohorts, especially when their first language is not well developed and the second language is used as a medium of instruction (Feng, 2005). However, only a few student-teachers in the present study were real ethnic minorities while the majority Han were from ethnic communities, so the questionnaires and interviews were only focused on the general perspectives of ELT proficiency required in most multi-ethnic communities instead of really emphasizing the specific bilingualism or multilingualism.

Conclusively, an adapted interrelation between the fourteen identified challenges and the four relevant training components were displayed as shown in Figure 5.1 according to the general findings. This developed interrelation played a critical guiding role for the following systematic phases of the training process based on the three following regards: ① the conclusive categories of codes and themes extracted from the questionnaires and interviews; ② my personal experience and present understanding of the situation; ③ the relevant research reviews and references.

In terms of the ELT proficiency at the beginning level in the context of the current educational situation, especially English teachers' pronunciation, spoken English and listening ability were ubiquitous and problematic issues in performing the practice (Tan, 2014; Wang & Mi, 2014). Similarly, it was difficult for them to design and organize good English teaching activities much less to include the development of integration in the bilingual curriculum based on my own teaching experience in previous ELT practice for both preschool and primary education majors (Shen & Zhao, 2010). In this way, fourteen areas of challenges which were highly rated with the percentage and frequency were finally refined and identified in the need analysis phase, and accordingly, the linguistic basis, lesson design, teaching techniques and teaching demonstration were synthesized as the training components and prioritized training objectives for the next training phase.

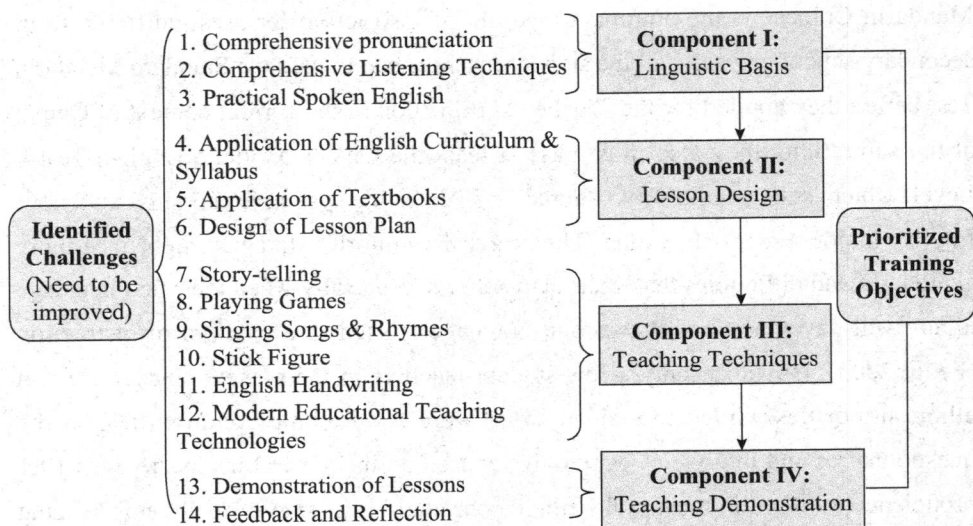

**Figure 5.1** Developing Interrelation between the Identified Challenges and the Prioritized Training Objectives

Additionally, it should be classified that certain items extracted from data, such as vocabulary, grammar, knowledge of British and American cultural backgrounds, knowledge of cross-cultural communication, reading ability, and writing ability at the same time were not included in the present study even though holding their equivalent percentages, but it did not absolutely indicate that they were not important or necessary for student-teachers' general ELT proficiencies. The reasons are as follows:

(1) In the critical period of language learning for children, its advantage is to build a corresponding language environment by imitating the voice and intonation to

form the language sense naturally; learning pronunciation well as the most important and basic factor in language acquisition, and to obtain a lot of language input of listening (Li, 2006; Wang, 2009).

(2) Children's English teaching emphasized not on the amount of vocabulary, but the ability of learning English and using it. If it was just the number of words we were valuing, they would be in a negative state sooner or later (Wang, 2016).

(3) Gimson (1962, cited in Wang, 2009) stated when a person spoke a language, he/she has to learn almost 100% pronunciation of the language, while he/she just needs to learn 50~90% grammar and 1% vocabulary. Phonetic learning directly affected the ability of oral expression and listening comprehension ability for the children's development, while reading and writing abilities were not emphasized in the early stage.

(4) Compared with adults, childhood have a key implicit period of learning, and a huge deformability of speech, strong imitative ability and reproductive ability could easily form good pronunciation and intonation, which have great advantages in second language acquisition (Tian, 2007).

(5) Last but not least, knowledge of British & American cultural background and cross-cultural communication are relatively hard to be examined and identified within such a limited training period especially for those who are non-English majors and not to mention their current lower situation of ELT proficiency or level.

**Research Question 2**: *"What are the specific components of training activities for student-teachers in teaching English effectively?"*

In respect of the specific components of training activities, each finding resulting from each training phase might constitute indispensable sub-sections for specific components of the training processes. Therefore, the immediately identified outcomes from the training design phase, the training development phase, the training implementation phase, the training evaluation phase, and the training modification phase were sequenced to interpret this research question based on the elaborative challenges identified in the need analysis phase.

The general goals of the proposed training aimed at improving basic professional qualities and practical teaching skills which based on ELT proficiency at the beginning level for current student-teachers to optimize their pre-service professional development towards the specific objectives. The specific training objectives in the phases of the training components were developed, revised and finalized in order to reflect realistically the necessity of the training. On one side, each item of the specific objective was derived from and identified by the quantitative and qualitative data during the phase of need analysis instead of listing randomly; on the other side, the suitability of the objectives was also considered based on the levels of current student-teachers' expertise which expected them to achieve under the parallel analysis of context in the present study. Therefore, corresponding instructional delivery and assessment criteria were determined at the 1~3 levels of *Knowledge, Comprehension* and *Application* by making a reference to Bloom's Taxonomy of cognitive domains (Huitt, 2011), which was oriented to be adequate and appropriate for them so far. That is, all the items of outcomes were determined as the specific objectives serving for each phase of the training components, and the degree of difficulty, the relationships between objectives also were overall reflected. In sum, several different activities performed sequentially in different phases of the ADDIEM training process initiated different outcomes, which constituted the specific components of the training processes as demonstrated in Table 5.1.

**Table 5.1    Phases, Activities and Outcomes within the ADDIEM Training Process**

| Main Phases | Specific Activities | Major Outcomes |
|---|---|---|
| **Need Analysis** *(2017,10~2018,8)* | - to design and conduct the questionnaires and interviews<br>- to consider characteristics of the training context<br>- to interpret and identify student-teachers' needs<br>- to inventory available training materials and resources<br>- to select appropriate instructional models of training | -identified challenges |
| **Training Design** *(2018,8~2018,9)* | - to distribute training modules<br>- to construct an instructional framework<br>- to set the training criteria of assessment<br>- to define detailed contents and activities<br>- to employ instructional techniques<br>- to draw a tentative schedule | -designed training objectives and training syllabus |
| **Training Development** *(2018,9~2018,10)* | - to design 14 different lesson plans<br>- to select appropriate materials and tools<br>- to determine a proper criteria of evaluation | -prepared lesson plans and instructional strategies |

Continued Table

| Main Phases | Specific Activities | Major Outcomes |
|---|---|---|
| **Training Development** *(2018,9~2018,10)* | - to develop assessment instruments<br>- to enroll trainees and provide training guides<br>- to make schedules and locate a classroom | -prepared lesson plans and instructional strategies |
| **Training Implementation** *(2018,10~2019,1)* | - to state current teaching and learning experience<br>- to make complete preparation<br>- to carry on real training activities<br>- to observe the classroom<br>- to conduct survey questionnaires<br>- to collect participants' feedback | -purposive recruitment of trainees<br>-successful delivery training |
| **Training Evaluation** *(2019,1~2019,2)* | - to confirm appropriate techniques of measurement<br>- to conduct the formative evaluation<br>- to conduct the summative evaluation<br>- to conduct final post-test evaluation<br>- to interpret training effectiveness | -complete formative and summative assessments |
| **Training Modification** *(2019,2~2019,3)* | - to review reflective notes<br>- to extract data from the survey and questionnaires<br>- to interpret data from class observations<br>- to review trainees' assignments<br>- to interview some trainees | -identified improvement and modification |

Determining general training goals, defining specific training objectives and organizing training activities were more often than not critically essential and particularly important considerations in training design and development to create a satisfying and effective learning experience (Brown & Green, 2016, p.102). Equally, the training syllabus generated from the training design phase, was considered as the critical and essential component based on Nation and Macalister's statement (2010). "*A negotiated syllabus involves the steps of: (1) negotiating the goals, content, format and assessment of the course; (2) implementing these negotiated decisions; (3) evaluating the effect of the implementation in terms of outcomes and the way the implementation was done (p.150).*" The following elements were "**negotiated**" in order to make the syllabus workable and effective; they were: negotiation procedures, training planning (for participation, procedures, and goals), training evaluation, and resources and materials (Nation & Macalister, 2010). That was just as the key rationale of the training syllabus design of the training process; and the above-shown training syllabus was negotiated to provide such a changeable instructional model for the following phase of training development.

Additionally, with a higher emphasis on the constantly increasing flexibility and accountability for current student-teachers' learning, the most successful instruction was that which resulted in growth and achievement for all the students. *"It would seem that using systematic processes to ensure that the identified needs of students direct all instructional decisions would be the most productive approach"*(Clare & Natalie, 2014, p.28). However, there was no ready norm which could be applied to such a context of the study; consequently, I designed a proposed instructional model "3Ps + 2Ds" as a referential instructional design framework by maximizing the identified challenges for all the student-teachers in such a context. The "3Ps + 2Ds" instructional model here refers to the following 5 abbreviations: *Preparation, Presentation, Practice, Demonstration and Discussion,* which were emplaced sequentially as the main body of each lesson plan. The proposed "3Ps + 2Ds" instructional model was expected to help: (1) clarify the goals for training; (2) identify training decisions on known trainees' needs; (3) locate and choose appropriate training resources; (4) understand the effect of the training materials or methods, and so on (Clare & Natalie, 2014, p.32).

With regard to another important outcome of the component, Serdyukov and Ryan (2008) expressed that *"good lesson plans are the foundation of successful student learning, accurate assessment, and effective classroom management"* (p.1). The development of 14 lesson plans according to the 14 areas of the indentified challenges was also a critical stage in the training design phase. The well-designed lesson plans helped set the sound implementation of the training program, and they also displayed a signal that such training was to be conducted in a professional manner (Serdyukov & Ryan, 2008). Therefore, once the specific training objectives and training syllabus had been designed in the preceding phase, the modular lesson plans were organized and prepared to outline the training program in terms of the sequence of activities and events, and to guide for the trainer that provided a step-by-step breakdown for conducting a sound training program (Serdyukov & Ryan, 2008).

The model of the lesson plan here might vary from other situations, but it shared the three common and essential features of a complete, well-organized lesson plan with objectives, procedures, and evaluation (Eby, Herrell & Hicks, 2002). The lesson objectives specified the training purposes, the lesson procedures described both *"what training experiences can be provided"* and the way which could be *"effectively organized"*, while the lesson evaluation described the way I had planned in advance to determine *"whether these purposes are being attained"* (Eby et al., 2002, p.145). An available well-prepared and individualized instruction facilitated to ensure that the products (all drafts of lesson plans) were responsive to the needs of the trainees and effective in achieving the desired training outcomes (Dick et al,, 2005, p.10). Accordingly, such instructional strategies/models/techniques: problem-based learning, open-ended learning, directed learning, cooperative learning, concept-attainment model, inductive learning, authentic teaching, simulations and games, and individualized instruction, and so on, were consulted, developed and embedded in different lesson plans in order to work best based on the trainees' needs, training goals and objectives.

Moore (2015) stated the evaluation served many roles in the teaching-learning process, and it should not be limited to only the *'desired outcomes'* but also must be *"sensitive to all factors"* potentially associated with the whole training (p.251). Consequently, all the outcomes of components generated from the preceding phases including the identified needs, the specific objectives, the negotiated syllabus, the selected instructional strategies, the designed materials, the prepared lesson plans, the enrolled trainees, and even the confirmed classroom, etc, were addressed again by guiding a dynamic and flexible evaluation system (Moore, 2015). I was sensitive to all the potential or possible instruments of measurements associated with the whole training process, and that was the main reasons why the following primary evaluation types: pretest, formative and posttest (summative) were applied to different phases of the training process by its natural and chronological position in terms of their special characteristics and purposes (Moore, 2015).

All in all, understanding the organization of training events, the determination of scope and sequence, the placement of teaching and learning experiences, the preparation of training syllabus and lesson plans, the description of delivery method and the application of evaluation criterion helped me identify what was necessary to create the specific components of training activities that were effective for a variety of student-teachers-from the average one to those who required either more support or greater challenges (Brown & Green, 2016, p.113).

**Research Question 3**: *"How does the training process develop and to what extent does the training module improve student-teachers' ELT proficiencies?"*

**Development of the Training Process**

One of the main purposes of the study was to develop a feasible training module to improve ELT proficiency among student-teachers in such a setting. As aforementioned, all the results from the whole training phases were not only the specific outcomes of the training program, but also the practical training process per se. So, I developed the ADDIEM training framework which involved the core research problem of ELT proficiency. The systematic framework was exhibited as a training blueprint throughout the whole ADDIEM training process of the study. In terms of the origins of the ADDIEM training process, it was rooted in the ADDIE model with a five-phase process (analyze, design, develop, implement, and evaluate) which is considered the most widely used methodology systematic training model and one of the most applicable used systematic instructional systems design models (Gagne et al, 2005; Allen, 2006; Reiser & Dempsey, 2007). Each ADDIE phase was purposeful and focused on the specific outcomes, and use of the ADDIE model can provide a well-organized, strategic plan for training and instructional design that ensures quality through consideration of all of the elements (Gagne et al., 2005; Clare & Natalie, 2014). In summary, I highlighted the particular phase of Modification into the ADDIEM training process in view of meeting uniformly rigorous standards for developing individual and effective training, because it allowed me to optimize the use of the training model and promote more rewarding and productive practice (Clare & Natalie, 2014). Moreover, I essentially expected to identify further and detailed modifications and improvements of the training by combining the trainees' practical performances, real feelings and constructive suggestions, my original intention and reflective notes with the experts' feasible recommendations and the contextual documents and orientation.

Overall, the ADDIEM training process was developed to *"lead and maintain the integrity of the training and development process"* effectively and systematically

(Richard & Elwood, 2009, p.244). In other words, each phase of the ADDIEM training framework played a critical role for the final training module, which mainly facilitated this training to have higher satisfaction and effectiveness to some extent.

### From the Trainees' Feedbacks

With regard to overall improvement for the trainees' ELT proficiency in the training module, the results obviously indicated a high and positive consistency from the data analysis of the training process. One hundred percent of the trainees affirmatively expressed their "*benefit from all of the training to a great extent*" (P#58). When asked "*What percentage of your satisfaction is based on the training content?*" 7.03% of the trainees rated their overall satisfaction in the range of 60~69%, 20.28% was in the range of 70~79%, 42.03% was in the range of 80~89%, and 30.66% was in the range of 90~100%. The majority of the trainees expressed that they had gained what to expect and basically reached their learning targets. Certainly, a few of the trainees reported the training did not meet their personal learning targets, nevertheless, they explained factual and understandable issues because of "*the limited training time* (P#46)". Furthermore, a higher percentage from the survey displayed a 97.87% rate of satisfaction of the training contents (targets, practicability, enlightenment, objectives, materials selection, time arrangement and courseware design) and 99.09% rate of satisfaction of trainer's performance (basic abilities in subject teaching, clarity of difficulty and key points, interactive control ability, materials preparation, progress and steps, attitudes and responsibility); and another comparison of the trainees' proficiency from the evaluation forms also showed a 93.61% rate of satisfaction of the their overall learning attitudes (concentration and attendance), 25.53% rate of satisfaction of their proficiency before training while 78.72% rate of satisfaction of that after training. All these results indicated the training components also produced a positive orientation of improvements for the student-teachers. Such data extracted from the multiple sources included the questionnaires, interviews, classroom observations, documents and my own reflective notes exactly served to validate both the qualitative and quantitative findings in terms of triangulation. That is to say, the techniques of triangulation strengthened conversely the reliability and validity of the results (Creswell, 2003).

With regard to the specific improvements, the main categories coded from the original data by revising, rereading and adjusting several times, such as: (1) Enhanced the trainees' learning interests and confidence; (2) Improved comprehensive English pronunciation; (3) Improved practical spoken English and comprehensive listening ability; (4) Well-acquired applying skills and techniques upon general instructional design; (5) Self-reflected awareness of disadvantages were respectively displayed in an existing high-low frequency as the specific aspects of improvements of the student-teachers' ELT proficiency.

*Category I: Enhanced Learning Interests and Confidence*

In the case of this category, the student-teachers first expressed their higher frequent feelings about advancing strong interests and confidence by asking the question "*What did you gain mainly from the training areas of the training?*" after training. Interest and confidence, belonging to the non-intelligence factors which played a crucial role in fulfilling the individual needs of language learners, were highlighted normally to raise the awareness of students' individual learning styles by arousing their potential in learning a target language and by enabling students to be in charge of their own learning (Pintrich & Schunk, 2002). Such aspects of the improvements recognized by the student-teachers themselves, conversely, might stimulate their own positive motivation to achieve and cultivate their sense of achievement in acquiring more ELT proficiency (Li, 2015). Exactly as Participant #42 realized that the training "*improved my learning interest about English, let me feel the charm of English classrooms.*" Participant #15 also expressed completely that the training "*It helped me learn so much knowledge which I cannot learn in daily life, let me understand English is so interesting, no more reciting boring English words, no more writing dull English sentences. Everything is useful and practical, and good for our professional development, I hope to participant more in the same training.*" While Participant #20 showed that "*I benefited from so many teaching techniques and methods, more importantly, I feel that learning English is such a relaxing activity.*" In terms of confidence, Participant #31 stated that the training "*let me know more about English teaching, at least I am not afraid of using it,...have a strong desire to learn English well.*" Participant #36 indicated "*I am not afraid of learning English, instead I am eager to learn more and more, it is interesting and practical.*" Then,

Participants #14, #17, #20, and #28 summarized feeling more confident to learn more English because the training was so unexpectedly relaxing and interesting, and it had an imperceptible transforming influence on them though it was a long-term process.

*Category II: Improved Comprehensive English Pronunciation*

The coming aspect of improvement of the student-teachers' ELT proficiency was that the training improved their comprehensive English pronunciation from the linguistic basis of the training component to some extent. More than a dozen participants affirmed that they had better comprehensive pronunciation after reviewing phonetic symbols and practice. Hence, it should be taken into account as one of the learning requirements with functional intelligibility and communicability designing in the ultimate goals for beginning levels (Morley, 1991; Li, 2014; Lamarca, 2016). Pronunciation was deemed the most important and difficult problem that non-native English majors had to face when studying English, even though they had had at least more than ten years of learning English based on the current situation with traditional teacher-centered instruction of Chinese ELT proficiency (Fraser, 2000; Zeng, 2008; Li, 2014). Exactly as Participant #50 reflected *"We just pay more attention to written achievements but neglect to learn the most fundamental English pronunciation from primary to university, now I can focus attention on it."* According to Harmer (2001), the lack of high quality, suitable teaching and learning materials, and the lack of time to practice pronunciation were the major reasons that cause lower attention to English pronunciation, so I intended to expose the authentic materials, an internet-linked APP software (phonetic symbols clicking and reading cards) which could be operated by a mobile phone whenever and wherever possible to help the student-teachers practice their pronunciation (Rasekhi, 2010). I just acted as a speech coach of pronunciation, gave feedback to them, and encouraged them to improve their pronunciation during the implementation of the training component inside and outside the classroom (Thanasoulas, 2002). The student-teachers also remarked that improper pronunciation could lead to negative impressions, misunderstandings and ineffective communication (Hope Speak, 2014), but now they *"mainly benefited from English pronunciation, the teaching resources and materials about how to pronounce helped a lot, and achieved personal learning targets (P#24)"*. Some of the student-teachers *"almost forgot all the phonetic symbols and feared to learn English pronunciation all the time before (P#2)"*, but now *"realized the correct approaches to pronounce problematic sounds intelligibly (P#35, P#51) and "learned it actively and initiatively, gained a lot from it"* (P#44, P#57).

*Category III: Improved Practical Spoken English and Listening Ability*

Listening and speaking were the essential skills which often affected the development of reading and writing abilities in learning a language (Yavuz & Celik, 2017). According to Phil (2007), both speaking and listening need to be especially and purposefully trained in order to become a well-rounded communicator. The traditional approaches of language teaching and learning, like the Grammar Translation Method, failed to properly care for the speaking and listening skills in the majority of classrooms which mainly emphasized reading and writing skills (Kaddour, 2016). Furthermore, exactly as Janice (2017) stated neither listening nor speaking would occur in isolation. That was, each one relied on the other to succeed in a conversation through interacting and negotiating verbally. In conclusion, one of the common instructional objectives identified in these two areas of the training was to expect the student-teachers to apply frequently used communicative expressions and classroom terminologies and to follow frequent instructions in daily activities based on the analysis of their prior knowledge and practical experiences in such a setting of the study. Recommended by Hosni (2014), some oral activities in the form of simple songs, rhymes, chants, games, stories and other conversational interactions were employed in the training to enable the student-teachers to have more fun and enjoy learning to effectively improve their listening and speaking skills. I designed plenty of activities related to listening and speaking, which were not only performed in these two lesson plans, but also covered in other areas during the whole implementation of training.

In terms of the routine teaching procedure of preparation, such as greetings and daily reports, asking and answering, repeating, and reviewing, and so on, were given 10~15 minutes to evoke more interactions centering on the hot, fashionable, interesting and well-known areas by all kinds of individuals, pairs, groups or class work. The majority of the student-teachers expressed to have made much progress, P#15, P#36,

#28 and #57 said specifically that they *"dare to open mouth to speak English because of being afraid of making mistakes"*. Now they *"acquired some listening techniques after practice (P#17)"*, and *"could focus on some key information instead of every aspect when listening (P#44)"*. Compared with their prior knowledge and practical experiences existing in the daily English learning and teaching, it was congruent that the student-teachers' difficulties in learning English attributed to being shy because of their limited vocabulary and afraid of making mistakes in front of the class (Farooqui, 2007). Some of the student-teachers confessed unhesitatingly that it just was such potential issues as simply shyness, nervousness, feeling afraid of making mistakes, not knowing how to pronounce certain words, having lower motivation or uneven participation that hindered them involving in the active and effective interactions (Ur, 1996; Rahman & Deviyanti, 2012). Some factual evidence from the classroom observation showed that few student-teachers kept quiet or in a low mood while engaging in the interactions all the time exactly because of the above-mentioned factors. Thus, giving more patience, allowance, especially encouragement could be induced as my individual instructional techniques or characteristics from the whole implementation of the training; after all, encouraging the student-teachers to practice more aimed at their practical improvement (Kaddour, 2016).

Lastly, I'd like to discuss *Problem-based Learning* (PBL), which was prioritized as one of the main instructional models to devote to the whole training according to the identified challenges and objectives. PBL was suggested as *"an active and effective learning model that might help the learners present or identify their problems, allow them to learn and hone authentic problem-solving skills, develop the cooperative competence and apply their prior knowledge and experiences"* for practical purposes in the present study (Clare & Natalie, 2014, p.284-288). Moreover, Ishrat (2007), Qutoshi and Poudel (2014), Skripsi (2015) and Kudryashova et al. (2016) concluded that the PBL could be adapted to maintain their interests, encourage their cooperation, apply their prior knowledge and intellectual skill, and demonstrate their communicative effectiveness to become problem-solving learners ultimately in the training, which was characterized by a student-centered approach and a teacher-facilitated role in listening and speaking training. In other words, such aspects of improvement of the student-teachers' ELT proficiency with regard to the practical spoken English and comprehensive listening ability were justified according to the proposed learning model especially in these two areas of the training to a large extent. Certainly, keeping more practice in listening and speaking both inside and outside the class was approved of improving the continual proficiency all the time (Skripsi, 2015).

*Category IV: Well-acquired Applying Techniques upon Instructional Design*
International Journal of Learning and Teaching. 9(3), 349-353.

Using fairy tales as a model to enhance learners' writing organization ski

Apart from the specific improvements of the student-teachers' ELT proficiency in respect of the linguistic basis of the training component, most aspects of improvements were closely related to and attributed to the Instructional Design (ID). On account of the coded results from the training, the participants expressed in succession that they benefited from knowing more about instructional design from the training. Specifically, they *"learned so many practical teaching methods and techniques (P#19, P#20, P#25, P#28, P#32, P#39)"*, such as how to *"select the teaching methods and organize teaching procedures directly (P#2)"*, *"transfer the requirements into practical classroom content by applying an instructional syllabus (P#9)"*, *"distinguish the difference between presenting and giving a lecture clearly (P#14)"*, *"demonstrate the teaching procedures and methods (P#16)"*, *"manage an effective classroom by using interactive methods (P26)"*, *"consider all factors in a lesson design based on a teaching syllabus (P#27)"*, *"select teaching materials and organize teaching content (P#29)"*, *"design the whole instructional framework and set key and difficult points (P#37)"* , *"make a practicable PPT (P#5)"*, and *"combine the games and interactions into practical teaching (P#48)"*, and so on. Similarly, it also deserved to be mentioned that *"the game-based method can focus all attention of the classroom (P#54)"*, *"felt less insipid and tired as well as more attractive and happy (P#57)"* And then *"we should arouse students' learning interests by using the teaching techniques of playing games and singing English songs in future practice (P#27, P#41) ."* Consequently, the ID could be said to be a system of creating more specific procedures or approaches for design, development, evaluation, maintenance and modification of instructional recourses and materials that facilitate more effective and efficient learning and performance (Richards & Lockart, 1994; Gustafson & Branch, 2002; Martin, 2011).

Some of the participants also realized the importance and necessity of the instructional design because "*it is so valuable for professional development* (P#35)". "*Design, presentation and evaluation are so important for a normal college student* (P#21) and "*it is also a required course for a normal college student* (P#16)". "*The techniques of the instructional design taught in the classroom may clearly lead me to design a more effective instructional activity* (P#14)", "*making full preparation is of great importance to have an instructional design* (P#39)". But anyway, "*we still need further improvement and more actual operation and practice* (P#25, P#27)". Generally speaking, instructional design is a system of developing well-structured instructional materials, using identified objectives and related teaching strategies, applying appropriate curriculum syllabi and textbooks, organizing well-prepared lesson plans, selecting proper teaching with techniques and technologies, launching systematic feedback, reflection and evaluation (Moore & Kearsley, 1996).

A few participants highlighted the teaching and learning resources and materials provided in and out of the class. "*The different and fruitful teaching resources and materials shared in the classrooms gave me various feelings* (P#26)". "*They are so close to our daily life* (P#58)", "*so practical for strengthening and improving our learning* (P#36)", and "*also valuable for our professional development* (P#35)". The teaching and learning resources and materials also were crucial to the success of student-teachers achievement and improvement in a way. One of the indispensable instructional components of lesson planning in teaching depends on the identification of teaching and learning resources and materials which could not only significantly increase student-teachers achievement but also add important structure to lesson planning and the delivery of instruction in the training (Hassan & Miraclea, 2009). Based on Hassan and Miraclea (2009), such properties of educativeness and relevance were prioritized and determined by the identified objectives of the training, various forms of the teaching and learning resources and materials, including audio-visuals, videos, handmade cards, pictures, worksheets, tutorials, linkages of networks, online books and articles, blogs, publications, charts, templates, maps, cases, screenshots, even WeChat public accounts, and so on, were distributed in accordance with the different activities in present training.

In sum, the authentic and effective resources and materials were applied to provide scaffolding for learning, stimulating the feedback and reflection, arousing and sustaining the curiosity and attention, enhancing the learning opportunities, promoting the input and output, enlarging the understanding of language, and activating intellectual emotional involvement (McGrath, 2002; Tomlinson, 2003, 2008; Hassan & Miraclea, 2009; Martin, 2011).

*Category V: Positive Self-reflected Awareness about Their Own Disadvantages*

A few student-teachers reflected faithfully that *"the training let us know our own shortcomings and weaknesses (P#1, P#2, P#35, P#46)"* and *"realize my weak basic knowledge and need of double effort (P#41)"*, *"I lack strong basic overall knowledge(P#23)"* so that *"every aspect should be improved in the future (P#31)"*, *"We still need a more practical operation and a further improvement in real situations (P#25, P#27, P#53)"*. As a result, they realized that they should make more effort to improve the following general aspects, such as *"English pronunciation, practice about spoken English, listening comprehension, practical knowledge of communication and classroom expressions, vocabulary, both sections of presentation and evaluation of instructional design, excellent learning and teaching techniques, flexible application of textbooks, overcoming nervousness, impatience, inferiority, lazy, timidity, and so on"*. As Confucius said, "By three methods may we learn wisdom: first, by reflection, which is the noblest; second, by imitation, which is the easiest; and third, by experience, which is the most bitter". The student-teachers' self-reflective awareness about their own disadvantages and weaknesses increased the motivation and participation to effectively address the identified challenges and prepare for their social practice conversely, which allowed space for their future growth and learning (Zimmerman, 2002; Mann, Gordon & MacLeod, 2009; Jordi, 2011).

The importance of reflection and reflective practice were frequently noted in the literature; indeed, reflective capacity was regarded not only as an essential characteristic and necessary component for successful professional development, but also as an important continuum to engage in personal self-reflection and correction toward the development of professionalism (Mann, Gordon & MacLeod, 2009; Copeland & Oliphant, 2014). The student-teachers' self-reflection in identifying their personal errors and making evidence-based decisions were closely involved in their learning processes, whereas self-awareness became one of the identified objectives of the training process (Elder et al., 2007). On the other hand, transitioning from the teacher-centered classroom model to a student-centered approach could also focus more on self-reflection, self-understanding, and transformative education (Silverman, 2008; Rosin, 2015). In summary, it should be highlighted that one of the components of "emotional intelligence" identified by Goleman (1996, cited in Graf & Birch, 2009, p.21) was self-awareness which maintained more importance to success and effective learning than traditional intelligence. Developing this emotional intelligence of learning or arousing the student-teachers to become "emotionally intelligent" in the practical training process of ELT proficiency just coordinated completely with the identified objectives of the training. It was obviously of great importance to urge every student-teacher to *"feel emotionally secure and psychologically safe"* in order to require such self-reflective processes and self-awareness practice in the overall curriculum design and the effective training (Ginnis, 2002, cited in Graf & Birch, 2009, p.26).

### From the Trainer's Perspective

In terms of my personal perspective as the trainer, I could objectively draw a conclusion that the whole implementation of the training was positive for the student-teachers' overall professional development based mainly on my reflective notes, classroom observation and the student-teachers' feedbacks. The following aspects might show evidence of the student-teachers' obvious improvement of ELT proficiency with regard to the two certain practical assignments.

Firstly, as discussed in RQ 2, it was identified that certain improvements were attained from viewing the trainees' manuscripts of English by comparing the *"entry point"* pretest and the *"exit point"* posttest based on the practical training under the special area of English handwriting, the majority of the trainees basically framed the identified objectives of writing English letters more legibly and more fluently by applying the basic writing skills and techniques in the certain training component of the teaching techniques (Eby, Herrell & Hicks, 2002). The following Figure 5.2 demonstrates a scanned sample of one trainee's English manuscript in both the pretest and posttest sides.

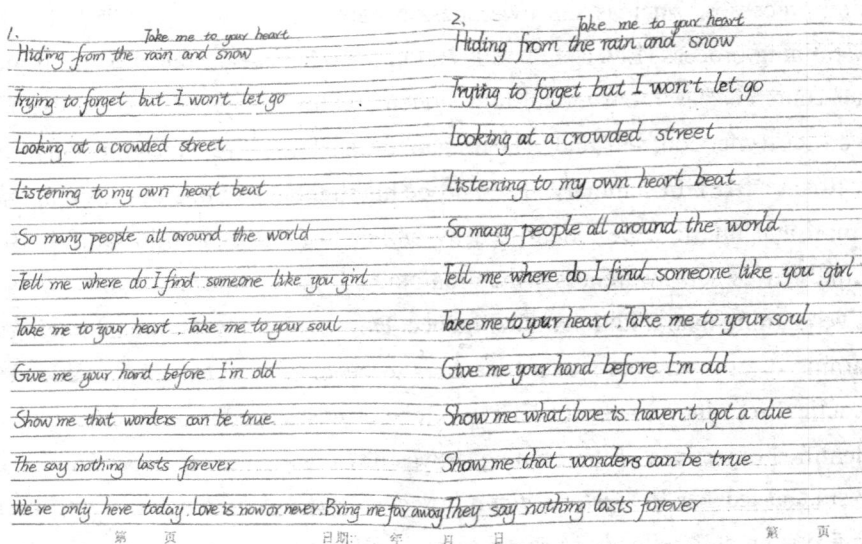

**Figure 5.2**　A Scanned Sample of One Trainee's English Manuscript

According to Spinelli (2011), I mainly assessed the student-teachers' handwriting legibility (the clarity and readability of handwriting) and fluency (the rate of written production) by observing and analyzing their writing samples. At the same time, by consulting the Zaner-Bloser Evaluation Scale which was a holistic method of assessing manuscripts, I determined whether the student-teachers' handwritings were significantly *below average*, *average*, or *above average* when compared with grade norms which highlighted the five main visual features as handwriting legibility components: letter form, alignment, size, spacing and slant (Amundson, 2005; Feder & Majnemer, 2007; Hadavandkhani et al., 2008; Spinelli, 2011, p.113). Regardless of increasing accessibility and dependency on modern electronic communication devices which has made communicating more universal, the ability to write and develop more legible and fluent handwriting remains the most important daily task especially for all levels of students (Drempt et al., 2011a; Santangelo & Graham, 2016). However, based on my individual long-term experience of teaching Chinese calligraphy in the current setting of the study, the factual situation was that I hardly bear the sight of the majority of students' illegibility and less-fluency of Chinese handwriting, not to mention their English handwriting even in some cases of English majors. The legibility (or illegibility) of children's handwriting in the beginning level of learning was frequently determined by their first teachers (Tseng, 1998). Letter formation was shown to be a key contributor to overall handwriting legibility in primary-aged children. Consequently, for the student-teachers in a normal university, mastering the ability to produce well-formed letters seemed an imperative and important competence for developing legible handwriting and successful completion of many classroom activities. While for children developing handwriting skills, improvements in all five legibility components above-mentioned would presumably improve the overall acceptability of handwriting to the student-teachers (Janes, 2018).

Another daily assignment was the lesson plan named *We Love Animals* designed by the trainees after delivering the 6th area of instructional design of the training. Similarly based on my personal teaching experience, I made an analysis of the current student-teachers that it was identified generally to lack of basic teaching skills, flexible classroom organizational ability and effective educational resources, always keeping traditional teaching methods and holding teacher-centered teaching patterns because of mainly being not qualified and systematic. Thus, I located my training objectives in this area to expect that the student-teachers could: (1) apply a relatively referenced instructional framework or templet to other different lessons; (2) state specific teaching objectives and strategies explicitly; (3) arrange appropriate and reasonable teaching processes or steps; (4) analyze beginning learners' abilities and levels; (5) review other lesson plans in peers or groups (Ali & Mina, 2014).

Designing good lesson plans is a primary teaching ability or technique for teachers in teaching and learning practice, in which the teachers provide a significant structure to represent their experiences effectively (Naegle, 2002; Neeraja, 2003). While an effective lesson plan commonly has three basic components: aims and objectives of the training, teaching and learning activities, and assessments to check students' understanding of the topic (Naegle, 2002). I preferred *the Demonstration Method* which could help the student-teachers to have a deeper understanding of the topic, and it could account for the principles of reflective thinking and impart maximum learning to them (Iline, 2013).

In view of the aforementioned consideration and implementation, my overall and objective feeling of evaluation about the trainees' submission of lesson plans was that the majority of the trainees basically understood how to place the framework of a lesson plan clearly, how to set the key and difficult points properly, and how to transfer the requirements into practical classroom content appropriately by applying an instructional syllabus and textbooks (Singh, 2008). Specifically, their instructional descriptions and instructions were relatively simple but clear, their teaching objectives were basically reasonable and coincidental with their teaching targets. The majority of the trainees added a certain procedure of *Teaching Reflective Notes* which was highlighted in the discussion section of *Self-reflected Awareness*, in which they could make a beginning to end self-checking to compare both proposed steps and performed achievements together. Therefore, it implied that they had fulfilled more or less about the requirements of the teaching pattern or standard based on the present educational situation and context.

## 5.3　Implications of the Study

To sum up the findings, the present study devoted itself to develop the training module to improve the pre-service student-teachers' ELT proficiency at the beginning level in multi-ethnic community schools. It was highly accepted not only on the effectiveness of the significant benefits for the student-teachers' current challenges but also on the practicability of applying the training program for further practice. Based on the findings and conclusions of the study, the following implications could be offered to concerned individuals and groups.

**To higher institutions:**

Facing the inconsistencies between the employees of preschool and primary school education majors and English majors under the special context of multi-ethnic areas in Yunnan Province, an acute shortage of qualified teachers exists in most bilingual community schools. Thus, the findings could be implied for pioneering the contemporary educational reform which is oriented to cultivate complex multi-skilled professionals in order to provide the theoretical and practical exemplification for establishing the appropriate curricula and majors in higher institutions. Thus, for normal universities, it is promising to initiate a new combination of preschool and primary education major (English oriented) for the current educational and teaching reform of curriculum and specialty construction in the future. In addition to constructing the new comprehensive professional development system of teacher preparation programs, building more stable bases of internships with suitable community schools also can help examine the student-teachers teaching practicum.

**To administrators and stakeholders:**

There were some research achievements about teacher training, professional development, pre-service and in-service training, but most traditional teacher education programs are premised on the conceptual level of theorization, policy, institutionalization and formalization upon general philosophy, pedagogy, psychology and sociology; and very few remained operationalized in practice. The findings could be implied for responsible administrators and stakeholders to add theoretical and practical experiences to the professional development of teacher education and training programs. Furthermore, it was useful to build a complete pre-service training system in which constituted effective and efficient teacher training programs based on the present context of multi-ethnic community in terms of ensuring the careful selection of training candidates, initiating the various strategies for the specific training assessments, demonstrating the constructed training components, theorizing the competence-based training activities, specifying the comprehensive training curricular designs, and finally achieving the national or local standards centered on beneficiaries of ongoing teacher professionalism.

## 5.4   Recommendations of the Study

Based on the research findings from the combination of quantitative data and qualitative data, the present "Training Module to Improve Proficiency in Beginning Level ELT among Student-teachers in Multi-ethnic Community Schools in Yunnan Province" was effective to some extent. Therefore, the following recommendations are given and presented in two perspectives: 1) for future practice; 2) for future research.

### 5.4.1 Recommendations for Future Practice

From a longitudinal review, three critical phases (i.e., identify the student-teachers challenges, specify the training objectives and develop the training process) are systematically and logically sequenced in the proposed ADDIEM training model of the present study. The following practical considerations are provided for other instructors who are designing or planning to develop a similar training program.

***Know the trainees' background knowledge***. The training module was developed in order to improve the learners' ELT proficiency. Therefore, this training module could be used, innovated or modified by other instructors who would like to improve the learners' ELT proficiency at any level. Instructors might design and develop more appropriate training activities in a specific training phase to gain different effects for different situations. As a result, the learners' basic majors, their academic levels, their learning interests, motivations and common targets, their prior knowledge of advantages and weaknesses, even their academic, social or emotional difficulties, and so on, should be understood thoroughly so that more impressive teaching materials, proper teaching methods, logical teaching procedures, appropriate grouping challenges and efficient classroom management, etc. can be well-designed, especially in the needs analysis and training design phases.

***Establish pleasant teaching and learning environment***. Creating a positive learning environment allows the learners to feel comfortable, safe and engaged, optimizes their learning, and also helps build a cohesive classroom community (Hue & Li, 2008). Therefore, make full use of the available teaching and learning resources and facilities firstly, such as multi-media classrooms with qualified equipment of a high-definition projector and modern acoustics (for audio-visual activities), a spacious and context-depended classroom with changeable desks and seats (for interaction, teamwork and game-playing activities), an accessible high-speed network (for demonstrating or sharing net resources), and other relevant hardware. In addition, software improvements should also be considered in terms of treating the learners respectfully, setting the rule enforcement equitably, exemplifying their behavioral and academic expectations clearly, addressing their needs intentionally, providing them constructive feedback and guidance frequently, motivating their confidence and encouraging their progress instantly, providing with opportunities to share their voices and experiences unconstrainedly, acknowledging the teacher's inescapable errors and the learners' negative emotions appropriately, making optimum use of the teaching and learning materials interactively, and being punctual and smiling for class from day one in the training development and implementation phases (Simonsen et al., 2008; Hue & Li, 2008).

*Ensure sufficient training time*. Based on the recommendations from the student-teachers, it was concerned frequently on the insufficiency of training duration, which was also critically required as the primary aspect to be revised carefully. During the whole implementation of the training process, total of 36 training periods covering 12 identified areas were proposed in the tentative schedule (It was originally expected that each area was delivered an average of 3 training periods each week, there were total of 12 available weeks within the current campus of 14 academic weeks generally.) But just as mentioned in the training syllabus, the partial training areas might be adjusted according to the practical situations without regard for some special delay, such as national holidays or festivals. The student-teachers frequently underlined the necessity of extending or increasing the training duration in matter of the following prioritized areas: English pronunciation, comprehensive spoken English and listening ability, lesson design, teaching techniques, and presentation and evaluation of lesson. In brief, such possible influencing factors should be taken into consideration, and an appropriate alternative scheme should be set to ensure sufficient and adjustable teaching periods regarding the different training components in order to meet the trainees' required competencies improvement, and ultimately to gain more evaluation effectiveness and satisfaction.

*Identify the trainer's traits and competencies*. With regard to the instructor's personal accomplishments under the increasingly diverse and personalized professional learning, the learners frequently would feel satisfied with the following challenges: (1) maintaining lasting passion, patience and creativity by performing lifelong learning with devoted responsibility and professional maturity, by paying careful attention to the possible challenges, and by holding creative expertise when presenting lessons, coaching the learners, supervising management and evaluating performance; (2) make both verbal and written communication effective by explaining the terms accessibly and meaningfully, by using professional yet friendly body languages and by listening actively; (3) use audio-visible learning by sharing more multimodal valuable artifacts, including texts, pictures, handmade cards, worksheets, videos, music and songs without any reservations; (4) think critically by creating comfortable and positive learning environments, by providing supportive services, and by setting clear behavioral and academic expectations. In sum, the instructors should be more conscientious in career engagement than the conventional classroom teaching (Simonsen et al., 2008; McIlveen & Perera, 2015).

*Consider relevant factors synthetically*. In this connection, it was recommended that: (1) more feasible studies should be done to identify the learners' imperative needs in practical ELT situations; (2) possible commitment for developing the training program was required between both trainer and trainees in terms of budget support and time guarantee; (3) suitable and systematic compilation of textbooks was expected for the current learners; (4) evidence-based management practice incorporating classroom and training programs should be enhanced (Simonsen et al., 2008); (5) equivalent criteria of recruitment for the learners' current levels of English proficiency, and a limited amount of trainees (no more than 45) with strict attendance regulations should also be modified, restricted and taken into account so as to gain more pertinence and effectiveness in further training practice.

## 5.4.2  Recommendations for Future Research

The present study offers the following two recommendations for further research.

*Attempt alternative instructional models.* The ADDIE instructional model adapted in this study could be altered into a more complete and creative instructional model for future research. It could also be recommended to shift the ADDIEM training framework to other majors or subjects, and partially help either directly or indirectly generalize the training framework to other multi-ethnic communities under a similar context as Yunnan Province. That is, future research may extend the challenges of other learner-centered instructional models or training frameworks according to different emphasis in different situations in terms of training needs, purposes, components, features, processes, settings and steps, but finally aiming at enabling more efficient creation of instructions or training.

For instance, one alternative recommendation is the **System Approach Instructional Design Model** by Dick and Carey (2005), which consists of ten inter-dependent components in procedural or sequential steps. The ten components of the model are: (1) assess needs to help identify learning goals; (2) conduct instructional analysis; (3) analyze learners and contexts; (4) write performance objectives; (5) develop assessment instrument; (6) develop instructional strategies; (7) develop and select instructional materials; (8) design and conduct formative evaluation; (9) revise instructional base from formative evaluation; (10) design and conduct summative evaluation. The construction of assessment items in this model sequentially follows the creation of the learning objectives, revised with data from the formative evaluation, and helps to ensure alignment of objectives and assessment. Another alternative is the **Kemp Instructional Design Model**. The Kemp model defines nine different components of an instructional design, and at the same time adopts a continuous implementation or evaluation model. This model emphasizes the interdependencies of each step in the process, highlights the importance of the evaluation, and recognizes more environmental factors in educational settings, and it is particularly useful for developing instructional programs that mix technology, pedagogy, and content to deliver effective, reliable and efficient learning (Morrison, Ross & Kemp, 2004). The assessment items in the Kemp model are created after the final revision of the objectives is subject to revision with data from the formative evaluation.

*Add different participants of in-service training*. The student-teachers studying on the campus of the setting were concerned about the present training program as the major trainees, but they were not the same particular participants who were invited to conduct the questionnaires and interviews of the study based on their different academic situations of learning developments in the practical training process. It was changed time and circumstances that the required challenges indentified by the previously engaged participants in the need analysis phase might differ in accordance with the perspectives cognized by the currently involved trainees in the training implementation phase. Accordingly, such English teachers who are working in kindergartens and primary schools (or higher secondary levels) are proposed to be the certain participants as well as trainees from day one for future researches. Based on this point, investigating the relationship between certain English teachers' expectations and their prior knowledge, and developing other relative areas such as comprehensive competencies of grammar and vocabulary, reading and writing abilities, which were not covered in present study, also deserve to be focused as imperative and influential factors in acquiring specific ELT proficiency (Hoz, Bowman & Kozminsky, 2001; Thompson & Zamboanga, 2003).

*Incorporate needs regarding language interferences*. To understand the problems of ethnic EFL learners, it is potentially necessary to deepen the research on bilingual or multi-lingual learners in multi-ethnic communities of Yunnan Province so as to be in an informed position to further develop a particular curriculum to meet the needs of multicultural learners in Dali University. It is argued that the study of ethnic minority learners through and beyond the lens of bilingual or multilingual education policy and practice will lead to a better understanding of their aspirations and learning experience and reveal the strengths, weaknesses and coping strategies of ethnic EFL learners in China (Wang, 2015; Shan, 2018). This attempt of incorporating language interferences may make a solid contribution to the design of more relevant language policies, teaching practices, learning resources and pave the way for further in-depth EFL research.

## 5.5 Summary

The purposes of the study were to investigate the student-teachers' professional development, especially the challenges facing their ELT proficiencies; develop training components to specify the training activities to improve their ELT proficiencies; and determine the effectiveness and make the appropriate modifications. The results from the quantitative and qualitative data displayed the identified student-teachers challenges, the specified training objectives and the developed training process, which were systematically and logically sequenced in the ADDIEM Training Process of the present study. Simultaneously, a detailed discussion was carried out respectively in each stage to justify the various results from the mixed data. Lastly, the constructive implications and recommendations of the study are presented for future practice and research.

# ACKNOWLEDGEMENTS

*"The harder work, the more luck. Life will be better when you cry a little, laugh a lot, be thankful and positive for everything."*

It is my sincere pleasure to gratefully acknowledge those who have contributed to completing my dissertation and offered me continued assistance, guidance, support, and help in the past four years of study.

Foremost to my principal advisor, assistant professor Dr. Janpanit Surasin, my co-advisor, Dr. Denchai Prabjandee, and the respected expert, associate professor Dr. Chalong Tubsree, I give my heartfelt thanks for their erudite and professional guidance, consideration and humanistic concerns. I benefited a lot from their profound academic expertise and individual charisma. I am also sincerely indebted to my respected Thai mother, Asst. Prof. Daranee Pummawan, who helped me thoughtfully in every physical and spiritual way.

To my dear parents and parents-in-law, I thank all of you for cultivating the character traits that allowed me to make my dreams a reality. Without your kind support and great love, I could not have completed my study abroad. I am also grateful to my beloved wife, who has offered me positive spiritual and emotional support throughout this long study journey.

Furthermore, I would like to thank those who facilitated the process of my study both in Burapha University and Dali University, Ms. Rattanasiri Khemraj, all of my dear colleagues and working teams for their greatest support, advice and encouragement.

Youxing Xiao
June, 2022

# REFERENCES

[1] Adamson B., & Feng A. W. A comparison of trilingual education policies for ethnic minorities in China[J]. Compare: A Journal of Comparative Education, 2008, 39(3):321-333.

[2] Ahn E. S., & Kim Y. H. An analysis of Korean domestic research trend in English education and bilingualism of young children[J]. Journal of Korean Child Care and Education, 2009, 5(1):81-101.

[3] Ahmed G. S. Foreign language teacher training in the Sudan: past, present and strategies for future recruitment policies[J]. International Journal of English Linguistics, 2011, 1(2):115-125.

[4] Ali J. N., Mina, H. The important role of lesson plan on educational achievement of Iranian EFL teachers' attitudes[J]. International Journal of Foreign Language Teaching & Research, 2014, 3(5):25-31.

[5] Amundson S. J. Prewriting and handwriting skills. In J. Case-Smith (Ed.), Occupational Therapy for Children (5th ed.)[M]. St Louis, MO: Elsevier, 2005: 587-614.

[6] Anthony J. L. A review of the literature: professional knowledge and standards for language teaching[J/OL].

[7] Antikainen A. Transforming A Learning Society[M]. Bern:Peter LangM, 2005.

[8] Ayşe Y. A., Kemal O. E. A Comparison of Pre-service English Language Teacher Training Systems in Turkey and Japan[J]. Journal of Faculty of Educational Sciences, 2012, 45(1): 83-105.

[9] Bachman L. Fundamental Considerations in Language Testing[M]. Oxford, UK: OUP,1990.

[10] Bakarman A. A. Attitude, Skill, and Knowledge: A New Model for Design Education. Proceedings of the Canadian Engineering Education Association[EB/OL].

[11] Baker C. The Care and Education of Young Bilinguals: An Introduction for Professionals[M]. Toronto: Multilingual Matters, 2000.

[12] Beckett G. H., MacPherson S. Researching the impact of English on minority and indigenous languages in non-western contexts[J]. TESOL Quarterly, 2005, 39(2): 299-307.

[13] Berry R. The role of language improvement in in-service teacher training programmes: killing two birds with one stone[J]. System, 2000, 18(1):97-105.

[14] Best J. W., Kahn J. V. Research in education (9th ed.)[M]. Boston: Allyn and Bacon, 2003.

[15] Borg S. Knowing and Doing: Teaching Grammar in In-service Training. In Liu, D. and Master, P. (eds.). Grammar Teaching in Teacher Education[M]. Alexandria, USA: TESOL, 2003.

[16] Borg W. R., Gall M. D. Education Research: An Introduction[M]. New York: Longman Inc, 2007.

[17] Breathnach C. Temporal determinants of language acquisition and bilingualism[J]. Irish Journal of Psychological Medicine, 2003,10(1): 41-47.

[18] Briggs A. J., Coleman M., & Morrison M. (Eds.)(3rd ed.). Research Methods in Educational Leadership and Management[M]. London: Paul Chapman Publishings, 2012.

[19] Briguglio C., Kirkpatrick A. Language Teacher Proficiency Assessment: Models and Options. Cited in Perth: NLLIA Centre for Literacy, Culture and Language Pedagogy[D]. Curtin University of Technology, 1996.

[20] Brooke M. Enhancing pre-service teacher training: The construction and application of a model for developing teacher reflective practice online[J]. Open Journal of Modern Linguistics, 2012,2(4):180-188.

[21] Brookfield S. D. Becoming A Critically Reflective Teacher. San Francisco: Jossey-Bass, 1995. Cited in Hue, M. T., & Li, W. S. Classroom Management: Creating a Positive Learning Environment[M]. Hong Kong: Hong Kong University Press, 2008.

[22] Brown A. H., Green T. D. The Essential of Instructional Design: Connecting Fundamental Principles with Process and Practice (3rd ed.)[M]. New York: Routledge, 2016.

[23] Brown H. D. Teaching by Principles: An Interactive Approach to Language Pedagogy[M]. Upper Saddle River, NJ: Prentice Hall Regents, 1994.

[24] Buchmann M. The Priority of Knowledge and Understanding in Teaching. In L. G. Katz & J. D. Raths (Eds.), Advances in Teacher Education[M], 1. Norwood, NJ: Ablex, 1984.

[25] Bulut S., Demircioğlu H., Yıldırım, A. Ortaokul ve Liselerde Fen ve Matematik öğretimi: Sorunlar ve öneriler. Paper presented at the Second National Science Education Symposium[D]. Middle East Technical University, Ankara. 1995.

[26] Burns A., & Richards J.C. (Eds). The Cambridge Guide to Second Language Teacher Education[M]. NY: Cambridge University Press, 2009.

[27] Caffrey J. R., Lockwood D. F., Koretz D. M., Hamilton L. S. Evaluating Value Added Models for Teacher Accountability[M]. Santa Monica, CA: RAND Corporation, 2003.

[28] Çakır A., & Güngör M. N. Pre-service teachers' evaluations of practices in teaching English to young learners in terms of 21st century teacher qualifications[J]. Journal of Language and Linguistic Studies, 2017, 13(1): 244-259.

[29] Calderhead J., & Gates P. Conceptualizing Reflection in Teacher Development[M]. London: Falmer Press, 1993.

[30] Caldwell J. C. Routes to Low Mortality in Poor Countries[J]. Population & Development Review, 1989, 12(2): 171-220.

[31] Cameron L.Teaching English to Young Learners[M]. New York, NY, 2001.

[32] Camuzcu S., & Duruhan K. Primary school teachers' needs for in-service training pertaining to the teaching-learning process[J]. e-International Journal of Educational Research, 2011, 2(1):15-29.

[33] Çakıroğlu E., & Çakıroğlu J. Reflections on teacher education in Turkey[J]. European Journal of Teacher Education, 2003, 26(2), 253-264.

[34] Carrier K. A. NNS Teacher trainees in western-based TESOL programs[J]. ELT Journal, 2003, 57(3): 242-250.

[35] Catherine D. E. The role of students and content in teacher effectiveness[J]. Research Quarterly for Exercise and Sport, 2015, 85(1):4.

[36] Chen C. Institutional legitimacy of an authoritarian state: China in the mirror of eastern Europe[J]. Problems of Post Communism, 2005, 52(4): 3-13.

[37] Chitpin S., Simon M., Galipeau J. Pre-service teachers' use of the objective knowledge framework for reflection during practicum[J]. Teaching and Teacher Education, 2008, 24:2048-2058.

[38] Clare R. K., Natalie B. M. Teaching Models: Designing Instruction for 21st Century Learners[M]. New York: Pearson Education, Inc, 2014.

[39] Copeland S. Oliphant E. BSW students personal reflection and self-correction: teaching implications[J]. International Journal of Business, Humanities and Technology, 2014, 4(3):45-53.

[40] Creswell J. W. Qualitative Inquiry and Research Design: Choosing among Five Traditions[M]. Thousand Oaks, CA: Sage,1998.

[41] Creswell J. W. Research Design: Qualitative, Quantitative, and Mixed Methods Approaches (2nd ed.)[M]. Thousand Oaks, CA: Sage, 2003.

[42] Creswell J. W. Designing and Conducting Mixed Methods Research[M]. Thousand Oaks, CA:Sage, 2007.

[43] Creswell J. W.Research Design: Qualitative, Quantitative, and Mixed Methods Approaches (3rd ed.)[M]. Thousand Oaks, CA: Sage, 2009.

[44] Creswell J. W. Educational Research: Planning, Conducting, and Evaluating Quantitative and Qualitative Research (4th ed.)[M]. Pearson Education, Inc, 2012.

[45] Creswell J. W., Clark P. V. L. Designing and Conducting Mixed Methods Research (2nd ed.)[M]. Thousand Oaks, CA: Sage, 2011.

[46] Cullen R. Incorporating language improvement in teacher training programmes[J]. ELT Journal, 1994, 48(2):163-171.

[47] Cummins J. Pedagogies of choice: challenging coercive relations of power in classrooms and communities[J]. International Journal of Bilingual Education and Bilingualism, 2009, 12(3):261-272.

[48] Dai C., The current status of trilingual education in Tibetan areas of China[J]. Overseas English, 2014,12(6):79-82.

[49] Dao F. D. An Analysis of the Education for 25 Indigenous Ethnic Minority Groups in Yunnan. In Li, Y. F., & Xu, Z. X. (Eds.), A Study of the Ethnic Minority Education and Development in Yunnan[M]. Kunming:Yunnan Press of Nationalities, 2005:11-20.

[50] DeKeyser R. M. The robustness of critical period effects in second language acquisition[J]. SSLA, 2000, 22:499-533.

[51] Deng B. C., Comparative study on English teacher education model of kindergartens[J]. Journal of Changchun Education Institute, 2009, 25(1):76-78.

[52] Deng M. The present situation and reflection of preschool bilingual teacher

training in Hunan province[J]. Teacher, 2010, 9: 27-28.

[53] Dennis S., & Susan. L. H., Five models of staff development[J]. Journal of Staff Development, 1989, 10(4): 1-39.

[54] Denzin N. K., & Lincoln, Y. S. The Handbook of Qualitative Research (2nd ed.) [M]. Thousand Oaks, CA: Sage, 2000.

[55] Dick W., Carey, L., & Carey, J. O. The Systematic Design of Instruction (6th ed.)[M]. Boston, MA: Pearson, 2005.

[56] Diógenes C. L. English-as-a-foreign-language teacher-training programs: an overview[J]. Linguagem & Ensino, 2001, 4(2):143-153.

[57] Dong Y. P., & Gui, S. C. Current foreign languages education in China[J]. Journal of Modern Foreign Languages, 2002, 4:2-16.

[58] Duxa S. Further Education Events for Teachers of German as A Second Language in Continuing Education and Their Impact on the Professionalism of Teachers[M]. Deutsch als Fremdsprache 57. FaDaF, 2001.

[59] Ebru M. K. A general investigation of the in-service training of English language teachers at elementary schools in Turkey[J]. International Electronic Journal of Elementary Education, 2016, 8(3): 455-466.

[60] Eby J. W., Herrell, A. L., & Hicks, J. Reflective Planning, Teaching, and Evaluation[M]. Upper Saddle River, NJ: Merrill Prentice Hall, 2002.

[61] Edmonds A., & Kennedy, T. An Applied Reference Guide to Research Designs[M]. Thousand Oaks: Sage, 2013.

[62] Elder W., Rakel, D., Heitkemper, M., Hustedde, C., Harazduk, N., Gerik, S., & Haramati, A. Using complementary and alternative medicine curricular elements to foster medical student self-awareness[J]. Academic Medicine, 2007, 82(9): 51-55.

[63] Eleonora V. R.Teacher Professional Development: An International Review of the Literature[M]. UNESCO: International Institute for Educational Planning, Paris, 2003.

[64] Enever J. Yet another early-start languages policy in Europe: Poland this time[J]. Current Issues in Language Planning, 2007, 8(2):208-221.

[65] Enisa M., & Melike, I. The needs of primary English teachers for an in-service teacher training program[J]. Turkish Online Journal of Qualitative Inquiry, 2016, 7(2): 1-30.

[66] Erdfelder E., Faul F., & Buchner A. GPOWER: A general power analysis

program. behavior research methods[J]. Instruments & Computers, 1996, 28: 1-11.

[67] Eslami-Rasekh, Z. Enhancing the pragmatic competence of NNEST candidates[J]. TESOL NNEST Newsletter, 2005, 7(1): 4-7.

[68] Eurydice. The Teaching Profession in Europe: Profile, Trends and Concerns. Teacher Supply and Demand at General Lower Secondary Level. Key Topics in Education in Europe[M]. Brussels: European Commission / Eurydice, 2002.

[69] Fahmy J., Bilton L. Planning a TEFL Education Program: Policies, Perspectives and Promise[M]. ERIC Document Reproduction Service, No. ED 369 281, 1992.

[70] Farooqui S., Developing speaking skills of adult learners in private universities in Bangladesh: problems and solutions[J]. Australian Journal of Adult Learning, 2007,47 (1): 94-110.

[71] Feder K. P., & Majnemer A. Handwriting development, competency, and intervention[J]. Developmental Medicine and Child Neurology, 2007, 49: 312-317.

[72] Feng A. W. Bilingualism for the minor or the major? An evaluative analysis of parallel conceptions in China[J]. International Journal of Bilingual Education and Bilingualism, 2005, 8(6): 529-551.

[73] Feng A. W. Intercultural Space for Bilingual Education. In A. W. Feng (Ed.), Bilingual Education in China: Practices, Policies, and Concepts[M]. Clevedon, England: Multilingual Matters, 2007: 259-279.

[74] Feng A. W., Adamson B. Trilingualism in education in China: models and challenges[J]. Multilingual Education, 2015,12: 37.

[75] Frankel R., Wallen E. How to Design and Evaluate Research in Education (4th ed)[M]. New York: McGraw-Hill Inc, 2000.

[76] Fraser H. Coordinating Improvements in Pronunciation Teaching for Adult Learners of English as A Second Language[M]. Canberra: DETYA, 2000.

[77] Freeman D. Observing teachers: three approaches to in-service training and development[J]. TESOL Quarterly, 1982, 6(1): 21-28.

[78] Freeman D., Johnson K. E. Reconceptualizing the knowledge-base of language teacher education[J]. TESOL Quarterly, 1998, 32(3): 397-417.

[79] Frede E. The role of program quality in producing early childhood program benefits[J]. Future of Children, 1995, 5(3): 115-132.

[80] Fu J. Research on bilingual teachers training in kindergarten[J]. Journal of Liaoning Educational Administration Institute, 2007, 24(11): 72-73.

[81] Fu L. L., & Zhong, W. X. Practice and exploration of curriculum reform for preschool children English education[J]. Journal of Hulunbeier College, 2013, 3(21): 96-99.

[82] Gagne R. M., Wager, R. W., Golas, K. C., & Keller, J. M. Principles of Instructional Design (5th ed.)[M]. Belmont, CA: Thomson Wadsworth, 2005.

[83] Gai X. Z. On trilingual education[J]. Journal of Dali College, 2003(6): 83-84.

[84] Ganser T. An ambitious vision of professional development for teachers[J]. In NASSA Bulletin, 2000, 84(618): 6-12.

[85] Gao X. J. Children's advantages in English learning and children's English teaching tactics[J]. Journal of Huahua University, 2009, 28(7):151-152.

[86] García O. Bilingual Education in the 21st Century: A Global Perspective[M]. Malden, MA: Wiley Blackwell, 2009.

[87] Giacomo D. Language Proficiency for English Teachers – An English Language Proficiency and Methodology Course for Teachers Who Speak English as A Second or Foreign Language[D]. Leeds Beckett University, 2016.

[88] Gibbon D., Mertins, I., & Moore, R. K. Handbook of Multimodal and Spoken Dialogue Systems[M]. Boston: Kluwer Academic Publishers, 2000.

[89] Gil J. A. . English in China: The Impact of the Global Language on China Language Situation[D]. Griffith Business School, Griffith University, 2005.

[90] Gimson A. C. An Introduction to the Pronunciation of English. London: Arnold. Cited in Wang, Y. J. An Effective Approach to Children's English Phonetics Teaching[J]. Bilingual Theory and Exploration, 2009, 6: 23.

[91] Ginnis P. The Teacher's Toolkit. Carmarthen: Crown House. Cited in Graf, M. & Birch, A. The Teaching Assistant's Guide to Understanding and Support Learning[M]. London: Cataloguing-in-Publication Data, 2009.

[92] Giorgio O. Teacher education in Italy, Germany, England, Sweden and Finland[J]. European Journal of Education, 2009, 44(2): 291-308.

[93] Goleman D. Emotional Intelligence. Why It Can Matter More Than IQ. London: Bloomsbury. Cited in Graf, M. & Birch, A. The Teaching Assistant's Guide to Understanding and Support Learning[M]. London: Cataloguing-in-Publication Data, 2009.

[94] Gong J. Lifelong learning-survival concept[J]. Continuing Education, 2005(2):

24-25.

[95] Graf M., & Birch, A. The Teaching Assistant's Guide to Understanding and Support Learning[M]. London: Cataloguing-in-Publication Data, 2009.

[96] Greene J. C. Mixed Methods in Social Inquiry[M]. San Francisco: John Wiley & Son, 2007.

[97] Greene J. C., & Caracelli, V. J. (Eds.). Advances in Mixed-method Evaluation: The Challenges and Benefits of Integrating Diverse Paradigms (New Directions for Evaluation, No. 74)[M]. San Francisco: Jossey-Bass, 1997.

[98] Gu L. The investigation of the bilingual pre-school teachers' English proficiency level and their training strategy[J]. Journal of Jining Normal University, 2016, 3(5): 115-118.

[99] Guskey T. Evaluating Professional Development[M]. Thousand Oaks, CA: Corwin Press, Inc, 2000.

[100] Gustafson K. L., Branch, R. M. What Is Instructional Design. In Reiser, R.A. & Dempsey, J.V. (Eds.). Trends and Issues in Instructional Design and Technology[M]. Columbus, OH: Merrill/Prentice Hall, 2002:17-25.

[101] Gülmez-Dağ G. Effectiveness of Early Childhood Teacher Education Programs: Perceptions of Early Childhood Teachers[D]. Middle East Technical University, 2012.

[102] Habeeb K. Teachers' Perceptions toward Implementing English as A Foreign Language at Kindergarten: What Can We Learn from the Case of Kuwaiti Kindergarten Teachers[D]. University of Arkansas, 2013.

[103] Habibi A., & Sofwan, M. Teachers of English for Young Learners: An Analysis on Their English Proficiency and Profile[C]. Presented at English Education Study Program-national Seminar, Faculty of Teacher Training and Education, Sriwijaya University, Palembang, 3rd October, 2015.

[104] Hadavandkhani F., Bahrami H., Behnia F., Farahbod M., Salehi M. Handwriting difficulties: introducing an instrument[J]. Iranian Rehabilitation Journal, 2008(6): 39-46.

[105] Hadley G., Yoshioka-Hadley H. The culture of learning and the good teacher in Japan: an analysis of student views[J]. The Language Teacher, 1996, 20(9): 53-55.

[106] Han T. M. Research on approaches and methods of strengthening practical teaching skills for preschool students[J]. Electronic Production, 2014(9): 194-

196.

[107] Harmer J. How to Teach English[M]. Beijing: Foreign Language Teaching and Research Press, 2000.

[108] Hassan S. & Miraclea, R. Learning to Identify Educational Materials. International Conference RANLP 2009 [M]. Borovets, Bulgaria, 2009:123-127.

[109] Hattie J. A. C. Visible Learning: A Synthesis of 800+ Meta-analyses on Achievement[M]. Oxford: Routledge, 2009.

[110] He Y. Z. Reforming teacher training modes to promote teachers' professional development[J]. Educational Research, 2014(1): 150-153.

[111] Henning E. Walking with barefoot teachers: an ethnographically fashioned casebook[J]. Teaching and Teacher Education, 2000(16): 3-20.

[112] Hesse-Biber S. N., Leavy P. The Practice of Qualitative Research[M]. Thousand Oaks, CA: Sage, 2006.

[113] Hiebert J., Gallimore R., Stigler J. W. The new heroes of teaching[J]. Education Week, 2003, 23(10): 42-56.

[114] Hightower A. M., Delgado R. C., Lloyd S. C., Witternstein R., Sellers K., Swanson C. B. Improving Student Learning by Supporting Quality Teaching: Key Issues, Effective Strategies[M]. Editorial Projects in Education, Inc, 2011.

[115] Hope Speak. The Importance of Correct Pronunciation[J]. Online published: December 16, 2014.

[116] Hosni S. A. Speaking difficulties encountered by young EFL learners[J]. International Journal on Studies in English Language and Literature (IJSELL), 2014, 2(6): 22-30.

[117] Hoz R., Bowman D., Kozminsky E. The differential effects of prior knowledge on learning: a study of two consecutive courses in earth sciences[J]. Instructional Science, 2001, 29: 187-211.

[118] Hu D. Y. Trilingual Education of Members from Ethnic Minority Nationalities in Yunnan[M]. Kunming: Yunnan University Press, 2008.

[119] Hu L. F., Chen Y. Q. Factors on bilingual teaching effect on the course of "introduction to e-commerce"[J]. Eurasia Journal of Mathematics, Science & Technology Education, 2017,13(8): 5273-5280.

[120] Hu Y. Y. China's English language policy for primary schools[J]. World Englishes, 2007, 27(3-4): 516-534.

[121] Huang C. W., Yu A. H. Acculturation and ethnic identity of minority undergraduates: a case study on Yunnan university of nationalities[J]. Journal of Chuxiong Teacher's College, 2009, 24(7): 47-56.

[122] Huang H. Y. Brain - based Teaching Strategies Used to Teach English as A Foreign Language (EFL) in Taiwan High Schools, Colleges, and Universities[M]. Dissertations & Theses - Gradworks, 2006.

[123] Huang J. A theoretical study on English teaching in Chinese ethnic minority regions[J]. English language teaching, 2013, 6(7): 168-175.

[124] Hue M. T., Li W. S. Classroom Management: Creating a Positive Learning Environment[M]. Hong Kong: Hong Kong University Press, 2008.

[125] Huitt W. Bloom et al.'s Taxonomy of the Cognitive Domain. Educational Psychology Interactive[M]. Valdosta, GA:Valdosta State University, 2011.

[126] Hundleby S., Breet F. Using methodology notebooks on in-service teacher training courses[J]. ELT Journal, 1988, 1(42): 34-36.

[127] Ida Ah C. M. Towards a reflective practice: the case of a prospective teacher in Hong Kong[J]. Journal of Mathematics Education 2010, 3(2): 25-39.

[128] Iline C. S. Impacts of the demonstration method in the teaching and learning of hearing impaired children[J]. IOSR Journal of Humanities & Social Science (IOSR-JHSS), 2013, 12(1): 48-54.

[129] Ishrat A. Q. The Importance of Speaking Skills for EFL Learners[D]. Alama Iqbal Open University, Pakistan, 2007.

[130] Janes M. D. An Investigation of Handwriting Legibility and Pencil Use Tasks in Healthy Older Adults[D]. Faculty of Health Sciences, University of Sydney, 2018.

[131] Jang Y. J. Status and Practical Ways of Teaching English to Children[C]. Proceeding of the Journal of Korea Open Association for Early Childhood Education Spring Conference, 2008:11-20.

[132] Janice J. B. Skills for Preschool Teacher (10th ed.)[M]. Pearson Education, Inc, 2017.

[133] Jasone C., Britta, H., & Ulrike, J. Towards trilingual education[J]. International Journal of Bilingual Education and Bilingualism, 2001, 4(1): 1-10.

[134] Jessner U. A Review of "Linguistic Awareness in Multilinguals: English as A Third Language"[M]. Edinburgh: Edinburgh University Press, 2006.

[135] Jiang Q. X. Liu Q. G., Quan X. H., Ma C. Q. EFL Education in Ethnic

Minority Areas in Northwest China: An Investigational Study in Gansu Province. Cited in A. W. Feng (Ed.), Bilingual Education in China: Practices, Policies and Concepts[M]. Buffalo: Multilingual Matters, 2007: 240-256.

[136] Ji H. L., Ju H. P., Zhang W. J. Study on bilingual education among preschoolers in Yunnan minority areas[J]. Journal of Yuxi Normal University, 2015, 31(10): 56-62.

[137] Jick T. D. Mixing qualitative and quantitative methods: triangulation in action[J]. Administrative Science Quarterly, 1979, 24: 602-611.

[138] Jie'ensi A. Trilingual education and bilingual education[J]. Gansu Education, 2004(4):10.

[139] Jin H. Y. The strategy of preschool English teachers training in normal universities[J]. Journal of Jilin Radio and TV University, 2016(4): 118-119.

[140] John M., Werner P., Randy L., Simone D. Human Resource Development. (4th ed.)[M]. Thousand Oaks, CA: Sage, 2006.

[141] John A. B. A better chance to learn: bilingual bi-cultural education[J]. United States Commission on Civil Rights Clearing House Publication, 1975, 51 (9): 1-22. Cited in Lv, L. The characteristics and implication of American preschool bilingual education[J]. Journal of Educational Development, 2016(5): 90-93.

[142] Johnson R. B. Mixed Methods Research Design and Analysis with Validity: A Primer[D]. Department of Professional Studies, University of South Alabama, 2014.

[143] Johnson R. B., & Chhetri, N. Exclusionary policies and practices in Chinese minority Eeducation: the case of Tibetan education[J]. Current Issues in Comparative Education, 2002, 2 (2):142-153.

[144] Johnson R. B., & Onwuegbuzie, A. J. Mixed methods research: a research paradigm whose time has come[J]. Educational Researcher, 2004, 33(7): 14-26.

[145] Jorda M. P. S. Third Language Learners: Pragmatic Production and Awareness[M]. Buffalo: Multilingual Matters, 2005.

[146] Jordi R. Reframing the concept of reflection: consciousness, experiential learning, and reflective learning practices[J]. Adult Education Quarterly, 2011, 61(2):181-197.

[147] Julia S. Language Documentation and Language Policy. In Peter K. Austin (ed.) Language Documentation and Description[M]. London: SOAS, 2010.

[148] Kachru B. B. Norms, Models and Identities. The Language Teacher Online[J/OL]. 1996, 20:10. Retrieved on August 15, 2017, from http://jalt-publications.org/tlt/files/96/oct/englishes.html.

[149] Kaddour K. I. Enhancing EFL Learners' Speaking Skill Through Effective Communicative Activities and Strategies: The Case of First Year EFL Students[D]. University of Tlemcen, 2016.

[150] Kamhi-Stein L. Teacher Preparation and Nonnative English-speaking Educators. In Burns, A. and Richards, J.C. (eds.). Second Language Teacher Education[M]. Cambridge, UK: Cambridge University Press, 2009:91-101.

[151] Kamhi-Stein L., & Mahboob, A. Language Proficiency and NNES Professionals: Findings from TIRF-Funded Research Initiatives[C]. Paper presented at the 39th Annual TESOL Convention, San Antonio, Texas, 2005.

[152] Khalil M. K., & Elkhider, I. A. Applying learning theories and instructional design models for effective instruction[J]. Adv Physiol Educ, 2016, 40: 147-156.

[153] Kim S. J. Television discourse on English education fever: narrative analyses of twelve current-affairs documentaries[J]. Korean Broadcasting Journal, 2008, 22(5): 7-52.

[154] Koehnecke D. S. Professional development schools provide effective theory and practice[J]. Education, 2001,121(3): 589-591.

[155] Köyalan A. Crosscultural reflections of teacher trainers on in-service training[J]. COLEJ: Contemporary Online Language Education Journal, 2011, 1: 130-143.

[156] Kristine T. Qualities of A Good Teacher in Early Childhood Development [EB/OL]. Retrieved on September 10th, 2017.

[157] Kudryashova A., Gorbatova T., Rybushkina S. & Ivanova, E.Teacher's roles to facilitate active learning [J]. Mediterranean Journal of Social Sciences, 2016, 7(1): 460-466.

[158] Kumari P. L. Significance of Solomon four group pretest-posttest method in true experimental research-a study[J]. Journal of Agriculture and Veterinary Science, 2013, 5(2): 51-58.

[159] Lafayette R. C. Subject Matter Content: What Every Foreign Language Teacher Needs to Know. In G. Guntermann (Ed.), Developing Teachers for A Changing World[M]. Lincolnwood, IL: NTC Publishing Group, 1993:124-158.

[160] Lamarca C. A. J. Explicit pronunciation instruction to improve Thai vocational college students' intelligibility[J]. HRD Journal, 2016, 7(1): 6-17.

[161] Lam A. English in education in China: Policy changes and learners' experiences[J]. World Englishes, 2002, 21(2): 245-256.

[162] Lam A. Bilingual or Multilingual Education in China: Policy and Learner Experience[M]. In A. Feng (Ed.). Bilingual Education in China: Practices, Policies and Concepts[M]. Clevedon, England: Multilingual Matters, 2007:13-33.

[163] Lan Z. Research Report on Teacher Training Model and Method Reform [R]. Retrieved on Febureay 14th , 2017.

[164] Lange D. L. A. Blueprint for A Teacher Development Program. In Richards, J. C. & Nunan, D. (Eds.), Second Language Teacher Education[M]. Cambridge, U.K.: Cambridge University Press, 1990.

[165] Li B. F. Research on Negative Factors of Multimedia Assisted Preschool English Teaching[D]. Faculty of Western Languages, Helongjiang University, 2012.

[166] Li D. G., Zhang, X. R., & Edwards, V. Innovation and Change in English Teaching in the Western Provinces of China: The Impact of Overseas Training[R]. Educational Development in Western China: Towards Quality and Equity. 2016:191-215.

[167] Li D. Y. The Functions of Non-intelligence Factors on University English Teaching[C]. International Conference on Arts, Design and Contemporary Education (ICADCE), 2015.

[168] Li G. X. The Comparative Research of Three English Teaching Models of Chinese Kindergarten[D]. Shanxi Normal University, 2007.

[169] Li J. F. Research on Endangered Languages in Southwest of China[M]. Beijing: Central University for Nationalities Press, 2006.

[170] Li L. F. Reflection on children's English education in ethnic minority areas[J]. Overseas English, 2012,16: 69-70.

[171] Li L. T. On the design and implementation of children English teaching[J]. Journal of Wuhan Institute of Educational Science, 2006, 4(12): 86-88.

[172] Li S. L., & Zhou, Z. Studies on EFL Teaching Reform in Minority Ethnic Areas[M]. Kunming: Yunnan University Press, 2005.

[173] Li W. Y. Primary School English Curriculum and Teaching[M]. Beijing:

Chinese People University Press, 2014.

[174] Li X. M., Chen W. Z., & Li B B. Exploration of training students' English teaching skills by integrating inside and outside courses[J]. Information of Culture and Education, 2015(19): 189-192.

[175] Li Y., Liu S. Y., & Ghil'ad Z. The impact of language policy on the development of bilingual education for minorities in China[J]. Higher Education of Social Science, 2014, 7(1): 51-56.

[176] Li Y. M. Some thoughts on foreign language planning in China[J]. Journal of Foreign Languages, 2010, 22 (258): 399-416.

[177] Lincoln Y. S., & Guba E. G. Naturalistic inquiry[M]. Newbury Park, CA: Sage,1985.

[178] Lin W. H. A Study on the Present Situation of Professional Qualities of Kindergarten English Teachers in Changsha[D]. Faculty of Education, Hunan Normal University, 2008.

[179] Liu D. Training Non-native TESOL Students: Challenges for TESOL Teacher Education in the West[M]. In Braine, G. (ed.). Non-native Educators in English Language Teaching[M]. Mahwah, USA: Lawrence Erlbaum. 1999:197-210.

[180] Liu H. Strengthening training of pre-service ability and promoting in-service sustainable development—a brief discussion on teacher training of preschool bilingual education[J]. Vocational Technology, 2011(5): 42-43.

[181] Liu Y. Teaching approach study on ESP guided by theory of multi-modal discourse[J]. Journal of Chengdu Aeronautic Polytechnic, 2012, 28(2): 32-35.

[182] Lorena V. How Do Foreign Language Teachers Maintain Their Proficiency? A Grounded Theory Approach[C]. MSU Working Papers in SLS, 2014(5): 5-31.

[183] Loughran J. J. Effective reflective practice: In search of meaning in learning about teaching[J]. Journal of Teacher Education, 2002(53): 33-43.

[184] Lv N. An investigation report on the employment status of preschool education students in recent years[J]. Time Education, 2016, 1(2): 51-59.

[185] Lv Y. Y., & Wang, W. L. The discussion on the feasibility of children bilingual English[J]. Journal of Hefei University of Technology: Social Sciences, 2007, 21(3): 160-163.

[186] Mann K., Gordon, J. & MacLeod, A.Reflection and reflective practice in health professions education: a systematic review[J]. Adv Health Sci Educ Theory Pract, 2009, 14(4): 595-621.

[187] Marshall C., & Rossman, G. B. Designing qualitative research (5th ed.)[M]. Thousand Oaks: Sage, 2010.

[188] Martin F. Instructional design and the importance of instructional alignment[J]. Community College Journal of Research and Practice, 2011,35: 955-972.

[189] Maxwell J. A. Qualitative Research Design: An Interactive Approach (2nd ed) [M]. Thousand Oaks, CA: Sage Publication, 2005.

[190] Maykut P., & Morehouse, R. Beginning Qualitative Research A Philosophic and Practical[M].Guide. London: The Falmer Press, 1994.

[191] McArthur T. Oxford Guide to World English[M]. Oxford University Press Inc. (NY,US), Hardback 2002, Paperback, 2003.

[192] McCaffrey J. R., Lockwood, D. F., Koretz, D. M., & Hamilton, L. S. Evaluating Value Added Models for Teacher Accountability[M]. Santa Monica, CA: RAND Corporation, 2003.

[193] McGrath I. Materials Evaluation and Design for Language Teaching[M]. Edinburgh: Edinburgh University Press, 2002.

[194] McIlveen P., Perera H. N. Career optimism mediates the effect of personality on teachers' career engagement[J]. Journal of Career Assessment, 2015, 23(13):35-43.

[195] Mendro R., Jordan H., Gomez E., Anderson M., Bembry K. An Application of Multiple Linear Regression in Determining Longitudinal Teacher Effectiveness[C]. Paper presented at the 1998 Annual Meeting of the AERA, San Diego, CA, 1998.

[196] Merita H. European portfolio for student-teachers of languages (EPOSTL) and insights from student-teachers' feedback[J]. Academic Journal of Interdisciplinary Studies, 2015, 4(3): 71-78.

[197] Miles M. B., Huberman A. M. Qualitative Data Analysis: A Sourcebook for New Methods (2nd ed.)[M]. Thousand Oaks, CA: Sage,1994.

[198] Ministry of Education. Curriculum for English Teaching in Compulsory Junior High School (experimental edition)[M]. Beijing, China, 2000.

[199] Ministry of Education. Curriculum for English Teaching in Full-time Senior High School (experimental edition)[M]. Beijing, China, 2000.

[200] Ministry of Education. National English Curriculum Standards[M]. Beijing, China, 2011.

[201] Ministry of Education. Teaching Guideline for Preschool Education[M].

Beijing, China, 2001.

[202] Ministry of Education. Guidelines on Actively Promoting English Teaching at Elementary Schools[M]. Beijing, China, 2001.

[203] Ministry of Education. College English Curriculum. Beijing, China, 2004.

[204] Ministry of Education. National Medium and Long-term Plan for Education Reform and Development(2010-2020), 2010.

[205] Miroslaw P. The Role of In-service Training for Language Teachers in the Domain of Language Competence[R].

[206] Moore M. G., Kearsley G. Distance Education: A Systems View[M]. New York: Wadsworth Publishing Company, 1996.

[207] Morain G. Preparing foreign language teachers: problems and possibilities[J]. ADEFL Bulletin, 1990, 21(2): 20-24.

[208] Morley J. The pronunciation component in teaching English to speakers of other languages[J]. TESOL Quarterly, 1991, 25(3): 481-520.

[209] Morrison G. R., Ross, S. M. & Kemp, J. E. Designing effective instruction (4th ed.). Cited in Obizoba, C. Instructional design models—framework for innovative teaching and learning methodologies[J]. The Business and Management Review, 2015, 6(5): 21-31.

[210] Morse J. M., & Niehaus, L. Mixed Method Design: Principles and Procedures[M]. Walnut Creek, CA: Left Coast Press, 2009.

[211] Muñoz C. Input and long term effects of starting age in foreign language learning[J]. IRAL, 2011, 49(2): 113-133.

[212] Murdoch G. Language development provision in teacher training curricula[J]. ELT Journal, 1994, 48(3):253-259.

[213] Natalia N. Language Teacher Proficiency or Teacher Language Proficiency? [R]. Simpson Norris Pty Ltd, 2017.

[214] NABE. The National Association for Bilingual Education is an American advocacy group that provides teacher training educational leadership and lobbying efforts on behalf of legislation regarding individuals learning English as a second language, 2012.

[215] Naegle P. The New Teacher's Complete Source Book[M]. USA: Scholastic Professional Books, 2002.

[216] National Bureau of Statistics of China. A Report of 2010 National Economy and Social Development of the PRC[R]. 2011.

[217] Nation I. S. P., & Macalister, J. Language Curriculum Design[M]. New York & London: Routledge, 2010.

[218] Neeraja K. Text Book of Nursing Education[M]. New Delhi: Jaypee Brothers N edical publishers, 2003.

[219] Newby D. et al. European Portfolio for Student Teachers of Languages- A Reflection Tool for Language Teacher Education[M]. Council of Europe Publishing, 2007.

[220] Nieswiadomy R. M. Foundations of nursing research (5th ed.)[M]. Upper Saddle River, NJ: Pearson Education Inc, 2008.

[221] Norris N. Language Teacher Proficiency or Teacher Language Proficiency? An Environmental Scan of Information Relating to the Competencies/Qualities/ Knowledge, Required to Be An Effective Language Teacher[C]. 1999.

[222] National People's Congress of the PRC. Constitution of the People's Republic of China[R]. 1982.

[223] Pan J. L. Study on the training mode of teaching skills for English student-teachers in local colleges[J]. Journal of Huanggang Normal University, 2012, 32(1):143-145.

[224] Phil B. The Importance of Spoken English Skills Training in the Business Setting[EB/OL].

[225] Pintrich P. R., Schunk D. H., Motivation in Education[M]. Englewood Cliffs, NJ: Prentice Hall, 2002,

[226] Postiglione G. A. China's National Minority Education: Culture, Schooling and Development[M]. New York: Falmer Press, 2000.

[227] Postiglione G. A. Introduction: State Schooling and Ethnicity in China. In G. A. Postiglione (Ed.), China's National Minority Education: Culture, schooling, and development[M]. New York: Falmer Press, 1999:3-19.

[228] Punch K. F. Introduction to Research in Education[M]. Thousand Oaks, London: Sage, 2009.

[229] Qutoshi S. B. Poudel T. Student centered approach to teaching: what does it mean for the stakeholders of a community school in Karachi, Pakistan?[J]. Journal of Education and Research, 2014, 4(1):19-33.

[230] Rahman A., Deviyanti R. The correlation between students' motivation and their English speaking ability[J]. Jurnal Ilmiah ESAI, 2012, 6(1): 1-18.

[231] Rani K., Jenna-Lynn B. S. An appraisal of students' awareness of "self-

reflection" in a first-year pathology course of undergraduate medical/dental education[J]. BMC Med Education. 2011(11):67.

[232] Rasekhi K. V. ESL/EFL Learners' Perception of Their Pronunciation Needs and Strategies[C]. 41st Annual State CATESOL Conference, Santa Clara, CA, April 23, 2010.

[233] Rasheed S., Zeeshan M., Zaidi A. Z. Challenges of teaching English language in a multilingual setting: an investigation at government girls secondary schools of Quetta, Baluchistan, Pakistan[J]. International Journal of English Linguistics, 2017, 7(4):149-157.

[234] Reiser R. A., & Dempsey, J. V. Eds. Trends and Issues in Instructional Design and Technology[M]. Saddle River, NJ, Pearson Education, 2007.

[235] Ren H. On cultivation of the preschool bilingual teachers[J]. China Education Innovation Heral, 2009(21): 225-226.

[236] Richards A. S., Elwood F. H. Foundations of human resource development (2nd ed.)[M]. Berrett-Koehler Publishers, Inc, 2009.

[237] Richards J. C. Competence and Performance in Language Teaching[M]. New York, NY: Cambridge University Press, 2001. Cited in Richards, J. C. Curriculum development in Language Teaching[M]. New York, NY: Cambridge University Press, 2011.

[238] Richards J. C. Key Issues in Language Teaching[M]. Cambridge University Press. Cambridge, United Kingdom, 2015.

[239] Richards J. C., & Lockhart, C. Reflective Teaching in Second Language Classrooms[M]. New York, Cambridge University Press, 1994.

[240] Richards L., Morse, J. M. User's Guide to Qualitative Methods (2nd ed.)[M]. Thousand Oaks, CA: Sage, 2007.

[241] Rivkin S. G., Hanushek E. A., Kain J. F. Teachers, schools, and academic achievement[J]. Econometrics, 2005(73): 417-458.

[242] Roberts J. Language Teacher Education[M]. London, UK: Edward Arnold, 1998.

[243] Robson C. Real World Research: A Resource for Social Scientists and Practitioner Researchers[M]. Oxford: Blackwell, 2002.

[244] Rosalba C., Orlando C. English teaching in Cali: Teachers' proficiency level described[J]. Lenguaje, 2013, 41 (2): 325-352.

[245] Rosin J. The necessity of counselor individuation for fostering reflective

practice[J]. Journal of Counseling and Development, 2015, 93(1): 88-95.

[246] Rossman G. B., Wilson B. L. Number and words: Combining quantitative and qualitative methods in a single large-scale evaluation study[J]. Evaluation Review, 1985, 9(5): 627-643.

[247] Rowan B., Correnti, R., & Miller, R. J. What large-scale survey research tells us about teacher effects on student achievement: Insights from the Prospects study of elementary schools[J]. Teachers College Record, 2002(104): 1525-1567.

[248] Rubin H. J., Rubin, I. S. Qualitative Interviewing: The Art of Hearing Data[M]. Thousand Oaks, CA: Sage, 1995.

[249] Sakulkoo S. Volunteering as Active Aging: A Study of Elderly Thai Who Are Member of the Brain Bank[D]. International Graduate Studies Human Resource Development Center, Burapha University, 2009.

[250] Samimy K., Brutt-Griffler, J. To Be a Native or Nonnative Speaker: Perceptions of Nonnative Speaking Students in A Graduate TESOL Program[M]. Cited in G. Braine (Ed.), Non-native Educators in English Language Teaching[M]. Mahwah, NJ: Erlbaum, 1999:127-144.

[251] Santangelo T., Graham, S. A comprehensive meta-analysis of handwriting instruction[J]. Educational Psychology Review, 2016, 28(2): 225-265.

[252] Sarma R. Research: In a methodological frame[J]. Journal of Arts, Science & Commerce, 2012, 3(1): 100-105.

[253] Schrier L. L. Understanding the foreign language teacher education process[J]. ADFL Bulletin, 1994, 25(3): 69-74.

[254] Schwandt T. A. The Sage Dictionary of Qualitative Inquiry (3rd ed.)[M]. Thousand Oaks, California: Sage Publication, Inc., 2007.

[255] Selvaraj B. English language teaching (ELT): Curriculum reforms in Malaysia[J]. Voice of Academia, 2010, 5(1): 51-60.

[256] Serdyukov P., Ryan, M. Writing Effective Lesson Plans: The 5-star Approach[M]. Boston: Allyn & Bacon, 2008.

[257] Shan F. F.Multilingual education in China: Taking the situation of Guizhou minority areas as an example[J]. Theory and Practice in Language Studies, 2018, 8(2): 197-202.

[258] Shen, X. M., & Zhao, F. The professional standards and development of preschool bilingual education teachers[J]. Studies in Preschool Education,

2010(5): 39-43.

[259] Shim D. B., Park S. Y. The language politics of "English fever" in South Korea[J]. Korean Journal, 2008, 48(2): 136-159.

[260] Shimizu K. Japanese college student attitudes towards English teachers: A survey[J]. The Language Teacher, 1995, 19(10): 5-8.

[261] Silverman E. Ongoing self-reflection[J]. American Journal of Speech-Language Pathology, 2008, 17(1): 92.

[262] Simonsen B., Fairbanks, S., Briesch, A., Myers, D., & Sugai, G. Evidence-based practices in classroom management: considerations for research to practice[J]. Education and Treatment of Children, 2008, 31(3): 351-380.

[263] Singh S. A study of teaching competences of school teachers in relation to their attitude towards ICT and teacher effectiveness[J]. International Journal of Information Technology & Computer Sciences Perspectives, 2015, 4(3): 1630-1634.

[264] Singh Y. K. Teaching Practice: Lesson Planning[M]. New Delhi: APH publishing corporation, 2008.

[265] Singleton D., & Muñoz, C. Around and Beyond the Critical Period Hypothesis. Cited in E. Hinkel (Ed.). Handbook of Research in Second Language Teaching and Learning[M]. New York: Routledge, 2011: 407-425.

[266] Skripsi A. The Effectiveness of Teaching Speaking Using Problem-based Learning to the Tenth Grade of SMKN 1 Kediri Academic Year 2015-2016[D]. University of Nusantara PGRI Kediri, 2015.

[267] Sovichea V. Perspectives of Teacher Training Towards An Information and Communication Technology Program: A Study of the National Institute of Education in Cambodia[D]. Faculty of Education, Burapha University, 2012.

[268] Spinelli C. G. Linking Assessment to Instructional Strategies: A Guide for Teachers[M]. Pearson Education, Inc., 2011.

[269] Springer K. Educational Research: A Contextual Approach[M]. Denver: John Wiley & Sons, 2010.

[270] Stake R. E. Qualitative Research: Studying How to Think Work[M]. Spring Street, NY: The Guilford Press, 2010.

[271] Stevens D., Cooper, J. Journal Keeping: How to Use Reflective Writing for Effective Learning, Teaching, Professional Insight, and Positive Change[M]. Sterling, VA: Stylu Publications, 2009.

[272] Strevens P. New Orientation in the Teaching of English[M]. Oxford: Oxford University Press, 1977. Cited in Sovichea, V. Perspectives of Teacher Training Towards An Information and Communication Technology Program: A Study of the National Institute of Education in Cambodia[D]. Faculty of Education, Burapha University, 2012.

[273] Susan E., Joce N. Professional learning in pre-service and in-service teacher education: contexts and issues Asia-Pacific[J]. Journal of Teacher Education, 2015, 43(3): 181-182.

[274] Swanson R. A., Holton, E. F. III. Foundations of Human Resource Development (2nd ed.)[M]. San Francisco: Berrett-Koehler, 2009.

[275] Tan, B. H. Chinese English and its implications for EFL teaching in China[J]. Education Journal, 2014, 3(6): 340-344.

[276] Tan D. R. Preschool Bilingual Education—A Case Study in Chinese Context[D]. Fujian Normal University, 2006.

[277] Tan X. Existing problems and countermeasures of preschool bilingual education teachers[J]. Journal of Suzhou Education Institute, 2014, 7(5): 79-80.

[278] Teddlie C., & Tashakkori, A. Foundation of Mixed Methods Research: Integrating Quantitative and Qualitative Approaches in the Social and Behavioral Sciences[M]. Thousand Oaks, CA: Sage, 2009.

[279] Teng X., Wen, Y. H. Bilingualism and Bilingual Education in China. Cited in Shimahira et al. (Ed.). Ethnicity, Race, and Nationality in Education: A Global Perspective[M]. Mahwah, NJ: Lawence Erlbaum Associates, 2005: 259-278.

[280] Teng Y. H. On the necessity and strategy of setting up preschool English major in normal universities[J]. Journal of Educational Institute of Jilin Province, 2013, 29(1): 19-20.

[281] Thanasoulas D. Motivation and motivating in the foreign language classroom[J]. The Internet TESL Journal, 2002, 8(11):56-64.

[282] Thompson R. A., Zamboanga B. L.Prior knowledge and its relevance to student achievement in introduction to psychology[J]. Teach Psychology, 2003 (30):96-101.

[283] Tian: F. A brief analysis of factors affecting English pronunciation learning[J]. Journal of Jining Teachers' College, 2007, 28(3): 31-32.

[284] Tomlinson B. Developing Materials for Language Teaching[M]. London: Continuum Press, 2003.

[285] Tsang M. C., Yang C. L., Qiu L. Ethnic Minorities Education in Yunnan: Developments, Challenges and Policies[EB/OL]. 2005.

[286] Tseng M. H. Development of pencil grip position in preschool children[J]. Occupational Therapy Journal of Research, 1998, 18: 207-224.

[287] Ur P. A Course in Language Teaching[M]. Cambridge: Cambridge University Press, 1996.

[288] Uysal H. H. Evaluation of an in-service training program for primary-school language teachers in Turkey[J]. Australian Journal of Teacher Education, 2012, 37(7): 14-29.

[289] Verma S., Paterson, M., Medves J. Core Competencies for Health Care Professionals: What Medicine, Nursing, Occupational Therapy, and Physiotherapy[EB/OL]. 2006.

[290] Wang G. Ethnic multilingual education in China: A critical observation[J]. Educational Linguistics, 2015, 30(2): 35-47.

[291] Wang L. Study on the training model of English teaching skills for preschool education major in higher vocational colleges[J]. Journal of Heilongjiang College of Education, 2012(31): 183-184.

[292] Wang L. A new model of preschool bilingual teacher training in English teaching[J]. Journal of Weifang Engineering Vocational College, 2014, 27(2):8-10.

[293] Wang S. P., Mi H. M. A strategic study of the demand for bilingual teachers for pre-school education[J]. Journal of Hebei Normal University(Educational Science Edition), 2014, 16(2): 105-109.

[294] Wang T. Y. How to develop children's English teaching activities effectively[J]. New Curriculum, 2016(1): 63.

[295] Wang Y. Imperatives of strengthening the study of preschool bilingual education in China[J]. Children Education, 2007(2): 52-55.

[296] Wang Y. J. An Effective Approach to Children's English phonetics teaching[J]. Bilingual Theory and Exploration, 2009(6): 23.

[297] Ward J. R., McCotter S.S. Reflection as a visible outcome for preservice teachers[J]. Teaching and Teacher Education, 2004(20): 243-257.

[298] Williams K., Woolliams M. Spiro J. Reflective Writing[M]. Basingstoke: Palgrave MacMillan, 2012.

[299] Williams M. Teacher Training for English Language Teachers. In G.R. Harvard

& P. Hodkinson (Eds.). Action and Reflection in Teacher Education[M]. Norwood, NJ: Ablex, 1994: 213-227.

[300] Wright S. P., Horn, S. P., Sanders W. L. Teachers and classroom context effects on student achievement: Implications for teacher evaluation[J]. Journal of Personnel Evaluation in Education, 1997(11):57-67.

[301] Wood F. H., Kleine P.E., Staff development research and rural schools: A critical appraisal[C]. Paper presented at the National Association of Rural Schools Conference, Lake Placid, N.Y.,1987.

[302] Wood F. H., Thompson S.R., Russell E. Designing Effective Staff Development Programs, Cited in Dillion-Peterson (Ed.). Staff Development Organizational Development[M]. Alexandria, Virginia: Association for Supervision and Curriculum Development, 1981.

[303] Wu N. H. A study of the adequacy of early English education[J]. Ministry of Education, 2002(16): 93-109.

[304] Wu Y. A. Research on the professional quality of excellent foreign language teachers[J]. Foreign Language Teaching and Research, 2005, 37(3): 199-205.

[305] Wu Z. D.Summary of the study of early children's English education[J]. Journal of Shenyang College of Education, 2005, 7(3): 109-112.

[306] Yan Z. Q. An Introduction of World English[M]. Beijing: Foreign Language Teaching and Research Press, 2002.

[307] Yang P. Advantages and principles of children's English learning[J]. Study of Preschool Education, 2007(4): 29.

[308] Yang R. X. A study on the bilingual education for ethnic minorities in Yunnan[J]. Education for Ethnic Minorities in China, 2005(2): 23-25.

[309] Yang Q. The Study on the Professional Qualities of Kindergarten English Teacher in Wuhan[D]. Faculty of Education, Huazhong Normal University, 2012.

[310] Yang S. J., Yang H. J., Lust B. Early childhood bilingualism leads to advances in executive attention: dissociating culture and language[J]. Bilingualism: Language and Cognition, 2011, 14(3):412-422.

[311] Yao D., Li Z. H. Research and exploration on pre-service training mode of preschool bilingual education[J]. Journal of HuBei Adult Education Institute, 2010, 16(2): 8-10.

[312] Yavuz F., & Celik G.Y. Using fairy tales as a model to enhance learners'

writing organization skill[J]. International Journal of Learning and Teaching, 2017, 9(3): 349-353.

[313] Ytsma J. Towards a typology of trilingual primary education[J]. International Journal of Bilingual Education and Bilingualism, 2001(4): 11–22.

[314] Yu X. Q. A study on the training mode of English educational proficiency of bilingual teachers in preschool education[J]. Innovation of Science and Education, 2012(5): 79-80.

[315] Yu Z. Y. The practice of bilingual education in kindergarten[J]. The Study of Preschool Education, 2000(4): 35-38.

[316] Yuan Y. C. Attitude and Motivation for English Learning of Ethnic Minority Students in China[M]. Shanghai: Shanghai Foreign Language Education Press, 2007.

[317] Yuan Y., Hu, D., Li, P., Zhu, H., Wang, J., & Shang, Y., et al. A Survey Report on Trilingualism and Trilingual Education in Yunnan[C]. Trilingualism in Education in China: Models and Challenges. Springer Netherlands, 2015.

[318] Yusuf M. Teachers of English at Public Elementary Schools in Palembang: Their Profile and Qualification[D]. Sriwijaya University, Palembang, Indonesia, 2007.

[319] Zeng M. The role of grammatical instruction within communicative language teaching among Chinese ESL students[J]. CELEA Journal, 2008, 31(1): 36-45.

[320] Zhang C. A preliminary study on the vocational skills training for bilingual students of preschool education major[J]. Chinese School Education, 2012, 24(1): 59.

[321] Zhang C. Y. Study on the Design of English Teaching Activities in Young Children[D]. Faculty of Education and Science, South China Normal University, 2007.

[322] Zhang H. M. On the training of preschool children's English teaching proficiency[J]. Research Exploration, 2017(3): 200-202.

[323] Zhang W. W. Teaching English in China: A Handbook for Native Speaker[EB/OL]. 2004.

[324] Zhang W. W. A Brief Introduction to Foreign Languages Education Policy in China[EB/OL]. 2012.

[325] Zhang W. W., Li S. L. An Investigation on Primary School English Teachers— in Case of Yunnan Province, China[C]. Paper Presented at the Annual Meeting

of the Yunnan Educational Association, 2010.

[326] Zhao Z. Z. Trilingual education for ethnic minorities: toward empowerment[J]. Chinese Education & Society, 2010, 43(1): 70-81.

[327] Zhou Q. F., Ni B. F. A study of English teaching model in higher vocational college under multimodal discourse framework[J]. Journal of Kaifeng Institute of Education, 2016, 36(6): 129-130.

[328] Zhu F. Y. The current situation of preschool English education and its requirements for teachers[J]. Journal of Inner Mongolia Normal University (Education and Science Edition), 2007(12): 67-69.

[329] Zhu X. M., Gao W., Liu J. D., et al. Concept, innovation and related theory of quality-oriented education[J]. Educational Research, 2006(2): 3-10.

[330] Zimmerman B. J. Becoming a self-regulated learner: An overview[J]. Theory Into Practice, 2002, 41(2): 65-70.

[331] Zuo J. Practice and exploration on English teaching skills cultivated by adopting "Three—dimensional mode" under the circumstance of the new curriculum standard[J]. Education and Teaching Research, 2012, 26(10): 22-25.

# APPENDICES

## APPENDIX A

## PARTICIPANT'S CONSENT FORM
## BURAPHA UNIVERSITY

**Title:** Development of A Training Module to Improve Proficiency in Beginning Level ELT of Student-teachers in Multi-ethnic Community Schools in Yunnan Province

**Researcher:** Youxing Xiao

I am a doctoral student at Faculty of Education, Burapha University, Thailand. This is a consent form for research participation.

The main purpose of this study is to investigate the kindergarten student-teachers' professional qualities, especially their English language teaching (ELT) proficiency, and to develop a feasible training module to improve their ELT proficiency and to determine the effectiveness of the training module in multi-ethnic communities of Yunnan Province. For doing so, this study examines the student-teachers who are majoring in preschool education and primary school education in the current campus of Dali University in Yunnan Province about their perceived English language and teaching proficiency, including their situation toward the English learning, and their attitudes and perspectives toward the present English education policies and practices. It also examines how some aspects of professional qualities are closely related to the ELT proficiency in English education in the multi-ethnic context of China. It is expected that this study will generate very important information for considering the future direction(s) of teacher professional development for teaching English efficiently for the beginning level.

This questionnaire inquires about: (1) English linguistic knowledge and skills; (2) beliefs and opinions about capacity as a kindergarten English teacher; (3) teaching techniques regarding English language teaching; (4) perception about current kindergarten English education policies and practices; (5) perceived English language and teaching proficiency and the necessary level of English proficiency for effective English teaching; (6) teaching practicum; (7) personal and relative background information and so on.

It is expected to take about 15~20 minutes to complete this survey. Please be sure to answer every single statement or question. Your response is very important to us. Please be assured that all of the information obtained from will be completely confidential.

Thank you for your participation!

Youxing Xiao
Faculty of Education and Science, Dali University
Tel: 13466162286
Email: youxingxiao@live.cn

# APPENDIX B

## Agreement Statement as Participant

Before I sign below, I have already got an explanation from Mr. Youxing Xiao ( 肖友兴 ) about the purposes, methods, procedures, and benefits of this study, and I understand all of the explanation. I agree to be a participant of this study.

I, Youxing Xiao ( 肖友兴 ), as the researcher of this study, have explained all about the purposes, methods, procedures, and benefits of this study to the participants honestly. All of the data/information of the participants will only be used for the purposes of this study. Please sign your name below to indicate your consent to participate in this study. You will be given a copy of this consent form to keep.

Thank you for your participation!

Signature of Participant: _____

　　　　　　　　　　　　　　　　　Date:

Signature of Researcher: _____

　　　　　　　　　　　　　　　　　Date:

# APPENDIX C

## QUESTIONNAIRE (For Student-teachers)

Dear all:

The main purpose of this study is to better understand the current status of preschool and primary school English education, especially student-teachers' English language teaching (ELT) proficiency. Please spare a few minutes to complete the following questionnaire carefully. Your information will be greatly valued and be kept strictly confidential. Thank you for your support and cooperation!

亲爱的同学们：

你好！本研究的主要目的是为更好了解幼小阶段的英语教育现状，尤其是幼小英语准教师的英语教学能力。请你花几分钟认真完成这份问卷，你所提供的信息将备受重视且被严格保密。谢谢你的支持与合作！

**Part I: Personal information 第一部分：个人信息**

1. Gender 性别：□ Male 男　　　□ Female 女
2. Age 年龄：＿＿＿＿＿＿＿
3. Minority 民族：＿＿＿＿＿＿＿
4. Grade 年级：＿＿＿＿＿＿＿
5. CET-4 score 大学英语四级分数：＿＿＿＿＿＿＿
   CET-6 score 大学英语六级分数：＿＿＿＿＿＿＿

**Part II: Trainees' general perceptions, beliefs, and current English language and teaching proficiency 第二部分：参与培训人员的观点、信念和目前的英语语言能力和教学能力**

Instructions: *Please read the following questions and tick (√) the appropriate rating that you feel/ think according to the scale of conformity provided.* 说明：请阅读以下问题，并根据所提供项目的一致程度，在你感觉／认为的符合级别栏内打"√"。

1 = Strongly Disagree;  2 = Disagree;  3 = Neutral;  4 = Agree;  5 = Strongly Agree

1、强烈反对；  2、反对；  3、中立；  4、赞同；  5、强烈赞同

### Area 1: Linguistic Basis 领域一：语言基础

| Items 项目 | 1 | 2 | 3 | 4 | 5 |
|---|---|---|---|---|---|
| 1. I believe a qualified kindergarten English teacher should have standard English pronunciation. 我认为一名合格的幼儿英语教师应该具备标准的英语发音。 | | | | | |
| 2. I feel I need to improve my English pronunciation. 我觉得我需要改善我的英语发音。 | | | | | |
| 3. I believe a qualified kindergarten English teacher should have a rich English vocabulary. 我认为一名合格的幼儿园英语教师应该具备丰富的英语词汇。 | | | | | |
| 4. I feel I need to improve my English vocabulary. 我觉得我需要提高我的英语词汇。 | | | | | |
| 5. I believe a qualified kindergarten English teacher should have good knowledge of English grammar. 我认为一名合格的幼儿英语教师应该具备良好的英语语法知识。 | | | | | |
| 6. I feel I need to improve my English grammar knowledge. 我觉得我需要提高我的英语语法知识。 | | | | | |
| 7. I believe a qualified kindergarten English teacher should have good background knowledge of British and American culture. 我认为一名合格的幼儿英语教师应该具备良好的英美文化背景知识。 | | | | | |
| 8. I feel I need to improve my background knowledge of British and American culture. 我觉得我需要提高我的英美文化背景知识。 | | | | | |
| 9. I believe a qualified kindergarten English teacher should have good knowledge of cross-cultural communication. 我认为一名合格的幼儿英语教师应该具备良好的跨文化交际知识。 | | | | | |
| 10. I feel I need to improve my knowledge of cross-cultural communication. 我觉得我需要提高我的跨文化交际知识。 | | | | | |
| 11. I believe a qualified kindergarten English teacher should have good English listening ability. 我认为一名合格的幼儿英语教师应该具备良好的英语听力能力。 | | | | | |

| Items 项目 | 1 | 2 | 3 | 4 | 5 |
|---|---|---|---|---|---|
| 12. I feel I need to improve my English listening ability. 我觉得我需要提高我的英语听力。 | | | | | |
| 13. I believe a qualified kindergarten English teacher should have good daily spoken English. 我认为一名合格的幼儿英语教师应该具备良好的日常英语口语能力。 | | | | | |
| 14. I feel I need to improve my daily spoken English. 我觉得我需要提高我的日常英语口语能力。 | | | | | |
| 15. I believe a qualified kindergarten English teacher should have good reading ability. 我认为一名合格的幼儿英语教师应该具备良好的阅读能力。 | | | | | |
| 16. I feel I need to improve my reading ability. 我觉得我需要提高我的阅读能力。 | | | | | |
| 17. I believe a qualified kindergarten English teacher should have good writing ability. 我认为一名合格的幼儿英语教师应该具备良好的写作能力。 | | | | | |
| 18. I feel I need to improve my writing ability. 我觉得我需要提高我的写作能力。 | | | | | |

## Area 2: Teaching Design 领域二：教学设计

| Items 项目 | 1 | 2 | 3 | 4 | 5 |
|---|---|---|---|---|---|
| 19. I believe a qualified kindergarten English teacher should know the teaching syllabus of preschool English intimately. 我认为一名合格的幼儿英语教师应该熟知学前英语教学大纲。 | | | | | |
| 20. I feel I need to acquire some knowledge of the preschool English teaching syllabus. 我觉得我需要获取一些学前英语教学大纲方面的知识。 | | | | | |
| 21. I believe a qualified kindergarten English teacher should know the English teaching methodology intimately. 我认为一名合格的幼儿英语教师应该熟知英语教学方法。 | | | | | |
| 22. I feel I need to acquire some knowledge of preschool English teaching methodology. 我觉得我需要获取一些学前英语教学方法方面的知识。 | | | | | |

Continued Table

| Items 项目 | 1 | 2 | 3 | 4 | 5 |
|---|---|---|---|---|---|
| 23. I believe a qualified kindergarten English teacher should analyze textbooks and content accurately. 我认为一名合格的幼儿英语教师应该准确地分析教材和内容。 | | | | | |
| 24. I feel I need to learn how to analyze the English textbooks and contents. 我觉得我需要学会如何分析英语教材和内容。 | | | | | |
| 25. I believe a qualified kindergarten English teacher should analyze the young learners accurately. 我认为一名合格的幼儿英语教师应该准确分析幼小的教学对象。 | | | | | |
| 26. I feel I need to learn how to analyze the young learners. 我觉得我需要学会如何分析幼小的教学对象。 | | | | | |
| 27. I believe a qualified kindergarten English teacher should set teaching objectives & strategy normatively and clearly. 我认为一名合格的幼儿英语教师应该规范清晰地设置教学目标和策略。 | | | | | |
| 28. I feel I need to learn how to set a teaching objective & strategy. 我觉得我需要学会如何设置教学目标和策略。 | | | | | |
| 29. I believe a qualified kindergarten English teacher should select and utilize media & materials reasonably. 我认为一名合格的幼儿英语教师应该合理地选择和使用多媒体素材。 | | | | | |
| 30. I feel I need to learn how to select and utilize media & materials. 我觉得我需要学会如何选择和使用多媒体素材。 | | | | | |
| 31. I believe a qualified kindergarten English teacher should encourage young learners to participate flexibly. 我认为一名合格的幼儿英语教师应该灵活调动幼儿的参与性。 | | | | | |
| 32. I feel I need to learn how to encourage young learners' participation. 我觉得我需要学会如何调动幼儿的参与性。 | | | | | |
| 33. I believe a qualified kindergarten English teacher should design a teaching plan normatively and skillfully. 我认为一名合格的幼儿教师应该规范熟练地设计教学计划。 | | | | | |
| 34. I feel I need to learn how to design a teaching plan. 我觉得我需要学会如何设计教学计划。 | | | | | |

### Area 3: Teaching Implementation 领域三：教学实施

| Items 项目 | 1 | 2 | 3 | 4 | 5 |
|---|---|---|---|---|---|
| 35. I believe a qualified kindergarten English teacher should select the right teaching methods reasonably. 我认为一名合格的幼儿英语教师应该合理地选择正确的教学方法。 | | | | | |
| 36. I feel I need to learn how to select the right teaching methods. 我觉得我需要学会如何选择正确的教学方法。 | | | | | |
| 37. I believe a qualified kindergarten English teacher should organize classrooms & teaching activities effectively. 我认为一名合格的幼儿英语教师应该有效地组织课堂教学活动。 | | | | | |
| 38. I feel I need to learn how to organize classrooms & teaching activities. 我觉得我需要学会如何组织课堂教学活动。 | | | | | |
| 39. I believe a qualified kindergarten English teacher should arrange the teaching process reasonably. 我认为一名合格的幼儿英语教师应该合理地安排教学进度。 | | | | | |
| 40. I feel I need to learn how to arrange the teaching process. 我觉得我需要学会如何安排教学进度。 | | | | | |
| 41. I believe a qualified kindergarten English teacher should evaluate teaching performance objectively. 我认为一名合格的幼儿英语教师应该客观地评价教学表现。 | | | | | |
| 42. I feel I need to learn how to evaluate teaching performance. 我觉得我需要学会如何评价教学表现。 | | | | | |

### Area 4: Teaching Techniques 领域四：教学技巧

| Items 项目 | 1 | 2 | 3 | 4 | 5 |
|---|---|---|---|---|---|
| 43. I believe a qualified kindergarten English teacher should master the technique of telling English stories. 我认为一名合格的幼儿英语教师应该掌握讲英语故事的技巧。 | | | | | |
| 44. I feel I need to master some techniques of telling English stories. 我觉得我需要掌握一些讲英语故事的技巧。 | | | | | |
| 45. I believe a qualified kindergarten English teacher should master the technique of playing English games. 我认为一名合格的幼儿英语教师应该掌握玩英语游戏的技巧。 | | | | | |

Continued Table

| Items 项目 | 1 | 2 | 3 | 4 | 5 |
|---|---|---|---|---|---|
| 46. I feel I need to master some techniques of playing games. 我觉得我需要掌握一些玩英语游戏的技巧。 | | | | | |
| 47. I believe a qualified kindergarten English teacher should master the technique of singing English songs & rhymes. 我认为一名合格的幼儿英语教师应该掌握唱英文歌曲和歌谣的技巧。 | | | | | |
| 48. I feel I need to master some techniques of singing songs & rhymes. 我觉得我需要掌握一些唱英文歌曲和歌谣的技巧。 | | | | | |
| 49. I believe a qualified kindergarten English teacher should master the technique of drawing stick figures. 我认为一名合格的幼儿英语教师应该掌握简笔画的技巧。 | | | | | |
| 50. I feel I need to master some techniques of drawing stick figure. 我觉得我需要掌握一些简笔画的技巧。 | | | | | |
| 51. I believe a qualified kindergarten English teacher should have pretty and neat English hand-writing. 我认为一名合格的幼儿英语教师应该能写一手漂亮整洁的英语书法。 | | | | | |
| 52. I feel I need to improve my level of English hand-writing. 我觉得我需要提高我的英语书写水平。 | | | | | |
| 53. I believe a qualified kindergarten English teacher should master the technique of playing tongue twisters. 我认为一名合格的幼儿英语教师应该掌握英语绕口令的技巧。 | | | | | |
| 54. I feel I need to master some techniques of playing tongue twister. 我觉得我需要掌握一些英语绕口令的技巧。 | | | | | |
| 55. I believe a qualified kindergarten English teacher should master the technique of using modern educational teaching technologies. 我认为一名合格的幼儿英语教师应该掌握现代教育教学技术的技巧。 | | | | | |
| 56. I feel I need to master some techniques of using modern educational teaching technologies. 我觉得我需要掌握一些现代教育教学技术的技巧。 | | | | | |

## Area 5: Comprehensive Aspects 领域五：全面评估

| Items 项目 | 1 | 2 | 3 | 4 | 5 |
|---|---|---|---|---|---|
| 57. I think it is necessary to acquire more professional knowledge about preschool education as a preschool English teacher. 我认为作为学前幼儿英语教师掌握更多有关学前教育的专业知识是有必要的。 | | | | | |
| 58. I think it is necessary to acquire more professional knowledge about English education as a preschool English teacher. 我认为作为学前幼儿英语教师掌握更多有关英语教育的专业知识是有必要的。 | | | | | |
| 59. I think it is important to have good linguistic proficiency as a preschool English teacher. 我认为作为学前英语教师掌握良好的语言能力是重要的。 | | | | | |
| 60. I plan to select a bilingual kindergarten to do my teaching practicum. 我打算选择一家双语幼儿园进行我的教学实习。 | | | | | |
| 61. I plan to teach children's English course when doing my teaching practicum. 我打算在开展教学实习时教授儿童英语课程。 | | | | | |
| 62. I'd like to attend the teacher-centered training activities. 我喜欢参加以教师为中心的培训活动。 | | | | | |
| 63. I'd like to attend the group-based training activities. 我喜欢参加小组合作式的培训活动。 | | | | | |
| 64. I'd like to attend the interaction-based training activities between teachers & students. 我喜欢参加师生间的互动式培训活动。 | | | | | |

# APPENDIX D

## QUESTIONNAIRE (For English Teachers)

Dear teachers:

The main purpose of this study is to better understand the current status of preschool English education, especially preschool English teachers' English language teaching (ELT) proficiency. Please spare a few minutes to complete the following questionnaire carefully. Your information will be greatly valued and be kept strictly confidential. Thank you for your support and cooperation!

亲爱的老师们:

你好！本研究的主要目的是为更好了解学前英语教育现状，尤其是幼儿英语教师的英语教学能力。请你花几分钟认真完成这份问卷，你所提供的信息将备受重视且被严格保密。谢谢你的支持与合作！

**Part I: Personal information 第一部分：个人信息**

1. **Gender** 性别：□ Male 男　　□ Female 女

2. **Age** 年龄：20-25，26-30，31-35，Over 35

3. **Minority** 民族：_____

4. **Educational Background** 教育背景：College 专科，Bachelor 本科，Master 硕士，Doctor 博士

5. **Your Major** 专业：Preschool Education 学前教育，English Education 英语教育，Other Major 其他（请写出）_____

6. **Your English Level** 英语水平：CET-4 大学英语四级，CET-6 大学英语六级，TEM-4 专业英语四级，TEM-8 专业英语八级，Other 其他_____

7. **Length of Employment** 工作年限：1-2 years 1-2 年，3-5 years 3-5 年，Over 5 years 5 年以上

**Part II: Preschool English teachers' general perceptions, beliefs, current English language and teaching proficiency** 第二部分：学前幼儿英语教师的观

点、信念和目前的英语语言和教学能力

Instruction: *Please read the following questions and tick (√) the appropriate rating where you feel/ think according to the scale of conformity provided.* 说明：请阅读以下问题，并根据所提供项目的一致程度，在你感觉 / 认为的符合级别栏内打 "√"。

1 = Strongly Disagree；2 = Disagree；3 = Neutral；4 = Agree；5 = Strongly Agree

1、强烈反对；2、反对；3、中立；4、赞同；5、强烈赞同

### Area 1: Linguistic Basis 领域一：语言基础

| Items 项目 | 1 | 2 | 3 | 4 | 5 |
|---|---|---|---|---|---|
| 1. I think I have standard English pronunciation. 我认为我具备标准的英语发音。 | | | | | |
| 2. I feel I need to improve my pronunciation of English. 我觉得我的英语发音有待改善。 | | | | | |
| 3. I think I have preferable rich English vocabulary. 我认为我具备丰富的英语词汇。 | | | | | |
| 4. I feel I need to increase my English vocabulary. 我觉得我的英语词汇量有待增加。 | | | | | |
| 5. I think I have preferable knowledge of English grammar. 我认为我具备较好的英语语法知识。 | | | | | |
| 6. I feel I need to improve my knowledge of English grammar. 我觉得我的英语语法知识有待提高。 | | | | | |
| 7. I think I have preferable knowledge of British and American cultural background . 我认为我具备较好的英美文化背景知识。 | | | | | |
| 8. I feel I need to improve my knowledge of British and American cultural background . 我觉得我的英美文化背景知识有待提高。 | | | | | |
| 9. I think I have preferable knowledge of cross-cultural communication. 我认为我具备较好的跨文化交际知识。 | | | | | |
| 10. I feel I need to improve my knowledge of cross-cultural communication. 我觉得我的跨文化交际知识有待提高。 | | | | | |
| 11. I think I have preferable English listening ability. 我认为我具备较好的英语听力。 | | | | | |

Continued Table

| Items 项目 | 1 | 2 | 3 | 4 | 5 |
|---|---|---|---|---|---|
| 12. I feel I need to improve my English listening ability. 我觉得我的英语听力有待提高。 | | | | | |
| 13. I think I have preferable daily spoken English. 我认为我具备较好的日常英语口语能力。 | | | | | |
| 14. I feel I need to improve my daily spoken English. 我觉得我的日常英语口语能力有待提高。 | | | | | |
| 15. I think I have preferable English reading ability. 我认为我具备较好地英语阅读能力。 | | | | | |
| 16. I feel I need to improve my English reading ability. 我觉得我的英语阅读能力有待提高。 | | | | | |
| 17. I think I have preferable English writing ability. 我认为我具备较好的英语写作能力。 | | | | | |
| 18. I feel I need to improve my English writing ability. 我觉得我的英语写作能力有待提高。 | | | | | |

## Area 2: Teaching Design 领域二：教学设计

| Items 项目 | 1 | 2 | 3 | 4 | 5 |
|---|---|---|---|---|---|
| 19. I think I know the teaching syllabus of preschool English intimately. 我认为我熟知学前英语教学大纲。 | | | | | |
| 20. I feel I need to acquire more knowledge of preschool English teaching syllabus. 我觉得我需要获取更多有关学前英语教学大纲方面的知识。 | | | | | |
| 21. I think I know the English teaching methodology intimately. 我认为我熟知英语教学法。 | | | | | |
| 22. I feel I need to acquire more knowledge of preschool English teaching methodology. 我觉得我需要获取更多有关学前英语教学法方面的知识。 | | | | | |
| 23. I think I can analyze English textbooks & teaching contents accurately. 我认为我能够准确分析英语教材和教学内容。 | | | | | |
| 24. I feel I need to improve my ability to analyze the English textbooks & teaching contents accurately. 我觉得在准确分析英语教材和内容方面的能力有待提高。 | | | | | |

| Items 项目 | 1 | 2 | 3 | 4 | 5 |
|---|---|---|---|---|---|
| 25. I think I can analyze the young learners accurately. 我认为我能够准确分析幼小的学习者。 | | | | | |
| 26. I feel I need to improve my ability to analyze the young learners accurately. 我觉得在准确分析幼小的学习者方面的能力有待提高。 | | | | | |
| 27. I think I can set a teaching objective & strategy normatively and clearly. 我认为我能够规范清晰地设置教学目标和策略。 | | | | | |
| 28. I feel I need to improve my ability to set a teaching objective & strategy. 我觉得我在设置教学目标和策略方面的能力有待提高。 | | | | | |
| 29. I think I can select and utilize media & materials reasonably. 我认为我能够合理选择和使用多媒体材料。 | | | | | |
| 30. I feel I need to improve my ability to select and utilize media & materials. 我觉得在选择和使用多媒体材料方面的能力有待提高。 | | | | | |
| 31. I think I can encourage young learners' participation flexibly. 我认为我能够灵活地吸引幼儿的参与性。 | | | | | |
| 32. I feel I need to improve my ability to encourage young learners' participation. 我觉得在吸引幼儿参与性方面的能力有待提高。 | | | | | |
| 33. I think I can design a teaching plan normatively and skillfully. 我认为我能够规范熟练地设计一份教学计划。 | | | | | |
| 34. I feel I need to improve my ability to design a teaching plan. 我觉得在设计教学计划方面的能力有待提高。 | | | | | |

## Area 3: Teaching Implementation 领域三：教学实施

| Items 项目 | 1 | 2 | 3 | 4 | 5 |
|---|---|---|---|---|---|
| 35. I think I can select right teaching methods reasonably. 我认为我能合理地选择恰当的教学方法。 | | | | | |
| 36. I feel I need to improve my ability to select teaching methods reasonably. 我觉得在合理选择恰当的教学方法的能力还有待提高。 | | | | | |
| 37. I usually speak English all the time in class. 我在课堂上采用全英文的教学方法。 | | | | | |

Continued Table

| Items 项目 | 1 | 2 | 3 | 4 | 5 |
|---|---|---|---|---|---|
| 38. I usually speak both Chinese and English in class. 我在课上采用中英结合的教学方法。 | | | | | |
| 39. I think I can organize classrooms & teaching activities effectively. 我认为我能够有效组织课堂教学活动。 | | | | | |
| 40. I feel I need to improve my ability to organize classrooms & teaching activities effectively. 我觉得在有效组织课堂教学活动方面的能力还有待提高。 | | | | | |
| 41. I think I can arrange teaching process reasonably. 我认为我能够合理地安排教学进度。 | | | | | |
| 42. I feel I need to improve my ability to arrange teaching process. 我觉得在安排教学进度方面的能力还有待提高。 | | | | | |
| 43. I think I can evaluate teaching performance objectively. 我认为我能够客观评价教学表现。 | | | | | |
| 44. I feel I need to improve my ability to evaluate teaching performance. 我觉得在评价教学表现方面的能力还有待提高。 | | | | | |

## Area 4: Teaching Techniques 领域四：教学技巧

| Items 项目 | 1 | 2 | 3 | 4 | 5 |
|---|---|---|---|---|---|
| 45. I think I know some techniques of telling English stories. 我认为我了解一些讲英语故事的技巧。 | | | | | |
| 46. I feel I need to improve the technique of telling stories. 我觉得在讲英语故事的技巧方面还有待提高。 | | | | | |
| 47. I think I know some techniques of playing English games. 我认为我了解一些玩英语游戏的技巧。 | | | | | |
| 48. I feel I need to improve the technique of playing games. 我觉得在玩英语游戏的技巧方面还有待提高。 | | | | | |
| 49. I think I know some technique of singing English songs & rhyme. 我认为我了解一些唱英文歌曲和歌谣的技巧。 | | | | | |
| 50. I feel I need to improve the technique of singing songs & rhyme. 我觉得在唱英文歌曲和歌谣的技巧方面还有待提高。 | | | | | |

| Items 项目 | 1 | 2 | 3 | 4 | 5 |
|---|---|---|---|---|---|
| 51. I think I know some technique of drawing stick figure. 我认为我了解一些画简笔画的技巧。 | | | | | |
| 52. I feel I need to improve the technique of drawing stick figure. 我觉得在画简笔画的技巧方面还有待提高。 | | | | | |
| 53. I think I can write pretty and neat English hand-writing. 我认为我能够书写漂亮整洁的英文书法。 | | | | | |
| 54. I feel I need to improve my English hand-writing. 我觉得在英文书写水平上还有待提高。 | | | | | |
| 55. I think I know some techniques of playing English tongue twister. 我认为我了解一些玩英语绕口令的技巧。 | | | | | |
| 56. I feel I need to improve the technique of playing tongue twister. 我觉得在玩英语绕口令的技巧上还有待提高。 | | | | | |
| 57. I think I know some technique of using modern educational teaching technologies. 我认为我了解一些使用现代教育教学技术的技巧。 | | | | | |
| 58. I feel I need to improve the technique of using modern educational teaching technologies. 我觉得在使用现代教育教学技术的技巧方面还有待提高。 | | | | | |

# APPENDIX E

## Interview Guide (For Parents)

1. Will (did) you send your child to a bilingual kindergarten? Why? 你会送（过）你的孩子去双语幼儿园吗？为什么？

2. What purposes do you hope your child has in learning English? Such as English words, English dialogue, spoken English, accurate pronunciation, English songs, and so on. 你希望你的孩子学英语是出于何种目的？比如学习英语单词、英语对话、英语口语、准确的发音、英语歌曲等。

3. What do you think of your present English level? Can you communicate with your child in English in daily life? How and when? 你自认为你目前的英语水平如何？你会在日常生活中跟孩子用英语交流吗？如何交流的？什么时候？

4. What do you think of the present English education in kindergarten based on your own understanding? 就你自己的理解，你如何看待当前的幼儿园英语教育。

4. Do you think it is necessary to develop English education in kindergarten? Why? 你认为在幼儿园开展英语教育是否有必要？为何？

5. How do you evaluate the English teachers in bilingual kindergarten based on your understanding? 就你自己的理解，你是如何评价双语幼儿园的英语教师的？

6. Do you think they are competent or qualified? Which qualities do you think highly of? 你认为他们都胜任或具有资格吗？你比较看重哪种素质？

7. What abilities do you expect an English teacher to have in a bilingual kindergarten? 你期望双语幼儿园的英语教师具备哪些能力？

8. What are your suggestions or opinions of preschool English teaching in kindergarten? 你对幼儿园英语教学有何建议或意见？

# APPENDIX F

## Interview Guide (For English Teachers)

1. What is your original major? Why did you choose to teach English in kindergarten? 你的初始专业是什么？为何选择在幼儿园教英语？

2. Do you like teaching English? What are the differences between the kindergarten level and other levels? 你喜欢教英语吗？在幼儿园教和在其他学校有何异同？

3. What are your greatest feelings (or experiences) while teaching in kindergarten? 在幼儿园教学你最大的感受（或经历）是什么？

4. How do you evaluate your present English educational and teaching knowledge? How about your English language proficiency, teaching abilities and techniques? 你如何评价你目前的英语教育教学知识？还有你的英语语言能力，教学能力和技巧如何？

5. Do you think whether you have passed the CET-4 or CET-6 (TEM-4 or TEM-8) is closely related with English teaching in kindergarten? And why? 你是否认为通过了大学英语四、六级（英语专业四、八级）和幼儿园英语教学有密切关系？为何？

6. Do you think you are competent for preschool English teaching? What do you think are the most important abilities or qualities as an English teacher in kindergarten? Why? What are the other abilities? 你认为你胜任目前的学前英语教学吗？作为一名幼儿园英语教师，你认为哪种能力或素质是最重要的，为何？别的能力还有哪些呢？

7. What are your main problems while teaching English? How did you solve them? 在英语教学过程中你最主要的问题时什么？你是怎样决的？

8. Did you attend any English teaching training? What kind of training? Did you benefit from the training? 你参加过任何英语教学培训吗？哪种培训？通过这些培训你都受益吗？

9. Do you think it is necessary to develop English teaching training? How long

do you think the training should be? And what kind of professional training do you prefer? 你认为开展英语教学培训是否有必要？ 你认为应该培训多长时间？ 你喜欢哪种形式的培训？

10. What are your suggestions or opinions on present preschool English teaching in kindergarten? 就当前幼儿英语教学你可有什么建议或意见？

# APPENDIX G

## Interview Guide (For Principals and Stakeholders)

1. What do you think about the necessity (or importance) of developing preschool English education in kindergarten? 你如何看待在幼儿园开展学前英语教育的必要性（或重要性）？

2. What are the standards (or conditions) for selecting a preschool English teacher? 你招聘学前英语教师的标准（或条件）是什么？

3. How do you evaluate the English teachers in your kindergarten? Are they competent? Are you satisfied with their qualities? 你如何评价你幼儿园的英语教师？他们胜任吗？ 对他们的素质你满意吗？

4. Do you think whether the employees' major will affect their English teaching? Which major do you think is more competent for English teaching in kindergarten? 你是否认为员工的专业将会影响到他们的英语教学？ 你认为哪一个专业更能胜任幼儿园英语教学？

5. How do you think of the effectiveness of developing English teaching activities in kindergarten? 你如何看待幼儿园英语教学活动的有效性？

6. Do you think it is necessary to develop English education and teaching training? What are your suggestions? 你认为开展英语教育教学培训有必要吗？ 对此你有何建议？

7. What are your general suggestion or opinions on preschool English education and teaching in kindergarten? 你对幼儿园学前英语教育教学的总的建议和意见是什么？

# APPENDIX H

## Course Syllabus

**Instructor Information:**

**Name**: Mr. Youxing Xiao, associate professor

**Office**: Teaching and Research Section of Teacher's Basic Skills

**Faculty**: Faculty of Education and Science, Dali University

**Country**: Yunnan Province, PRC.

**Phone No.**: 134661622××

**Email**: youxingxiao@live.cn

**Wechat**: youxingxiao23

**QQ**: 641459510

**Course Name:**

ELT Proficiency Training for Pre-service Teachers

职前教师英语教学技能培训

**Applied Grade and Majors:**

**Grade**: 2016, 3rd year, will take the teaching practicum

**Majors**: Preschool Education, Primary Education

**Class Information:**

**Semester**: 2nd semester of 2018~2019 academic year

**Weeks**: 12

**Periods**: 36 (3 periods/week)

**Time**: 10:00-12:10 (40 minutes/period)

**Classroom**: Room 201, the 1st Teaching Building

**Campus**: Ancient Town Campus, Dali University, Dali District

**Course Description:**

This training course is comprised of four modules: (1) Linguistic Basics; (2) Lesson Design; (3) Teaching Techniques; (4) Teaching Demonstration. Each module consists of different topics and there are the totals of 14 topics. The course aims to improve basic professional qualities and practical teaching skills which are based on English Language Teaching (ELT) proficiency at the beginning level for student-teachers to optimize their pre-service professional development, especially to strengthen the instructional demonstration before they do the teaching practicum.

**Course Limitations:**

I combined all the results extracted from both questionnaires and interviews with the Conceptual Framework of the present study, some topics related with language teaching competences such as vocabulary, grammar, reading and writing ability, British & American cultural background knowledge, and cross-cultural communication knowledge, will not be covered in the course design because of considering the factor of applicability and practicality for the need of the trainees to be teaching at the beginning level, but it doesn't imply that they are not important and necessary for trainees.

**Course Objectives:**

This course provides four operational training modules and 14 topics that will promote trainees' professional development towards the following objectives. Upon successful completion of this training course, trainees are expected to be able to improve the following capabilities:

***Module I: Linguistic Basics***

-Comprehensive pronunciation

-Comprehensive listening techniques

-Practical spoken English

***Module II: Lesson Design***

-Application of English curriculum and syllabus

-Application of textbooks

-Design lesson plans

### *Module III: Teaching Techniques*

-Application of teaching techniques such as story-telling, playing games, singing songs and rhymes, stick figure, handwriting, and modern educational teaching technologies

### *Module IV: Teaching Demonstration*

-Demonstration of lessons

-Feedback and reflection

## Course Instructional Framework:

*Problem-based Learning Model* will be adopted as the main instructional model according to the course characteristics and objectives. *Problem-Based Learning Model* is an active and effective learning model that helps learners present or identify their problems, allows them to learn and hone authentic problem-solving skills, develop the cooperative competence and apply their knowledge and experiences for practical purposes in present study (Clare & Natalie, 2014, p.284-288).

For the stage of teaching procedures, a "3Ps+2Ds Model" is designed to present the steps and activities according to the ultimate training objectives. 3Ps refers to Preparation, Presentation and Practice while 2Ds refers to Demonstration and Discussion.

## Attendance:

Trainees recruited from the purposed sample are required to participant in the training course from the beginning to the end according to the agreement statement. Trainees may be excused due to an illness or other special reasons, and they must attend the final training test or assessment in principle. If there are some circumstances that may interfere with the trainees' ability to attend class, it can be discussed with the instructor.

## Course Assessment:

### *Standard Evaluation:*

**Total:** 100 points (100%) = Participation 10% + Classroom Performance 30% + Periodical Tests 60%

**Assignments:**

*Participation (10%)*: The trainees must come to class on time, guarantee full attendance from beginning to end of training except for special cases, participate in all the activities actively and positively since it will enhance the trainees' professional development.

*Classroom Performance (30%)*: In terms of learning attitudes, attention, interests, confidence, and other factors, trainees' actual performances in the classroom will be recorded as one of their results evaluations such as proper reaction, active participation, quick question-answer, clear expression, critical thinking, creative ideas, etc.

*Periodical Tests (60%)*: It is the primary evaluating tools to check the effectiveness of trainees' demonstration or application upon each topic among the whole training modules, that is, there is a formal or informal test that focuses on some certain points of a lesson which will be taken after each lesson. It provides an overall and accountable standard to assess and improve training module for further course study.

**Course Survey Evaluation Forms:**

Trainees will be asked to fill out the *Evaluation Form for Training Effect*, *Evaluation Form for Training Instructor's Abilities*, and *Survey of Training Satisfaction*. These three survey evaluation forms provide theoretical and practical accordance and reasons based on the actual improvements, effects, and satisfaction which trainees achieve after the course training, which helps the instructor adjust and modify every phase of training for further course study.

**Additional Encouragement, Rewards and Penalties:**

Choose 3~5 outstanding trainees from each training section, award some learning stationery (personal paper-cutting collection) or give certificates from the faculty to encourage good performance. Those who act with abominable attitudes, intended absence, cheating on tests or plagiarism in any form will result in disqualification.

**Tentative Teaching Schedule:**

| Section | Week | Date | Duration | Topics | Assignments |
|---|---|---|---|---|---|
| | | **Proposed Pre-test** | | | |
| Module I | 1 | Oct. 23, 2018<br>Oct. 30, 2018 | 3 | 1. Pronunciation (a)<br>Pronunciation (b) | Practical operation |
| | 2 | Nov. 6, 2018 | 3 | 2. Listening Ability | Practical operation |
| | 3 | Nov. 13, 2018 | 3 | 3. Spoken English | Practical operation |
| Module II | 4 | Nov. 20, 2018 | 3 | 4. Application of Syllabus<br>5. Application of Textbooks | Practical operation |
| | 5 | Nov. 27, 2018 | 3 | 6. Lesson Plan | Practical operation |
| Module III | 6 | Dec. 4, 2018 | 3 | 7. Story-telling | Practical operation |
| | 7 | Dec. 11, 2018 | 3 | 8. Playing Game | Practical operation |
| | 8 | Dec. 18, 2018 | 3 | 9. Song & Rhyme | Practical operation |
| | 9 | Dec. 25, 2018 | 3 | 10. Stick Figure<br>11. English Hand-writing | Practical operation |
| | 10 | Jan. 8, 2019 | 3 | 12. Modern Educational Teaching Technology | Practical operation |
| Module IV | 11 | Jan. 15, 2019 | 3 | 13. Demonstration of Lesson | Practical operation |
| | 12 | Jan. 22, 2019 | 3 | 14. Feedback and Reflection | Practical operation |
| | | **Proposed Post-test** | | | |

The teaching dates and topics might be adjusted according to practical situations.

# APPENDIX I

## SAMPLE OF Lesson Plan 1

**Topic:** Comprehensive Pronunciation
**Time:** October 23, 2018  10:10-12:10
**Duration:** 3 periods (2 hours)
**Classroom:** J1-202

### Background & Principles:

Pronunciation is the most important and difficult problem that non-native English speakers have to face when studying English. Improper pronunciation can lead to negative impressions, misunderstandings and ineffective communication (Hope Speak, 2014).

Learners with good English pronunciation are likely to be understood even if they make errors in other areas, whereas learners with bad pronunciation will not be understood, even if their grammar is perfect (Abbas, 2012).

The learning requirements of beginning levels' English pronunciation are mainly reflected in alphabetical pronunciation, spelling rules and stress. Clear pronunciation and natural intonation are the ultimate learning goals (Li, 2014).

On the one hand, teachers should choose better English phonetic materials for students, on the other hand, teachers should also have a higher pronunciation level. To a large extent, English teachers' pronunciation level has a direct impact on students (Li, 2014).

### Teaching Context Analysis
### Analysis of Student-teachers:

Pronunciation is not comprehensive, silent English, affected by local dialects and Mandarin Chinese.

**Teaching Subject Contents**

Comprehensive Pronunciation:

-Phonemes

-Word Stress

-Intonation

**Teaching Objectives**

**General Objectives:**

This course is intended to help Chinese EFL students to improve their English pronunciation, including such elements as the correct pronunciation of individual phonemes and words in English as well as the rhythmic patterns of the English language and patterns and functions of English intonation, so that the students will be able to communicate more effectively with good pronunciation and intonation.

**Specific Objectives:**

Students will be able to:

-pronounce English phonemes correctly

-correct problematic sounds which most Chinese learners have

(e.g. [θ]-[ð]-[s],[d]-[t], [ʃ]-[tʃ]...)

-apply rules about accents, stress and intonation correctly

**Key Points and Difficult Points**

**Key Points:**

To distinguish similar phonemes between English and Chinese sounds correctly.

**Difficult Points:**

To demonstrate appropriate pronunciation approaches and apply good activities to learners.

**Teaching Methods**

Activity-based Approach (Churchill, 2003)

**Teaching Medias and Materials**

1. PowerPoint; 2. Multi-media classroom; 3. Videos; 4. Alphabet cards; 5. Worksheets

**Teaching Procedures** (3Ps + 2Ds)

<u>Preparation</u> (15 minutes)

**Activity 1: Greeting & Introduction**

(1) T greets Ss daily;

(2) T chooses 4-5 Ss to introduce themselves in English.

**Activity 2: Audio-visual Moment**

(1) T asks Ss to sing the traditional version of the ABC song.

(2) T plays a video of a different version of the ABC song. Ss sing along.

(3) T changes to another English song with the same tone of ABC song with lyrics, Ss follow to sing.

*Designing Intentions:*

*-to focus Ss' attention*

*-to ease their learning condition*

*-to motivate their learning interests*

*-to build an active learning environment*

*-to know some general information about their pronunciation*

<u>Presentation</u> (20 minutes)

**Activity 3: Problems Checking [t]-[θ], [w]-[v], [r]-[l], stress and intonation**

(1) Ss compare the following sentences, tell the reasons.

*"I'm going to the hospital* <u>today</u>*."* and *"I'm going to the hospital* <u>to die</u>*."*

*"There are* <u>pears</u> *in the garden."* and *"There are* <u>bears</u> *in the garden."*

(2) Ss first read and discriminate the difference of each pair words on slides, check with partners, and write down the uncertain words. Then T demonstrations.

*tinker-thinker  tank-thank  team-theme  wit-with  mat-math*

*taught-thought  tick-thick  tree-three  boat-both  fort-fourth*

*vest-west  verse-worse  versed-worst  veal-weal  vale-whale*

*vet-wet  vine-wine  vain-wane  very-worry*

*right-light  rate-late  road-load  rain-lane  rout-lout*

*row-low  read-lead  rack-lack  rhyme-lime  room-loom*

(3) Ss first read aloud the following sentences on the slide, T asks them to pay attention to word stress in the sentence based on their own understanding.

*I shall have to try and get some cash from our bank at lunchtime.*

*Then we can let them have the money that they want as soon as they like.*

*What are they asking us to pay them?*

Then, T demonstrates and shows the right word stress.

*I shall have to <u>try</u> and <u>get</u> some <u>cash</u> from our <u>bank</u> at <u>lunch</u> time.*

*<u>Then</u> we can <u>let</u> them have the <u>money</u> that they <u>want</u> as <u>soon</u> as they <u>like</u>.*

*<u>What</u> are they <u>ask</u>ing us to <u>pay</u> them?*

(4) T explains that different word stress will depend on different speakers to indicate the important words in the sentence.

(5) Ss practise more examples of words and sentences.

*dessert-desert    present v.-present n.  too-two-to  buy-by  cell-sell  sea-see  dear-deer  die-dye  eye-i  fair-fare  flower-flour  hair-hare  hole-whole*

*know-no  piece-peace  right-write  some-sum  steal-steel  their-there*

-*Oh! You didn't break the window. I believe you* (trustful and distrustful attitude)

-*London bridge is falling down!* (surprised, happy, sad, and none of my business felling)

-*Open the window, please!* (requesting and ordering speech)

-*I bought a black bike.* (different stress on each word)

***Designing Intentions:***

-*to help Ss recognize their problems (problematic sounds, intonation)*

-*to realize the importance of standard pronunciation and its demonstration*

-*to enhance Ss' learning self-awareness for the next process*

Practice (25 minutes)

**Activity 4: General Practice**

(1) T operates a network instructional tool (音标点读卡 *Phonetic Symbols Clicking and Reading Cards*) via internet. Ss are asked to review and repeat the International Phonetic Symbols one by one.

(2) T picks 4~5 Ss randomly to repeat (*individual work*), others check(*class work*), T corrects mistakes if Ss have.

(Phonetic Clicking and Reading Cards *is a network inter-linkage, each card has both face and back sides. The face side displays a big phonetic symbol with a standard female sound, while back side displays a vivid image and word pronunciation corresponding to the face phonetic symbol, also elaborates the name and approaches of how to articulate in Chinese. It also can be collected and kept in personal Wechat APP, open and use it at any proper time. See the following screenshot*)

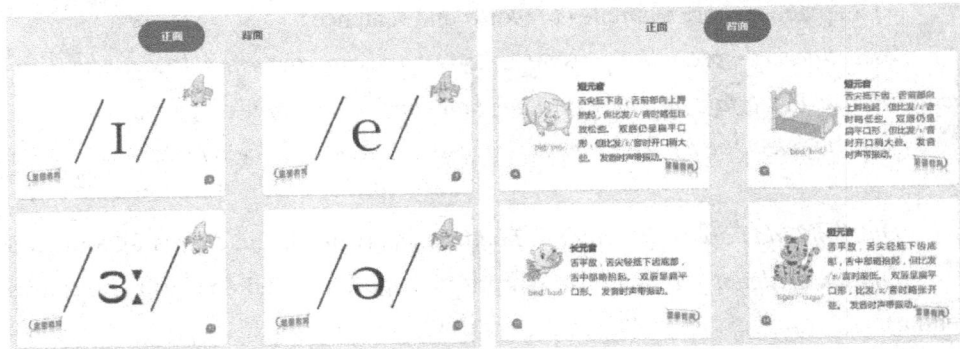

**Activity 5: Focusing Practice—Sound "[θ], [ð], /ʃ/, /tʃ/"**

(1) Ss practise saying the following ordinal numbers. T checks randomly.

*1st - first 2nd - second 3rd - third 4th - fourth 5th - fifth*

*6th - sixth 7th - seventh 8th - eighth 9th - ninth 10th – tenth*

*11th - eleventh 12th - twelfth 13th- thirteenth 14th - fourteenth 15th - fifteenth*

*16th- sixteenth 17th- seventeenth 18th- eighteenth 19th- nineteenth 20th- twentieth 21st- twenty-first 22nd-twenty-second 23rd- twenty-third*

*30th- thirtieth 31st- thirty-first ...*

(2) Ss practise the following problematic sound /θ/. T checks randomly.

*-initial position:* thank - theatre - theory - thermometer - thick - thief
- thin - thing - think - third - thirsty - thirty - thought
- thousand - thread - three - throw - thumb /θʌm/- Thursday
*-mid-position:* anthropology - author - athlete - birthday - enthusiasm - ethnic
- filthy - healthy - hypothesis - mathematics - method - monthly - wealthy
*-final position:* bath - birth - breath - cloth - death - earth - faith
- fourth - growth - health - length - month - moth - mouth - north
- south - teeth - tooth - truth - worth

(3) Ss practise the following problematic sound /ð/. T checks randomly.

*-initial position:* than - that - the - their - them - then - there - these - they
- this - those - though - thus
*-mid-position:* although - another - either - neither - other - together - whether
*-final position:* with - within - without

(4) Ss practise the following problematic sound /tʃ/. T checks randomly.

*-initial position:* change - charge - cheap - check - cheese - chew - choose
*-mid position:* achieve - kitchen - future - picture - purchase - teacher
*-final position:* approach - catch - each - lunch - much - pitch - research

(5) Ss practise the following problematic sound /ʃ/. T checks randomly.

*-initial position:* shine - ship - shoe - shop - should - show
*-mid-position:* action - passion - patient - position - station
*-final position:* dish - push - wash - wish

(6) S compare the pair sound /ʃ/- /tʃ/. T give feedback.

chair - share; cheap - sheep; cheat - sheet; cheese - she's
chew - shoe; choose - shoes; chip - ship; chop - shop
catch - cash/cache; match - mash; watch - wash; which/witch - wish


### Designing Intentions:

-to help Ss discriminate and consolidate correct pronunciation of each phonetic symbol

-to provide Ss some available network resources to facilitate self-learning and teaching

-to focus on practising Ss' problematic sound "[θ], [ð], /ʃ/, /tʃ/"

*-to help Ss conclude the rule of pronunciation*

Demonstration (30 minutes)

**Activity 6: Singing a Song and Acting (TPE, Total Physical Exercise)**

(1) Ss consolidate singing a song "If You Are Happy" by following the Video. T divides class into 4~5 groups, every group discusses and presents the alphabet song in their own ways (sing, dance and act, etc.). T evaluates and selects the most excellent group.

(2) T shows the 26 English phonemes cards prepared in advance, leads Ss to make and create other relative teaching aids by hands after class, such as headwear, masks, gloves, finger dolls, and other cards or pictures which may facilitate teaching pronunciation.

**Activity 7: Carrot Down**

T distributes 12 Chinese zodiac headsets on which write 12 different English phonemes to different 10 Ss randomly, those Ss play "*Carrot Down*" game. See the example:

*"A down, A down, A down then  C down"*

*"C down, C down, C down then _ down"*

*" _down, _down, _down then _ down"*

...

***Direction:*** A represents a certain student who wears the corresponding headwear. Starting from A, A crouches while saying "A down, A down, A down then B down ", then A can points to anyone in the group, if C is pointed, C will take a turn to follow saying "C down, C down, C down then ", and crouches at the same. The game continues to check Ss' reactive ability and their correct pronunciation of English phonemes.

**Activity 8: Tongue Twisters (from easy to difficult)**

(1) Ss practise the following tongue twisters:

*Big, black, bug, blood.*

*Big black bugs' blood.*

*Quick kiss.*
*Quicker kiss.*
*Quickest kiss.*
*Good blood, bad blood,*
*good blood, bad blood,*
*good blood, bad blood.*

*Six sharp smart sharks.*
*Nine nice night nurses nursing nicely.*

*One-One was a racehorse.*
*Two-Two was one, too.*
*When One-One won one race,*
*Two-Two won one, too.*

(2) Ss take the challenge to practice the following tongue twisters:
*A big black bear sat on a big black bug.*
*Big black bugs bleed blue black blood but baby black bugs bleed blue blood.*
*How many cookies could a good cook cook if a good cook could cook cookies?*
*I wish I were what I was when I wished I were what I am.*

*I wish to wish the wish you wish to wish,*
*but if you wish the wish the witch wishes,*
*I won't wish the wish you wish to wish.*

*She sells sea shells on the seashore.*
*The seashells she sells are seashells she is Sure.*

*I thought a thought.*
*But the thought I thought wasn't the thought I thought I thought.*

*Whether the weather be fine or whether the weather be not.*

*Whether the weather be cold or whether the weather be hot.*

*We'll weather the weather whether we like it or not.*

**Designing Intentions:**

*-to develop Ss' cooperative learning ability and practical creativity*

*-to improve Ss' demonstrative and reactive ability*

*-to motivate Ss' learning interests*

*-to build an active learning environment*

*-to help Ss apply to young learners*

Discussion (20 minutes)

**Activity 9: Finding and Matching (Five Vowels Aa--Ee--Ii--Oo--Uu)**

(1) T hands out worksheets to Ss.

(2) Ss read aloud and write the phonetic symbol of each pair group in blanks, and then discuss with partners to find the different sounds of the same vowel.

(3) Ss finish the matching tasks in following square in pairs and conclude.

(4) Ss present the rules and T gives feedback.

**Can you summarize some rules about consonants pronunciation?**

_____

**Designing Intentions:**

*-to consolidate Ss' learning performance*

*-to enhance Ss' problem-solving ability and cooperative ability*

*-to help Ss' conclude pronunciation rules*

*-to apply pronunciation of the vowel sounds to young learners*

**Assignments:** (Omit) _____

**Learning Resources**: (Omit)

**References:** (Omit)

**Reflection:** (Omit)

# APPENDIX J

## Sample of Lesson Plan 2

**Topic:** Listening Competence
**Time:** November 6, 2018
**Duration:** 3 periods (2 hours)
**Classroom:** J2A-202

### Backgrounds & Principles:

An effective classroom leader or lecturer is not only a knowledgeable and skilled teacher he or she is a good active listener. Good listening skills are needed to develop empathy and understanding with the students and to assess whether they understand what they are being taught. Listening skills also help in negotiating with students and defusing any potential classroom conflicts (ACS Distance Education).

Teaching students listening skills gives them a key advantage when it comes to linguistic interaction. It is generally recognized that listening comprehension plays a key role in facilitating language learning (Vandergrift, 1999, p.168). Listening comprehension also plays a critical role in both communication and in language acquisition. (Bozorgian & Pillay, 2013).

Listening is an essential skill which develops faster than speaking and often affects the development of reading and writing abilities in learning a new language (Yavuz & Celik, 2017).

### Teaching Context Analysis
### Analysis of Students:

Low listening competence, limited communicative ability, lack of listening techniques, dumb English.

## Teaching Objectives

-to follow frequent instructions in daily activities

-to demonstrate an understanding of audio-visual materials

-to use listening techniques correctly (recognizing, pointing, coloring, drawing, doing, asking, guessing, predicting, etc.)

## Key Points and Difficult Points

**Key Points**: To apply frequent classroom languages and instructions to real situations.

**Difficult Points**: To develop listening comprehension.

## Teaching Methods

Audio-visual Method, TPR

## Teaching Materials

1. PowerPoint; 2. Multi-media; 3. Short videos; 4. Worksheets

**Teaching Procedures** (3Ps + 2Ds)

Preparation (15 minutes)

### Activity 1: Greeting and Answering

(1) T greets Ss daily;

(2) T asks the following questions in English and Ss answer.

*-Is there anybody who has been to foreign country? Which country?*

*-If there is a chance, which country would you like to go? Why?*

*-Please raise your hand if you are wearing blue clothes/T-shirts?*

*-Whose student card ends with a 5? ...*

### Activity 2: Cocking Your Ears

T plays a video with simple and clear speaking by a native speaker. Ss listen and tell what they can understand.

*Designing Intentions:*

*-to focus Ss' concentration*

*-to build a relaxed learning environment*

*-to train Ss' listening comprehension*

<u>Presentation</u>(20 minutes)

**Activity 3: Missing Words**

(1) T gives worksheets to Ss, some words are taken out of the lyrics in blanks.

(2) T plays the video without lyrics, Ss listen and fill in the blanks.

(3) T plays another video with the complete lyrics, Ss listen and check.

(4) Ss sing the song together.

**Take Me To Your Heart《吻别》**

Hiding from the _____ and _____. Trying to forget but I won't let go.

Looking at a crowded _____. Listening to my own _____ beat.

So many people all around the _____.

Tell me where do I find someone like you _____.

Take me to your _____、Take me to your _____. Give me your _____before I'm old.

Show me what _____ is haven't got a clue. Show me that _____ can be true.

They say _____ lasts forever. We're only here _____.

_____ is now or never. Bring me far away.

Take me to your _____. Take me to your _____. Give me your _____ and hold me.

Show me what _____ is be my guiding star. It's _____ take me to your heart.

Standing on a _____ high. Looking at the _____ through a clear blue sky.

I should go and see some _____. But they don't really _____.

Don't need too much _____ without saying anything.

All I need is _____ who makes me wanna sing.

***Designing Intentions:***

*-to present a kind of listening approach from learning English songs/videos*

*-to introduce a listening strategy for specific information*

*-to arouse Ss' learning interests with a familiar musical melody*

Practice(25 minutes)

**Activity 4:Listening and Doing (TPE)**

T gives the classroom instructions, Ss listen and do the corresponding actions quickly.

-*Stand up!* -*Turn left!* -*Turn right!* -*Sit down!*

-*Close your eyes!* -*Open your eyes!*

-*Touch your mouth!* -*Touch your ear!*

-*Point to the window!* -*Point to the blackboard!*

-*Put up your hands!* -*Put down your hands!*

-*Look at me!* -*Look at him/her!*

-*Clap your hands!* -*Stamp your feet!*

-*Show me your thumb!* -*Show me your book!*

**Activity 5: Simon Says**

T adds "Simon says" before a classroom instruction, Ss listen and do actions same as Activity 4. But if T does not add "Simon says" before an instruction, Ss just keep silent. T changes randomly.

-*Simon says: "Stand up, please!"*

-*Turn right!*

-*Simon says: "Turn left!"*

-*Sit down, please!*

-*Simon says: "Sit down, please!"*

*...*

***Designing Intentions:***

*-to practise following classroom instructions*

*-to test Ss reactive ability*

*-to practise an available listening game*

*-to train Ss's listening skill of focusing on speaker's words*

*-to demonstrate the TPR approach*

Demonstration(30 minutes)

**Activity 6:Listening and Drawing**

(1)T hands out paper to class. Prepares a picture with a few objects which are simple to draw.

(2) T reads out detailed instructions, T tells Ss as following:

-*I'm going to read out a few instructions and as I talk, you have to draw.*

-*You don't have to worry about how good your drawing is.*

-*It's not an art class, it's English class! Just draw quickly.*

-*I am just checking to see whether you follow the instructions given in English.*

-*Is this clear? Is there a question, or is the activity clear to everybody?*

(3)T ensures Ss' full understanding about the instructions, then T starts to illustrate, Ss listen and draw on the paper according to what is heard.

-*Right, so you all have pens with you. Can you show your pens?*

-*OK, draw a bear on the left side of the page first.*

-*Now, draw a butterfly around the bear.*

-*After you have drawn the butterfly, draw a girl sitting on the ground to the right of the bear.*

-*Draw a basket to the right of that girl.*

-*Then draw some apples in the basket.*

-*Draw a cake next to the basket ...*

(4) As Ss draw, T walks around the classroom to encourage them by saying:

-*Nice bear!*

-*Beautiful butterfly!*

-*Good, the girl is on the right side of the page.*

-*So big apples!*

-*Oh, the cake is next to the basket.*

...

(5) After finishing drawing, Ss compare their pictures with each other.

Ss note any differences and compare with the real picture.

(Ss maybe laugh as they look at each other's drawings because of the difference. Someone may draw on the wrong side of the page.)

**Activity Extending:**

*Listening and Drawing* can be adapted into group or pair work, one student describes to classmates or group members, others listen and draw.

***Designing Intentions:***

*-to helps Ss practise language in context (etc. prepositions)*

*-to involve all Ss*

*-to motivate Ss' learning interests*

*-to build an active learning environment*

Discussion(30 minutes)

**Activity 7: BBC News**

(1) Ss watch a video which tells about the terrible Typhoon Mangkhut (*happened on September 16, 2018*), the video has no subtitles.

(2) T first writes the following 7 questions on the blackboard as Ss watch.

*-How many dead doll in Philippines?*

*-What reason causes them to die?*

*-What is the wind speed?*

*-What is the number of injured in Hong Kong?*

*-What is the height of water levels?*

*-How many flights have been canceled?*

*-How many passengers have been affected?*

(3) T plays the recording of BBC news, and Ss listen, try to find the answers, and check the answer in pairs.

(4) T selects 4~5 Ss to check their answers.

(5) T plays the recording, Ss confirm their answers again.

**Activity 8:Discussing and Sharing**

(1) Based on all above activities, T asks Ss what activity is their favorite? And why? What other listening techniques have they used before?

(2) Ss share voluntarily.

*(pointing, coloring, drawing, doing, asking, guessing, predicting...)*

(3) Ss listen, appreciate and follow to sing the song.

**The River is Flowing**

The river is flowing, flowing and growing 河，在流淌；河，在成长

The river is flowing, back to the sea 河，在流淌，流回到大海

Mother Earth carry me, the child that I will always be 地球母亲带着我，我永远是她的孩子

Mother Earth carry me, back to the sea 地球母亲带着我，带我回家

The river is flowing, flowing and growing 河，在流淌；河，在成长

The river is flowing, back to the sea 河，在流淌，流回到大海

*Designing Intentions:*

*-to help Ss focus on listening to key points or specific information*

*-to help Ss prepare or predict the following topic in text.*

*-to help Ss practise listening techniques.*

*-to help Ss analyse language/text*

*-to help Ss conclude listening tips*

**Teaching Evaluation/Assignments:**

T gives a mp3 song to Ss. Ss learn to sing the folk song *Twinkle, Twinkle Little Star* by native English speakers. Ss are required to focus on "linking" pronunciation and the "soft-T". T checks next class.

Lyrics:

*Twinkle, twinkle little star,*

*How I wonder what you are.*

*Up above the world so high,*

*Like a diamond in the sky.*

*Twinkle, twinkle, little star,*

*How I wonder what you are.*

**Testing Points:**

★ Soft sound "T" of little ★ Focusing: "what-you" CH sound ★ Linking: "up-above"

★ Linking: "world-so" ★ Linking: "Like a" ★ Pronunciation: "diamond"

**Network Learning Resources**: (omit)

**References:** (omit)

**Reflection:** (omit)

# APPENDIX K

## IOC Evaluation Form (Lesson Plans)
### (For Experts)

### I. Basic Information
### -General Objectives of Training Course:

This training course provides four operational training modules and 14 topics that will promote trainees' professional development towards the following objectives. Upon successful completion of the training course, trainees are expected to be able to improve the following capabilities:

*Module I: Linguistic Basics*

-Comprehensive pronunciation

-Comprehensive listening competence

-Practical spoken English

*Module II: Lesson Design*

-Application of English curriculum and syllabus

-Application of textbooks

-Design of lesson plan

*Module III: Teaching Techniques*

-Application of teaching techniques, such as story-telling, playing games, singing songs and rhymes, stick figure, handwriting, and modern educational teaching technologies

*Module IV: Teaching Demonstration*

-Demonstration of lessons

-Feedback and reflection

### 3Ps+ 2Ds Instructional Model:

During this phase of teaching procedures, a "3Ps+2Ds Instructional Model" is designed to present the teaching steps and activities systematically according to the ultimate training objectives. 3Ps refers to Preparation, Presentation and Practice while 2Ds refers to Demonstration and Discussion.

## II. Directions:

Please fill in the blanks and put a check in the appropriate place.

+1 means the item that is in congruence with the training course.

0 means the item that is uncertain to be in congruence with the training course.

-1 means the item that is not in congruence with the training course.

Thank you very much!

Truly yours,

Mr. Youxing Xiao (Jack)

### Evaluation Form for Lesson Plan 1

## Module I: Linguistic Basics

**Topic 1:** Comprehensive Pronunciation

*More details can be seen in Lesson Plan 1.*

| Evaluation Items | +1 | 0 | -1 | Comments |
|---|---|---|---|---|
| **Objectives: At the end trainees will be able to**<br>-pronounce 26 English letters correctly<br>-demonstrate ABC song<br>-summarize rules about accents, stress and intonation<br>-correct problematic sounds which Chinese learners have | | | | |
| **Teaching Methods:** Activity-based Approach | | | | |
| **Teaching Medias and Materials:**<br>1. PowerPoint; 2. Multi-media classroom;<br>3. Videos; 4. Alphabet cards; 5. Worksheets | | | | |
| **Learning Resources:**<br>音标点读学习卡<br>**English Central.**<br>**From Text To Speech.** | | | | |

Continued Table

| Evaluation Items | +1 | 0 | -1 | Comments |
|---|---|---|---|---|
| **BBC Learning English.** http://www.bbc.co.uk/ learningenglish/english/features/pronunciation **Corpus Linguistics.** http://ec-concord.ied.edu.hk/ | | | | |
| **Teaching Procedures and Activities:** <br> Preparation: <br> 1. Greeting and introduction: *Warm-up* <br> 2. Audio-visual moment: *Sing ABC Song* <br> Presentation: <br> Problem checking: *Discriminate Stress* <br> Practice: <br> General practice: *Phonetic Symbols Clicking on Line* <br> 2. Focusing practice: *[θ]-[ð], [d]-[t], [ʃ]-[tʃ]* <br> Demonstrate: <br> 1. Sing a song and acting: *Present ABC Song in Groups* <br> 2. Carrot down: *Letter Game* <br> 3. Tongue twister: <br> *Challenge Your Pronunciation* <br> Discussion: <br> Finding and matching: <br> *Summarize Pronunciation Rules of the Five Vowels* | | | | |
| **Assignments:** <br> Ss complete vowels and consonants test after class: <br> *Consolidate the 48 Phonetic Symbols* | | | | |

What comments/suggestions can you provide to improve the lesson as a whole?

**Expert's Signature:**

**Date:**

# APPENDIX L

## The Evaluation Form of Satisfaction

1 = Not Satisfied;

2 = Just So So;

3 = Basically Satisfied;

4 = Satisfied;

5 = Very Satisfied

| Items | No. | Key Points | 1 | 2 | 3 | 4 | 5 |
|-------|-----|-----------|---|---|---|---|---|
| **Training Contents** | 1 | Course Targets | | | | | |
| | 2 | Course Practicability | | | | | |
| | 3 | Course Enlightenment | | | | | |
| | 4 | Course Objectives | | | | | |
| | 5 | Teaching Content Selection | | | | | |
| | 6 | Teaching Time Arrangement | | | | | |
| | 7 | Teaching Courseware Design | | | | | |
| **Trainer's Performances** | 8 | Basic Teaching Abilities in Subject | | | | | |
| | 9 | Teaching Clarity of Difficult & Key Points | | | | | |
| | 10 | Classroom Instruction and Linguistic Expression Ability | | | | | |
| | 11 | Teaching Interactive Control Ability | | | | | |
| | 12 | Teaching Materials Preparation | | | | | |
| | 13 | Teaching Progress and Steps | | | | | |
| | 14 | Teaching Attitudes and Responsibility | | | | | |

Continued Table

| Items | No. | Key Points | 1 | 2 | 3 | 4 | 5 |
|---|---|---|---|---|---|---|---|
| **Trainees' Feelings** | 15 | Your Whole Learning Attitudes (Concentration, Attendance) | | | | | |
| | 16 | Your Proficiency before Training | | | | | |
| | 17 | Your Proficiency after Training | | | | | |
| | 18 | Your Whole Learning Satisfaction | | | | | |

## General Evaluation

1. Write down your benefits or feelings in 1~3 sentences.

2. What do you think should be improved for the training?

# APPENDIX M

## Evaluation Form for the Training
## (Modules I, II, III & IV)
## 培训评价表（模块一、二、三、四）

1. Do you think the training content is beneficial for you? What percentage of your original expectation is based on the training content? 你认为培训内容对你有益吗？你对该培训内容的预计期望值百分比是多少？

( )Yes ( )No ____%

2. How do you think of the teaching activities in the classroom? How about the participation? Any suggestions? 你如何评价课堂教学活动？参与性如何？有何建议？

_____

_____

3. What do you think of the teaching process and arrangement? Any suggestions? 你如何评价教学进度安排？有何建议？

_____

_____

4. What do you think of "3Ps +2Ds" teaching model? Any suggestion? If you design the teaching model, what is your challenge? And why? 你对"Preparation 准备 +Presentation 引入 +Practice 练习 +Demonstration 示范 +Discuss 讨论"的教学模式评价如何？有何建议？如果你来设计该教学模式，你觉得你的挑战性在哪里？为何？

_____

_____

5. What do you think of the teacher's language expression and teaching instruction? Any suggestions? 你如何评价教师的语言表达及教学指令？有何建议？

_____

_____

_____

6. What do you think of the teaching materials and resources? Any suggestions? 你认为教学材料和教学素材如何？有何建议？

_____

_____

_____

7. What do you think of the teaching PPT? Any suggestions? 你如何评价教学课件？有何建议？

_____

_____

_____

8. What do you think of the teaching method? Any suggestions? 你如何评价教学方法？有何建议？

_____

_____

_____

9. What did you gain mainly from the 3 teaching topics（English pronunciation, listening and speaking）? Did you reach your learning objectives? What other aspects need to be improved? 对于三个教学主题(英语语音，英语听力，英语口语)，你的主要收获是什么？你的个体学习目标达到了吗？哪些方面还需要完善？

_____

_____

_____

10. What is your most impressive or favorite teaching activity (stage, material)? 你印象最深刻或是最喜欢的教学活动 (环节、材料) 是什么？

_____

_____

11. What other content is related with the 3 topics? Do you still want to learn based on your own situation? 结合你自身情况而言，你还想获取跟这三个主题相关的别的哪些学习内容？

_____

_____

_____

12. Generally speaking, do you have any suggestions or comments about the training or teacher? 整体而言，你可有任何想对本模块培训或是老师想说的话？

_____

_____

_____

*Thank for your cooperation!* 谢谢合作！

# 一封泰国妈妈写给中国儿子的信

A special note written specifically for Mr. XIAO YOUXING, one of the most outstanding Burapha TEGL alumni, who was my former TESL student and my Chinese son.

Dear Jack,

Looking backward for about 15 years, I still remember clearly when I first got to know you as a newcomer of the TESL Second Batch. I noticed a young guy who was very attentive and participated actively in the class. As the Chair of the TESL Program, I had to take good care and gave some good academic and personal advice for the students. We became closer and closer when we got to know more of each other. Later on, you became part of my family and had also joined some family activities with us. As a student, you had great responsibility and good effort for your study. Apart from the study, I had provided you opportunities to attend and participate in both national and international conferences in your field, as well as a school visit to observe the learning/teaching Chinese language at the primary education level in Thai famous schools in Bangkok. We learned and shared academic and cultural aspects among other students and teaching staff both inside and outside the class. We enjoyed preparing traditional Chinese food and demonstrating Chinese performance for a special Chinese festival. With your perseverance, persistence, and devotion to your study, undoubtedly, you were one of the fast-track students who graduated within time allocation for Master's Degree Program. We think you were fully equipped with the things needed for your job when you graduated and started your job at your home country.

Later on after a few years passed by, I was very glad to know that you decided to go back to Burapha University to further your PhD studies. With your academic maturity, knowledge acquisition, and purposive determination, you put a great effort and worked hard for your coursework and dissertation. Finally, you achieved your academic accomplishment, and your academic work is going to be published. We all are happy that your perseverance has given you a big reward and that you are part of knowledgeable and worthy human resources who can contribute much to your organization.

As a mother to say to her son, I would like to say loudly to you, "I am very proud of you, my dear Chinese son."

With love and warm wishes,

*Daranee Pummawan*

Asst. Prof. Daranee Pummawan

Chair,

TESL Program,

Burapha University, Thailand.

我尊敬的优雅的泰国妈妈 Daranee Pummawan 女士

# 致 谢

十年前有缘结识澳大利亚学者毕百灵博士 (Dr. Brian Billard) 和毕丽丝博士 (Dr. Liz Billard) 夫妇。他们夫妇俩均就职于澳大利亚昆士兰大学，毕百灵博士是一名从事物理研究的科学家，而毕丽丝博士是一名从事艺术教育研究的教育学者。

为了共同理想，毕百灵夫妇二人于 2002 年来到中国，到了云南大理剑川县的一个偏远贫困村石龙村开展白汉双语教育研究，研究成果丰硕。

2015 年，为了进一步推广毕百灵夫妇在大理剑川关于双语课程开发、教师培训以及有效教学的研究成果，我和我的团队有幸和毕先生之间有了合作，期间我和毕百灵先生在大理有过五次见面以及无数次的邮件来往。他每次只身远航来到大理，我都荣幸能有机会给他当过随行的半英半汉的翻译人员，虽然是蹩脚的口译，但却一直受到毕老先生的信任和鼓励；也很荣幸能陪同毕先生前往大理剑川沙溪镇石龙村开展过一次实地调研，他对偏远贫困地区学校教师及儿童的关注总是打动着我的内心，每每看到他宽大厚实的背影和稳重矫健的步伐，我都感到心中充满了无限的力量。

毕先生曾许诺只要他身体硬朗就保证每年至少来一次大理以完成他的心愿，因为他有太多的教育理想需要去实践，有太多的教育成果要来分享。2018 年是我与毕先生在大理的最后一次见面，那时的他已经七十多岁了。2019 年毕先生再来大理时，我因回老家照料生病住院的父亲，遗憾没能与毕先生见面，那年也是毕先生来大理的最后一年了。回望所发生的一切，毕先生那张慈祥亲切的面孔无时无刻都历历在目，他对教育的至深情怀永远是那么的打动人心。我曾无数回感悟我们最初的二人团队（Jack & Julie）曾经的坚持，也曾无数次感怀毕先生夫妇对教育的敬业和执着，毕先生真的是将他的毕生都投入到他所热爱的教育事业中。最后一次和毕先生的邮件往来是 2023 年的 1 月 11 日，从信中得知，毕先生夫人毕丽丝因病手术后状态不容乐观，我也不敢再问，唯有在心中默默祈祷，希望他们一切顺遂顺愿。

坦白地说，我的博士论文研究主题及思路就是受到毕先生夫妇投身教育所感而引发的，这段经历必将是我人生中难忘的一段美好回忆。

"越努力，越幸运。"

读博期间所经历的各种，也更加让我学会了对身边所遇之人都要怀以感恩之心，因为他们都是我生命中的贵人。除了这些贵人，还有给予我体质生命和精神生命的亲人，特别是我的亲生父亲和岳父大人。"树欲静而风不止，子欲孝而亲不在"，感觉都没有行施丝毫孝道，两位父亲就在同年相继病逝，留给我的是心中的万分遗憾和那份身为男人的责任感；还有在人生最低谷期一直鼓励我给予我精神支持的发妻，结婚以来我个人一直前前后后在攻读硕士和博士，期间有太多浓情的话语积压在心间至今都未曾开口言出，如今也只有默默将自己身为人夫和身为人父的双重责任顶起来，以示对爱妻的感恩与致歉。

最后，我还要由衷感谢那些为我完成论文做出贡献的人和在过去四年间持续给予我指导、支持和帮助的人。首先，感谢我的导师 Janpanit Surasin 教授和 Denchai Prabjandee 博士以及受人尊敬的 Chalong Tubsree 教授，感谢他们的博学专业的人文关怀和学术指导；其次，真诚感谢我尊敬的"泰国妈妈"Daranee Pummawan 女士，这位优雅老太太在我攻读硕士、博士期间真是给予了我太多无微不至的物质帮助和精神关怀，每次去到泰国都要亲自为我接风，请我吃遍了学校附近的地道泰国美食。近八十岁的她还时不时驾车带我去海边兜风，带我去品尝当地有名的夜市海鲜，带我去体验泰国华文学校的传统文化习俗活动，带我去见一些知名的教育行业大咖，还带我参加了一些专业领域的全国性学术会议，等等；最记得老太太家中那棵菠萝蜜（jackfruit）树，每年菠萝蜜成熟一定会给我留一个最大的菠萝蜜果实，因为那是 Jack（我的英文名）的"专属水果"；还要感谢大理大学教师教育学院、外语学院的领导和泰国东方大学教育学院领导以及研究生院的 Rattanasiri Khemraj 女士，以及我所有亲爱的同事和工作团队给予我莫大的支持、建议和鼓励。

感谢拥有，感恩一切！

图一　陪同 Brian Billard 博士赴云南大理剑川县石龙村开展调研

图二　我的博士生导师泰国东方大学 Janpanit Surasin 教授